CRITICAL INTERNATIONALIZATION OF HIGHER EDUCATION

This edited collection explores ethical global engagement in higher education internationalization. Framed by organizational change theory and critical internationalization approaches, chapter authors discuss the systemic inequities in who is served and for what purposes, while also providing new insights on what drives the why, what, and how of internationalization. This volume features contributions from scholars across disciplines, presenting original research and theoretical insights on topics within higher education internationalization, including teaching and learning, mobility, university service, collaborative partnership, student recruitment, evaluation, and leadership. Ultimately, this volume provides higher education leaders, professionals, and graduate students with ethical policies and practices that champion internationalization of higher education for its capacity to meet contemporary global challenges while also maintaining its foundational educational mission.

Melanie Agnew is an organizational development consultant with over 25 years of higher education leadership experience at both departmental and dean levels. She specializes in internationalization, guiding cultural transformation, facilitating leader development, integrating discipline-specific change frameworks, and in partnering with multiple stakeholder groups internal and external to the organization.

Jos Beelen is Professor of Global Learning at The Hague University of Applied Sciences, Netherlands. He is a Visiting Professor at Coventry University, UK, at Western Norway University of Applied Sciences, Norway, and at the University of the Free State, South Africa.

CRITICAL INTERNATIONALIZATION OF HIGHER EDUCATION

From Internationalization Drift to Ethical Global Engagement

Edited by Melanie Agnew and Jos Beelen

NEW YORK AND LONDON

Designed cover image: Getty Images

First published 2026
by Routledge
605 Third Avenue, New York, NY 10158

and by Routledge
4 Park Square, Milton Park, Abingdon, Oxon, OX14 4RN

Routledge is an imprint of the Taylor & Francis Group, an informa business

© 2026 selection and editorial matter, Melanie Agnew and Jos Beelan individual chapters, the contributors

The right of Melanie Agnew and Jos Beelan to be identified as the authors of the editorial material, and of the authors for their individual chapters, has been asserted in accordance with sections 77 and 78 of the Copyright, Designs and Patents Act 1988.

All rights reserved. No part of this book may be reprinted or reproduced or utilised in any form or by any electronic, mechanical, or other means, now known or hereafter invented, including photocopying and recording, or in any information storage or retrieval system, without permission in writing from the publishers.

Trademark notice: Product or corporate names may be trademarks or registered trademarks, and are used only for identification and explanation without intent to infringe.

ISBN: 978-1-138-65428-0 (hbk)
ISBN: 978-1-138-65429-7 (pbk)
ISBN: 978-1-315-62333-7 (ebk)

DOI: 10.4324/9781315623337

Typeset in Sabon
by SPi Technologies India Pvt Ltd (Straive)

CONTENTS

List of Contributors	*viii*
Foreword	*xiii*
Preface	*xv*
Acknowledgements	*xxiv*

PART 1
Foundations of Critical Internationalization: Addressing Systems of Drift   **1**

1 Cultural Readiness for Internationalization (CRI)   3
  Melanie Agnew

2 Critical Approaches to Internationalization of Higher Education   26
  Jos Beelen

3 University Governance and Internationalization: Navigating Disciplinary Cultures and Power Dynamics   46
  Melanie Agnew

PART 2
Strategic Dimensions of Internationalization: Critical and Cultural Readiness Approaches 71

4 A Critical Approach to Internationalization of Teaching and Learning 73
   Jos Beelen

5 Exploring Incoming Mobility through a Critical and Inclusive Internationalization Lens 91
   Eva Janebová, Christopher Johnstone, and Thi Nguyen

6 A Critical Approach to Research into Internationalization from a Global South Perspective 114
   Lynette Jacobs, Nelia Oosthuysen, Cornelius Hagenmeier, and Tafadzwa Ruzive

7 International Development, Higher Education's Third Mission and the Internationalization of Service: Toward an International Community-Centered University Service Model 134
   Julian Prieto and Annie Everett

8 Collaborative Partnerships: Epistemic Fluency, Transcultural Competence and the Sustainability of Identity 165
   Anne Carr, Gabriela B. Bonilla Chumbi, Matias Abad, Patricia Tineo, Pilar Constanzo, Antonina Bulyna, Jorge R. Lemos Shlotter, Athena Alchazidu, Katerina Chudova, William A. Booth, Olena Yasynetska, Oleh Shlapakov, Bahar Aksu, and Oguzhan Yilmaz

9 Assessing Risks and Monitoring International Student Recruitment Partners: Toward Ethical Engagement with Education Agents 183
   Pii-Tuulia Nikula

10 Beyond Metrics: A Critical Framework for Evaluating
   Higher Education Internationalization   197
   Melanie Agnew, Christopher Fuglestad, and
   Megan Lochhead

11 Leadership: A Call to Action   219
   Melanie Agnew and Moreen Carvan

12 Conclusion: Looking Back, Looking Forward   247
   Melanie Agnew and Jos Beelen

Index   255

CONTRIBUTORS

Matias Abad is a full professor at Universidad del Azuay (Ecuador), where he teaches at the School of International Studies. He is a PhD candidate in Business Administration at Universidad Nacional de Rosario and holds a Master's degree in Latin American Studies from Universidad de Salamanca.

Melanie Agnew is an organizational change consultant with 25 years of academic and administrative leadership in higher education. She partners with institutions to transform their aspirations into achievable strategies and sustainable outcomes. Her aim is to help individuals, teams, and organizations through personal and collective changes that are most important to them.

Bahar Aksu is a lecturer in TESOL at Erzincan Binali Yıldırım University, Türkiye. Her research mainly focuses on second language acquisition, phonetics, and sociolinguistics.

Athena Alchazidu is a professor assistant from the Language Centre at Masaryk University, Brno, Czech Republic. Her field of academic interest includes Cultural studies, particularly Latinamerican History, Culture, and Society. In her research, she focuses on the literary and oral traditions, including indigenous orality and other traditional manifestations proper to indigenous ethnic groups and minority communities.

Jos Beelen is Professor of Global Learning at The Hague University of Applied Sciences. He is a Visiting Professor at Coventry University, at

Western Norway University of Applied Sciences and at the University of the Free State. Jos leads a research group that explores internationalization at home, particularly the skills of lecturers to develop and teach internationalized curricula.

William A. Booth is a Lecturer in Latin American History at University College London paying particular attention to socialism and communism during the Cold War era.

Antonina Bulyna is Assistant Professor at the Department of English Philology, deputy head of the International Relations Department at Uzhhorod National University (UzhNU), in Ukraine. She holds a Master's Degree in Philology with honors in "Language and Literature" (English) obtained from UzhNU, with 17 years of work experience. She researches queer, alienation, grotesque; English language and literature.

Anne Carr is Associate Professor at the University of Azuay, Cuenca, Ecuador and member of the international Studies Faculty with teaching, research, and service interests in critical internationalization, interdisciplinary collaboration, and epistemic justice issues in inclusive teaching and learning.

Moreen Carvan is an associate professor and Vice President for Academic and Faculty Affairs at Rosalind Franklin University of Medicine and Science in the USA. Her teaching, research, and practice of systems of science education and higher education span four decades of lived experience at the local, state, and national levels.

Katerina Chudova is Head of the Language Centre Unit at the Faculty of Law, Masaryk University, with 20 years of teaching experience. She specializes in legal English, AI and gamification in language teaching, and academic internationalization. She leads workshops and coordinates summer schools on creativity and professional development in education.

Gabriela B. Bonilla Chumbi is a PhD student in Education at Universidad del Azuay (Cuenca - Ecuador). She holds a bachelor's degree in International Studies and a master's degree in International Business. She teaches courses in the areas of International Cooperation and International Relations. In her research, she focuses on migration, cross cultural communication, and international cooperation.

Pilar Constanzo is a specialist in Higher Education and Doctor in Tourism. She has been working for 29 years in tourism activities, as academic director, faculty, and as consultant for different projects. She is a part-time professor at the School of Tourism of the Pontificia Universidad Católica Madre y Maestra in the Dominican Rebublic.

Annie Everett earned her Ph.D. candidate in Higher Education from The Pennsylvania State University in 2025. Her work prioritizes research *with* international college students enrolled in U.S. institutions, focusing on issues related to accreditation and the assessment of student learning, curriculum development and instructional praxis, and academic inclusion in diverse educational environments. https://orcid.org/0000-0002-6012-9979

Christopher Fuglestad is an international education practitioner with over a decade of experience in global health, risk, and safety. He holds BA degrees in International Studies and French, a Master of Professional French Studies in International Education, and serves as an Assistant Editor for the Critical Internationalization Studies Network (CISN).

Cornelius Hagenmeier is Head of Internationalisation at the Mittweida University of Applied Sciences and Research Fellow of the University of the Free State in South Africa. He is an internationalisation of higher education expert and jurist with strong ties to both the South African and German legal systems.

Lynette Jacobs is serving as the interim Director of the Office for International Affairs at the University of the Free State in South Africa, where she also leads research on internationalisation of higher education.

Eva Janebová is the Founding Director of the Mestenhauser Institute for International Collaboration and an Assistant Professor at Palacky University. She serves as Chair of Publications Committee at EAIE and on the International Advisory Board of Morgan State. Among other, she co-authored "Mapping the Dimensions of Inclusive Internationalization" in *Inequalities in Study Abroad* and "The Challenge of Culture" in <u>Mestenhauser and the Possibilities of International Education</u>.

Christopher Johnstone is an Associate Professor in the University of Minnesota's Comparative and International Development Education program. He teaches classes on global higher education and the Sustainable Development Goals. He has conducted research or performed evaluations on six continents on topics of inclusive education and the internationalization of higher education.

Megan Lochhead is an educational leader specializing in outcomes-based curriculum design at the University of British Columbia Okanagan in Canada. With over a decade of experience, she provides strategic leadership to improve student learning and educational outcomes. Megan is pursuing her PhD, researching innovative approaches to assessing personal responsibility in undergraduate science.

Thi Nguyen is a PhD candidate and course instructor at the University of Minnesota-Twin Cities. Her research interests include critical internationalization studies, sustainability education, and student identity development in transnational contexts. Prior to her doctoral studies, Thi was a graduate admissions counselor at the Middlebury Institute of International Studies.

Pii-Tuulia Nikula is Associate Professor at Eastern Institute of Technology in New Zealand. Most of Pii-Tuulia's research explores ethical issues and sustainability questions associated with the international education sector. Her work on education agents has been published in international journals and books.

Nelia Oosthuysen is the portfolio leader for Research and Systems Management in the Office for International Affairs at the University of the Free State, South Africa. She holds a Master of Commerce (MCom) in Computer Science and a Postgraduate Certificate in Education. She combines her digital skills and analytical expertise to analyze research trends and support the internationalization project at the UFS.

Julian Prieto earned his Ph.D. in Education Policy and Leadership with a dual title in Transdisciplinary Research on the Environment and Society from The Pennsylvania State University in 2025. His research focuses on the science diplomacy of climate change, internationalization of higher education, and the role of scientific diasporas in research partnerships. https://orcid.org/0000-0002-4983-9291

Tafadzwa Ruzive is a Post Doctoral fellow in the Office for International Affairs of the University of the Free State, South Africa. He is specializing in Higher Education Internationalization policy dynamics as well as the operationalization of Credit Systems in Higher Education. Tafadzwa harnesses knowledge and experience from Development Finance and System Dynamics to develop innovative policy and practice to further the higher education internationalization agenda.

Oleh Shlapakov is Associate Professor at the Horlivka Institute for Foreign Languages of State Higher Education Institution "Donbas State Pedagogical University" (Dnipro, Ukraine) PhD (2011); research interests: sociolinguistics, psycholinguistics, speech genres, translation studies, and history of translation.

Jorge R. Lemos Shlotter is a research professor at Universidad Católica de Salta (Argentina) and a student in Higher Education PhD program. He holds a Master Degree in TEFL of UNEATLÁNTICO (Spain). He carries out research in Higher Education Internationalization, Systemic-Functional Grammar, and Linguistics lectures on these fields in conferences.

Patricia Tineo is a research professor at the Pontificia Universidad Católica Madre y Maestra (PUCMM) in the Dominican Republic. Master in Service Leadership and Innovation (PUCMM- RIT), graduated with honors in Hotel Administration (PUCMM), with more than 30 years of work experience. Carries out different types of research, studies and training, preparation of manuals, diagnoses, evaluations, and audits.

Olena Yasynetska is an Associate Professor Horlivka Institute for Foreign Languages, Ukraine with an MA in Linguistics (USA, 2005) and a PhD in Translation Studies (Ukraine, 2009). She has been teaching English and Translation since 1999, specializing in Applied Translation Studies, supervising translation internships, and guiding student research.

Oguzhan Yilmaz is a faculty member at Erzincan Binali Yıldırım University in Türkiye. He conducts research in the field of children's literature, with a particular focus on problem-oriented themes such as war and migration.

FOREWORD

Sharon Stein
Associate Professor, Professor of Climate Complexity and Coloniality, Department of Educational Studies, Faculty of Education, University of British Columbia (Canada), Musqueam Territory.

Over the past decade, critical approaches to internationalization have received increasing attention from higher education scholars. These interventions have been accompanied by a parallel shift toward interdisciplinary and internationalized research focused on leadership development in higher education. Together, these changes have encouraged deepened consideration of the power imbalances in resources, representations, and relationships within the context of higher education internationalization. Beyond research, these more critical approaches to international engagements, knowledge production, and flows of scholars and students have infused policy and practice as well, yet it is often more difficult to assess in what ways and to what effect. Indeed, even when higher education institutions adopt a more public critical stance to their internationalization efforts, these shifts can be symbolic and tokenistic, changing the "window dressing" on what remains an otherwise neoliberal and neocolonial approach.

This edited volume speaks directly and clearly to these matters, asking how internationalization and critical approaches to internationalization, in particular, have and can infuse higher education practice. The contributing authors bring nuanced and power-informed analyses to the internationalization of research, teaching, service, governance, evaluation, and leadership. In doing so, they draw readers' attention to the enduring inequities that characterize this work and identify both barriers and pathways to meaningful transformation. They also offer generative frameworks and examples of "next practices" for those engaged in this work.

These chapters remind us of the enduring imperative and difficulties of shifting colonial institutional cultures and activities toward educational approaches prioritizing reciprocity and respect for global differences and meeting the priorities of systemically marginalized communities. This is no surprise, given that—as many contributors point out—internationalization is often driven by a search for revenues given declining public funding and the pressures of global rankings, international reputation-building, and student recruitment. Higher education is also facing the impacts of increased protectionism and xenophobia in Western nations. As anxious publics feel the crunch of austerity, housing and food insecurity, and inflation, international students and scholars become easy scapegoats for their frustrations.

For instance, in my context in what is currently known as Canada, the government has recently instituted caps on international study permits. International students have been unfairly blamed for housing shortages, and public support for international student migration is rapidly declining. International students, treated in the post-World War II era paternalistically as objects of "charity" (development) by universities and then as sources of "cash" (income) in an era of public funding decline, are now framed as "competition" (Stein & Andreotti, 2016). Notably, each of these categories—cash, charity, and competition—is grounded in an enduring modern/colonial global imaginary in which Western people are viewed as more advanced and important than their non-Western peers, and Western knowledge is treated as universally valuable and relevant. Even in their spirited defenses of international students' right to mobility, many institutions and scholars fall back into a logic that treats the students as sources of cash or charity, rather than offer a more educational or equity-oriented response.

When I founded the Critical Internationalization Studies Network in 2018, I did so out of recognition of the need for more spaces in which scholars and practitioners could address the complexities and challenges of bringing critical perspectives to our research, teaching, and practice. Now, more than ever, we need robust, rigorous conversations with multiple perspectives on possible futures of internationalization in a world that is increasingly uncertain, unequal, and polarized. New pressures, such as the impacts of climate change and increasing global conflict, add further challenges as well as renewed urgency to our ability to engage these conversations with emotional maturity, relational rigour, and self-reflexivity.

As Agnew and Carvan note in their contribution to this book, "How one thinks about internationalization will ultimately support or impede organizational change. In short, organizational change requires its membership to learn to do things differently." These and the other contributing authors to this book encourage scholars and practitioners of internationalization, and higher education in general, to learn to do things differently. Beyond symbolic gestures of inclusion, they invite us to ask how we can shift the very fabric of our institutions toward more equitable, ethical, and educational priorities and outcomes. Those of us invested in livable futures on our finite, fragile planet would be wise to take up this invitation.

PREFACE

Melanie's Journey

I remember like it was yesterday that first faculty meeting of the term so many years ago. Upon walking into the faculty conference room, the tension was far too obvious as many sat with quiet apprehension, others avoiding eye contact, and some squirming in their seats. The palpable disquiet in the room was a result of one of the line items on the agenda.

The agenda item seemed deceptively simple: "define urban mission". Yet this item would reveal the complex intersections of many related factors of university culture and the social, political, and economic forces bearing on this institution. As it turned out, the eventual debate, demonstrated the ongoing struggles of power, colonialism, disciplinary divergence, structural constraints, professional identity and territory, and epistemic and paradigm differences. All because of a single agenda item.

This definitional deadlock revealed more than just academic territory disputes—it exposed how neoliberal forces shape institutional priorities and how colonial legacies persist in academic structures. Power dynamics came into play quite quickly and visibly. Market pressures drove tensions around institutional identity, while conflicts emerged between traditional academic values and market-oriented planning. These dynamics manifested in heated debates over what "counted" as urban engagement, all underscored by persistent power and gender dynamics that formed the foundation of the continuing debate. What crystallized for me in that charged climate was not just the difficulty of organizational change, but its fundamentally disruptive nature in systems built to resist it.

As I observed these dynamics, my own experience as a Canadian immigrant navigating American culture provided an unexpected lens. These personal and professional intersections of culture, power, and change would ultimately shape my research on internationalization of higher education. The cultural transitions I faced as a young professional woman—from understanding a new health care system to adapting to different workplace norms, to raising my children in another country some 2000 miles away from my extended family, my would-be support system—paralleled the institutional struggles with change that I was witness to and a part of.

Our university's adoption of an urban mission forced us into difficult and oftentimes uncomfortable conversations about its meaning and implications. As these discussions unfolded, a crucial question came to mind: "Who is being served, and for what purposes?" These deliberations revealed individual and group values, beliefs, and assumptions about institutional change that would eventually become central to my research.

As these faculty meeting debates unfolded, I was immersed in doctoral studies in Higher Education Leadership, taking courses on topics such as Organizational Theory and Internationalization of Higher Education. Each faculty meeting became a case study in how neoliberal ideologies and market-driven approaches in education increasingly colonize academic spaces.

A pivotal moment crystallized these power dynamics when the question of "water" came into the debate in defining urban education. One professor declared, "Water is water wherever it is in the world!" Without missing a beat, another professor asserted, "Water takes on different meanings in regions where water is scarce and polluted", suggesting that water in less developed regions of the world might think differently about water than we did in our city that offered us unlimited filtered clean drinking water. I witnessed how privileged Western epistemologies can often silence marginalized perspectives and lived experiences.

Through these encounters, I began to see how internationalization often operates as a conduit for neocolonial practices in higher education. The seemingly innocent question of "Who is served, and for what purpose?" revealed darker truths about how market ideologies reduce international students to commodities, how institutional self-interest can corrupt cultural exchange, and how our well-intentioned practices often perpetuate global inequities. This critical awakening challenged not just the assumed benevolence of internationalization, but its role in maintaining power imbalances in perpetuating global inequities.

Jos Joins the Journey

The relevance of these critical insights was starkly illustrated at the 2022 European Association for International Education (EAIE) conference in

Barcelona. Alongside Stephanie Doscher, Jos Beelen and I presented on *Internationalization Drift*—a concept describing how market and government forces pull internationalization away from its foundational educational aims and how this phenomenon perpetuates harmful global patterns of education. Using Sharon Stein, Andreotti, Bruce, and Suša's (2016) framework of four articulations of internationalization—Global Knowledge Economy, Global Public Good, Anti-oppressive, and Relational Translocalism—we conducted a revealing exercise with conference participants.

Through a simple but powerful body-voting activity, we first asked participants to physically position themselves to indicate their *institution's* motivational drivers for engaging in internationalization. We then asked participants to vote for their *personal* motivational driver. The discrepancies between institutional and personal motivations were telling, as was the divide between the four articulations. Of approximately 60 participants, 85% of the participants perceived their institution's motivations were aligned with the Global Knowledge Economy while personal motivations revealed roughly 75% of participants aligned with the Global Public Good articulations.

This glaring incongruence between institutional and personal motivations revealed the extent to which they may differ on a much higher scale, locally, regionally, and globally. This is important for several reasons. It suggests that:

1 International higher education has a strong market orientation and educational aims are perceived as a low institutional priority.
2 There is often incongruence between what an institution says it does (espoused mission) and what it does (enacted mission).
3 There is incongruence in values between the individual and their institution, highlighting potential areas of intrapersonal conflict as well as conflict and resistance concerning organizational mission and change.
4 There are alarmingly few individuals voted in the Anti-oppressive (three people) or the Relational Translocalism (one person) articulations in response to both the personal and institutional motivations to engage in internationalization. The low representation reveals the extent to which individuals and institutions work to perpetuate systems of oppression in higher education.

Jos and I realized that we had a common research agenda concerning *internationalization drift* of higher education and understood the important implications for research, policy, and practice. Thus, we set out to identify other authors who could offer a critical analysis of internationalization of higher education policy and practice, and who might have the time and resources to commit to this project.

That first faculty meeting, with its charged atmosphere and seemingly straightforward agenda, was more than an introduction to the university's cultural, political, and structural challenges—it was a microcosm of the deeper issues I would later confront through my professional work and research. The tension, debates, and clashing perspectives revealed how power dynamics, entrenched beliefs, and varying motivations influence decision-making and change. These early encounters laid the foundation for what would become the Cultural Readiness for Internationalization change model, described in Chapter 1. The CRI model is a framework that emerged from witnessing firsthand how institutional transformation demands more than just new policies. It requires excavating and confronting the deeply rooted power structures that silently shape our academic spaces.

As I reflect on my path from that conference room meeting to my current research, I recognize how my own experiences as a scholar, administrator, immigrant, mother, and wife have deepened my understanding of these challenges, reinforcing the critical importance of examining not just what we do in our internationalization efforts, but why and how we do it, and most importantly, who we serve in the process. Through this lens, I've come to see how institutions, driven by both personal and collective missions, must thoughtfully navigate the push and pull between their ideals and external market forces, always mindful of the voices and perspectives that might otherwise be silenced in the process.

What to Expect in this Volume

This volume outlines a comprehensive exploration of higher education internationalization framed within organizational theory, critical frameworks, and real-world case studies. Throughout the chapters, you will encounter the introduction of the term "internationalization drift" and discover practical recommendations for ethical policy and practice that address this phenomenon.

We begin by building a strong theoretical foundation through three interconnected chapters. The first introduces you to the Cultural Readiness for Internationalization (CRI) change model, providing frameworks for organizational culture and change theory and systems theory to guide subsequent discussion. The second chapter delves into critical approaches and frameworks, equipping you with essential analytical tools. The third chapter examines the complex power dynamics within university governance including a robust discussion on how internationalization manifests differently across academic disciplines. This discussion offers important considerations for engaging faculty-as-stewards of internationalization.

The volume then transitions to a substantive collection of case studies and frameworks, where contributing authors apply organizational change theory and critical frameworks to examine key aspects of internationalization. You'll explore internationalization of the curriculum at home, investigate student mobility programs framed in inclusive internationalization, and analyze research and scholarship initiatives juxtaposing Global North and Global South perspectives. The discussion extends to international development as service, collaborative partnerships, risk management, monitoring systems, evaluation methods, and a leadership call-to-action. Each of these topics is examined through a critical lens, revealing both challenges and opportunities.

Every chapter in this second section follows a thoughtful progression. You'll see how different aspects of the CRI change model apply to real-world situations, engage with critical analysis of specific cases or frameworks, and discover practical implications for ethical policy and practice that you can apply to your own work.

To make the most of this volume, readers should have some foundational understanding of internationalization principles, cultural transformation processes, critical approaches, and the interplay of the triple helix in higher education. This background will enhance your ability to engage with the complex ideas and analyses presented.

By the time you complete the reading of this volume, you will have gained a deep understanding of the CRI model as an effective tool for driving organizational culture change in internationalization efforts. You'll develop a sophisticated understanding of critical approaches to internationalization and recognize the subtle power dynamics at play within higher education institutions. Importantly, you will comprehend how market and government forces shape internationalization initiatives and develop a framework for implementing ethical policies and practices in your own context.

This edited collection, *Critical Internationalization of Higher Education: From Internationalization Drift to Ethical Global Engagement* advocates for dismantling neocolonial practices in international education. Each chapter utilizes organizational and critical frameworks to demonstrate ways in which motivations to engage in internationalization can yield considerations for implications for research and ethical practices. We recommend reading Chapters 1–3 as together they provide the reader with organizational and critical theory models and frameworks for which to discern additional meaning from the remaining chapters.

The remaining chapters provide case studies and other research on the major strategies of internationalization. The final chapter urges our professional community to work together in building collective capacity for leadership essential for positioning higher education in response to global challenges while staying true to their core educational purpose.

Chapter 1 explains and demonstrates the effectiveness of the CRI model in realizing transformational culture change supporting internationalization. The conceptual framework of the CRI model draws on ideology, organizational culture, and university culture (a specific subset of organizational culture) and is situated in systems theory. The CRI model acknowledges the need for universities to take a critical approach to internationalization to balance and engage multiple diverse stakeholders across local, national, and global contexts. Claude Version 3 was used in Chapter 1 to reduce word count.

Chapter 2 presents critical approaches and calls to values within international higher education as they developed over time. This chapter also contains a case study of critical internationalization in the Netherlands, where critical actions are undertaken in a higher education landscape that has increasingly become neoliberal and where universities' autonomy clash with regulation in a right-wing political climate.

Chapter 3 explores the complex relationship between university culture, governance structures, and internationalization of higher education. It analyzes university governance and power dynamics through four primary structural sub-cultures—hierarchical, anarchical, monarchical, oligarchic—that shape institutional operations and decision-making processes. Academic disciplines are discussed in relation to faculty engagement highlighting the significant variation across hard and soft disciplines. Key challenges, including the marginalization of humanities and threats to academic freedom, are discussed emphasizing the need to balance economic pressures with broader educational aims while fostering inclusive environments that value diverse perspectives.

Chapter 4 discusses internationalization of the curriculum at home and explores to what extent internationalized teaching and learning have become focused on outcomes rather than on activities. The chapter explores misconceptions, the type of leadership action that is needed to achieve internationalization in departments, who the stakeholders are, and what the role of the disciplines is. Virtual Exchange and Collaborative Online International Learning (COIL) have become prominent within internationalized curricula and have been generally positively received but there are questions about the inclusive character of these virtual forms of learning and their exact role in the internationalization of teaching and learning.

Chapter 5 connects two contemporary concepts in internationalization literature: critical internationalization and inclusive internationalization. The organizing framework draws from Janebova and Johnstone's (2020) "Dimensions of Inclusive Internationalisation". Janebova and Johnstone's work was itself informed by previous attempts at mapping critical internationalization (Stein et al., 2016) and utilizes social cartographic methods to both seek connections and draw boundaries between concepts and dimensions. The chapter concludes with case examples of mobility within the Czech context. As a full-fledged member of the European Union (EU) since 2004, Czechia's higher education institutions have enjoyed unfettered access to Bologna and other EU member state opportunities. Despite this, mobility in the Czech framework has been inconsistently implemented. The authors analyze various aspects of Czech mobility through their framework of inclusive internationalization, which is informed by criticality of the field.

Chapter 6 aims to critically examine the current state of internationalization research in higher education, juxtaposing discourses from the Global North and the Global South over the past decades. The authors then consider how a recent contextual definition of internationalization of Higher Education in South Africa is impacting the discourse and how the stratified discourses can come together. Through a focus on South Africa within the broader Global South and discourse at large, the authors reflect on the progress made to advance local agendas as well as global agendas in this space.

Chapter 7 explores the intersection of international development, higher education's third mission, and critical scholarship on the internationalization of service. Drawing on frameworks like the U.S. Cooperative Extension System and the Cultural Readiness for Internationalization (CRI) (Agnew & VanBalkom, 2009) change model, we highlight the importance of ethical, community-centered service frameworks. Emphasizing equitable partnerships, inclusive decision-making, and robust accountability, the chapter advocates for a transformative discourse in global engagement, guiding higher education institutions toward more just and ethically grounded international service activities.

Chapter 8 explores a transdisciplinary research partnership project involving universities across eight countries, focusing on student identity and migration. Through virtual sessions, the study examined how students negotiate identity in an era of global mobility. Utilizing innovative methodologies like "Migrants' Suitcase Stories", the project created a platform for cross-cultural dialogue, developing students' epistemic fluency and understanding of global migration challenges.

Chapter 9 examines risk assessment and monitoring in ethical internationalization of higher education, focusing on institutions' use of for-profit education agents to recruit international students. When institutions contract these third parties, various agency problems and ethical challenges arise. The chapter analyzes how institutions can balance financial goals with ethical considerations while protecting student interests. It evaluates institutions' capacity to maintain ethical practices with agents through risk assessment and monitoring, concluding with recommendations for research and practice.

Chapter 10 introduces a critical evaluation model for higher education internationalization. It examines tensions between educational missions and market-driven approaches, drawing on existing frameworks, 1) internationalization articulations and 2) the Cultural Readiness for Internationalization (CRI) change model. The critical evaluation model was developed to address "internationalization drift", highlighting how global education increasingly prioritizes economic goals over cultural exchange and mutual understanding, potentially perpetuating systemic inequities and persistent power imbalances.

Chapter 11 traces higher education's evolution from medieval origins to its contemporary role, positioning internationalization as an emerging fourth macro mission. The authors analyze universities' transformation from teaching-focused institutions to complex organizations serving multiple societal purposes. Examining the shift from scholasticism through postmodernism, they demonstrate how internationalization has drifted from educational foundations toward market-driven goals. The chapter concludes by calling for collective leadership to guide higher education in addressing global challenges while maintaining its educational mission.

Chapter 12 synthesizes major themes and insights across the book, tracing higher education internationalization's evolution from medieval origins to its current market-driven state. Through multi-level analysis, it reveals how market ideology has compromised academic missions and created systemic inequities. The authors advocate for transformative leadership and propose internationalization as higher education's fourth mission to address ecological, social, and cultural divides while fostering sustainable and equitable global engagement.

We have taken a critical stance on internationalization of higher education in this manuscript to demonstrate, in part, the extent to which market-driven ideology is often prioritized over foundational educational values. In doing so, we have highlighted implications for ethical policies and practices in each chapter to guide practitioners in their internationalization work.

One of the joys of collecting this volume was that we worked with contributors with positions ranging from PhD students to postdocs, Assistant Professors, and Full Professors, all with their specific takes on the topic. They are affiliated with institutions in Argentina, Canada, the Dominican Republic, the Czech Republic, Ecuador, New Zealand, The Netherlands, South Africa, Turkey, Ukraine, the United Kingdom, and the United States of America. But they represent not only their institutions but also their backgrounds, which may be local but also from the other side of the world, which makes this book a colorful kaleidoscope of international higher education.

This book speaks to all who are leaders and champions of internationalization of higher education for its capacity to meet contemporary global challenges while maintaining its foundational educational mission.

This book serves three primary audiences—campus leaders responsible for internationalization (including senior leadership, deans, department chairs, faculty, and international office staff); professionals working across organizational boundaries who drive internationalization through visioning, policy, planning, and assessment; and graduate students researching international education. It provides frameworks and evidence-based practices to advance ethical internationalization while countering market-driven trends, reaching out to both formal leaders and informal champions passionate about reversing internationalization drift on their campuses.

ACKNOWLEDGEMENTS

Melanie's Acknowledgements

This work would never have come to fruition without the unwavering support and endless patience of my loving partner, Doug, and our wonderful children, Lauren and partner Ben, Lindsey, and Sandon and his partner Justine. Their encouragement and understanding throughout this journey have been my foundation. While they may share my relief at seeing this project completed, their steadfast belief in me made all the difference. I am profoundly grateful to have such an incredible family by my side.

And to my radiant granddaughter, Cecelia Bay, who represents the next generation of our family, to the grandchildren yet to come, and to all future generations: this book is primarily for you.

I am deeply indebted to Eveke de Louw, Beth Dobkin, Katy Heyning, Sabine Klahr, Hilary Landorf, Donna Pasternak, Michael Santarosa, and Francine Tompkins for their thoughtful review of my work. Their perceptive feedback and timely contributions significantly enhanced the quality of this manuscript. I am also grateful to Joan Kunicki, Sandra Rincón, and Jane Marko, who have served as critical friends and lifelong supporters of my work. Finally, I owe a special debt of gratitude to Moreen Carvan and Duffie VanBalkom, whose mentorship and professional guidance have profoundly shaped my thinking and approach. Their wisdom and generosity in sharing their expertise have been invaluable to my professional journey.

Jos' Acknowledgements

Collaborating on this book gave me an opportunity, once again to work with some of my closest colleagues, Lynette Jacobs at the University of the Free State, Eva Janebová at the Mestenhauser Institute, and Christopher Johnstone at the University of Minnesota.

I would also like to mention the members of my research group Global Learning at The Hague University of Applied Sciences. Working with them and seeing them grow as researchers is a great source of both satisfaction and inspiration.

My colleagues at EAIE have been an inspiration for many years, particularly those involved with first the Special Interest Group Internationalisation at Home, then the Expert Community and now the Thematic Committee Teaching, Learning and Curriculum.

Finally, engaging with these critical perspectives made me think about the future of higher education and indeed the future in general in which my children, grandchild, and my niece Elaine will live.

Together

We would also like to express our deepest admiration for the dedicated researchers and practitioners in higher education internationalization, at any level, who work tirelessly to advance our field while preserving its core educational values. This means a lot to us. Their commitment to principled leadership continues to inspire and guide our collective work.

PART 1

Foundations of Critical Internationalization

Addressing Systems of Drift

1
CULTURAL READINESS FOR INTERNATIONALIZATION (CRI)

Melanie Agnew

Introduction

The evolution of higher education from its medieval origins through its emerging role in the 21st century reveals a complex transformation, particularly in its internationalization mission. While universities have evolved from teaching-focused institutions to complex organizations serving multiple societal purposes, the debate surrounding internationalization's definition and purpose continues to evolve in significant ways.

The 900-year evolution of higher education's macro missions from scholasticism through humanism to postmodernism[1] provides an essential context for understanding contemporary internationalization debates. Modern critiques highlight how market forces and governmental policies have shifted internationalization of higher education away from its educational foundations, creating the current threat of *internationalization drift*.[2] The multiplicity of goals within higher education creates tensions that are evident in ongoing scholarly discourse, particularly in critiques of how internationalization is conceptualized and implemented. Internationalization drift calls for collective leadership from the internationalization community to guide higher education's evolution in meeting contemporary global challenges and simultaneously maintain its foundational educational mission.

Marginson's (2023) critique of Knight's widely accepted definition highlights this drift, arguing that it is "overly normative and insufficiently explanatory, uses a truncated geography, claims a universality that cannot be achieved, and when applied in the practices of Euro-American higher education has regressive effects in the non-Euro-American world" (p. 3).

DOI: 10.4324/9781315623337-2

The paradox lies in how Knight's definition, despite these shortcomings, has shaped the field since the 1990s and been broadly adopted by scholars and professional organizations.

The four key issues Marginson identifies—problematic purpose, alignment with neoliberal governmental policies, use of seemingly universal terms that protect neoliberal agendas, and the perpetuation of global higher education hierarchies—reflect how internationalization has drifted from its educational foundations. These problems are expressed as self-interest motivations that primarily benefits Western/Northern interests while neglecting others. As an alternative, Marginson proposes that definitions should be conceptually sound and practical for both researchers and practitioners, "broadly illuminating reality, enabling people to make up their own minds about issues of justice" (p. 10).

How internationalization is defined shapes policies, practices, and research in the field. To improve cross-border higher education, institutions should maintain coherence in their policies and practices while providing clarity in explanations of their goals (Marginson, 2023; Sporn, 1996). It is important that they shape reciprocal relationships more effectively and equitably, and integrate international, global, and worldwide perspectives at multiple scales (Marginson, 2023; Stein et al., 2016).

A promising solution emerges through the Cultural Readiness for Internationalization (CRI) model (Agnew & VanBalkom, 2009), an organizational change framework that positions institutional culture and context at the heart of its design. The CRI model offers a bottom-up top-supported and structured approach to address internationalization drift. It helps institutions align their international initiatives with their unique internal culture in relation to their external, enabling environment. This approach maintains internal coherence in policies and practices while acknowledging and working within complex institutional dynamics. The need to address internationalization drift while respecting institutional uniqueness makes the CRI model particularly relevant in today's higher education landscape.

Through critical and organizational frameworks like the CRI model, institutions can create more reciprocal relationships that are effective and equitable, integrating international, global, and worldwide perspectives at multiple scales while addressing the challenges of internationalization drift.

The Cultural Readiness for Internationalization (CRI) Change Model

The CRI change model is situated in the dynamic interplay between internal culture and the external environment (Figure 1.1). It asserts that creating favorable conditions can create an institutional culture that is "ready" to advance internationalization, given the context in which it exists. The CRI

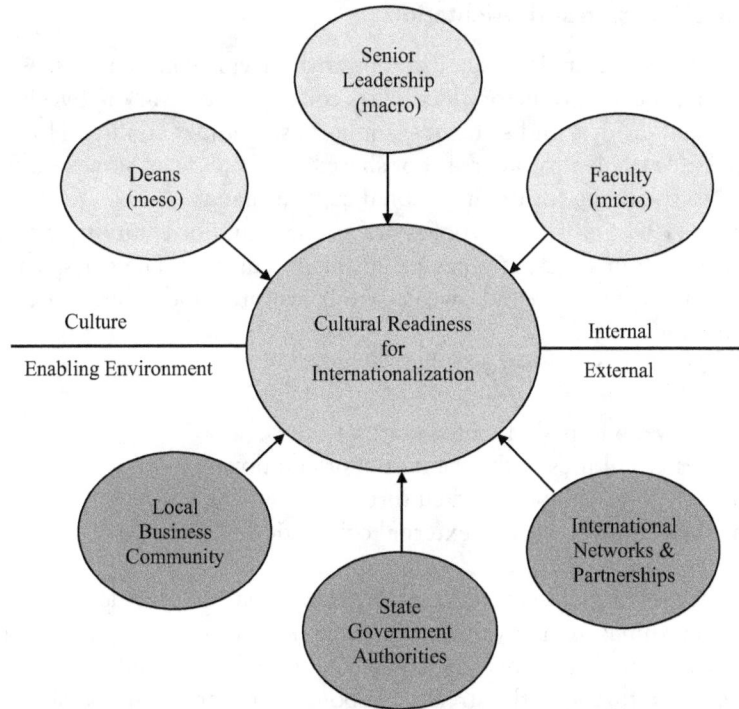

FIGURE 1.1   Cultural Readiness for Internationalization Change Model.

model was developed to operationalize cohesion and orientation of university culture, to view the process and measure the progress of internationalization, and to ensure sound strategy in the coordination and integration of internationalization policies and practices. Because the CRI model considers institutional culture and context, it has high utility for all institutional types and sizes, and any organization planning strategic change using a cultural framework.

The CRI model utilizes three levels of analysis framed in ideology, organizational culture, and university culture within an institution of higher education (internal)—the macro (senior leadership), the meso (deans), and the micro (faculty). The internal analysis is conducted simultaneously in relation to the external, or enabling, environment. The enabling environment considers the motivations, goals, and drivers of market, government, and international organizations. This multilevel representation of internationalization offers a convenient yet purposeful orientation to understanding and advancing internationalization. The CRI model therefore is highly adaptive, flexible, and considers context and culture in the dynamic processes of organizational change supporting internationalization.

Cultural Cohesion and Orientation

Universities are complex organizations with diverse communities. Within them, multiple contradictory ideologies coexist, values vary between individuals and groups, and structural supports sometimes conflict. However, it is possible to identify a core set of shared values that can serve as a foundation for planning for organizational culture change.

Sporn (1996) created a typology of strength and orientation of culture inclusive of four different types of university cultures. The classifications within the typology include weak–strong cultures and internal–external orientations.

The typology is framed as follows:

- incohesive, internally focused cultures,
- incohesive cultures with an external orientation
- cohesive, internally focused cultures
- cohesive cultures with an external orientation

The weak–strong classification of organizational culture describes how unified a group is in their values, beliefs, goals, and actions. Cohesion measures how strongly members are connected to each other and committed to shared goals. It reflects the strength of bonds between group members and their collective approach to taking action and experiencing together its consequences (Chen & Starosta, 1996; Johnson & Johnson, 2009; Tajfel & Turner, 1979; Triandis, 1995).

Sporn's (1996) "weak–strong" terminology has been adapted to "incohesive-cohesive" to better describe the extent to which individuals share values, beliefs, and attitudes regarding internationalization as depicted in Table 1.1. Additionally, the framework examines whether a culture has an internal orientation (focused on their immediate program, department, or school, campus) or primarily an external orientation (responding to outside factors). In higher education, the external environment includes political, economic, social, technological, and competitive factors beyond the institution's direct control. The CRI model operationalizes Sporn's typology by examining both the cohesion level (cohesive/incohesive) and orientation (internal/external) of organizational cultures in the internationalization process.

Incohesive, internally focused cultures have divergent values, beliefs, and attitudes. In higher education, the different values and beliefs are rooted in the various disciplines and expressed in a variety of schools/colleges, departments, programs, and curricula. The culture is focused internally, lacking the external orientation needed to adequately respond and engage with the stakeholders within the external environment.

TABLE 1.1 Typology of Cohesion and Orientation of Culture

Cohesive	Uniform values, beliefs, and attitudes manifested in a shared pattern of behavior where internal activities are concerned. A cohesive, internally focused culture can be identified in the shared beliefs concerning academic freedom, autonomy, tenure and promotion, and shared governance. Uniform values; stable in a stable environment	Shares the same values, beliefs, and attitudes but whose activities are externally oriented. A culture manifesting an external orientation is flexible, adaptive, and negotiates its normative practices as it responds to the external environment. Most adaptive to change
Incohesive	Has divergent values, beliefs, and attitudes. The different values and beliefs are rooted in the various disciplines and expressed in a variety of schools/colleges, departments, programs, and curricula. Most resistive to change	Subcultures have divergent values, beliefs, and attitudes but are focused on the external environment. For some institutions this might mean, for example, that a sub-culture of some faculty is supportive of focused internationalization while others may not be, but the institution is unable to harness existing energies in a focused manner to achieve greater internationalization. Divergent values; responsive to environment
	Internal	External

In an *incohesive culture with an external orientation*, the subcultures have divergent values, beliefs, and attitudes and are focused on the external environment. For some institutions this might mean, for example, that a sub-culture of some faculty is supportive of focused internationalization while others may not be, but the institution is unable to harness existing energies in a focused manner to achieve greater internationalization. Adaptation in response to environmental conditions can still take place with the presence of a sub-culture but an aligned university culture will need to be developed while the external orientation is retained.

A *cohesive, internally* focused culture dominates uniform values, beliefs, and attitudes manifested in a shared pattern of behavior where internal activities are concerned. Within a stable external environment, this is satisfactory to the academic membership until the environment becomes unstable placing new demands on institutional membership. The new demands will challenge existing beliefs, values, and attitudes. Higher education's cohesive, internally focused culture is challenged by the dynamic environment that disrupts its historical normed patterns of behavior causing destabilization within the academic community.

Finally, *a cohesive and externally* oriented culture shares similar values, beliefs, and attitudes but whose activities are externally oriented. A culture manifesting an external orientation is flexible, adaptive, and negotiates its normative practices as it responds to the environment. With little doubt, this culture type is most conducive for successful adaptation to the external environment in which it exists and to which it belongs.

The assumptions associated with this typology are that university cultures with high cohesion are more successful than cultures with low cohesion and externally oriented cultures can more readily adapt to a changing environment than internally oriented cultures. Developing an organizational culture that will invite innovative change and adapt to environmental forces requires strategic plans that are guided by an understanding of the existing institutional culture. Failing to understand university culture relative to the cohesion and orientation jeopardizes the institution's capacity for strategic and meaningful global engagement.

Sporn's typology of university culture, as adapted in the CRI change model, provides a valuable framework for understanding how institutional cohesion and orientation impact a university's ability to adapt and internationalize. The four culture types—ranging from incohesive and internally focused to cohesive and externally focused—offer important insights into the challenges and opportunities institutions face in their internationalization efforts. This framework suggests that universities with high cohesion and external orientation are best positioned to navigate the complex global landscape of higher education.

Ideologies

The first consideration in the CRI change model is ideology. Different ideological perspectives simultaneously motivate engagement in internationalization of higher education institutions. These various approaches are driven by diverse rationales, each grounded in the underlying values and assumptions held by individuals and groups within the academic community. Stier (2004), for example, organized and critiqued ideologies into three categories—instrumentalism, educationalism, and idealism. Stein et al.'s (2016) created and critiqued four articulations—global knowledge economy, global public good, anti-oppressive, and relational translocalism. An analysis of ideologies and articulations of internationalization reveal ways in which some of them can reproduce harmful global patterns despite good intentions. Goals drivers, motivations, and aims of Stein et al.'s (2016) articulation of internationalization are highlighted in Table 1.2.

Ideology is expressed through individual and group behavior. One can identify the underlying assumptions that influence rationales at the individual, institutional, regional, and national levels. For example, in viewing internationalization for the global knowledge economy, Stein et al. (2016) identifies personal motivation focused on self-interest activity such as improving a curriculum vitae (CV) and developing differential human capital for success in a global labor market. Taking another perspective, in viewing internationalization as an anti-oppressive approach, the main personal motivation includes such aspects as acting in solidarity with marginalized people and groups in pursuit of social justice.

Figure 1.2 illustrates how ideologies are underpinned by assumptions. In the first example, personal motivations related to internationalization for the knowledge economy, the self-interest assumptions may be that the academic work will enhance a CV and that a more enhanced CV will strengthen a tenure file in preparation for a promotion. In the second example in Figure 1.2, personal motivations related to anti-oppressive internationalization, the underlying assumptions may include improving the lives of others, rooting out inequities and embracing differences, and/or creating a stronger sense of community. Examining underlying assumptions is necessary to understand motivations at the individual, institutional, regional, and national levels—all that may be operating simultaneously at various strengths.

Stein et al. (2016) proposes mapping social relationships, networks, and dynamics to invite engagement and problematize conversations concerning internationalization. This approach can spark new discussions and challenge existing perspectives on internationalization. Shared beliefs about society, underpinned by ideology, shape what is considered important and influence individual and group interactions. These collective understandings can limit the questions we ask and the solutions we accept. By mapping social structures, we can surface overlooked issues and foster new dialogues. This process allows groups to develop shared language and imagine alternative futures for internationalization efforts. Ultimately, social cartography can be a tool for organizational change by linking current conditions to future aspirations and encouraging fresh perspectives.

TABLE 1.2 Stein et al.'s (2016) Four Articulations of Internationalization

	Internationalization for the Global Knowledge Economy	Internationalization for the Global Public Good	Anti-oppressive Internationalization	Relational Translocalism
Main goal	Improve individual and national economic advantage within global "knowledge society"	Democratize access to modern institutions; expand opportunities for social mobility	Work in partnership for systemic change toward global justice, anti-colonial and anti-racist approach	Center interdependence, expand imaginaries of existence beyond what is currently possible, but cautious of escapism
Secondary goals	Income generation (particularly to address deficits generated by public defunding)	Make the dominant/existing system fairer and more inclusive	Theorize links between different systemic oppressions; problematize and contest "inclusion"	Decenter and disarm; contextualize and deprioritize the logic of modernity and global capitalism; pluriversality
Institutional driver	Branding and prestige; novel resource streams; performance and productivity	Equitable balance between international/local students; advancing liberal democratic ideals	University as critic and conscience of society; enactment and protection of academic freedom	Protect spaces of dissent; revitalize marginalized knowledge; experiment with alternatives; trace existing patterns of violence
Main personal motivation	Improve CVs; develop differential human capital for success in global labor market	Self-betterment; benevolent social entrepreneurship and public responsibility (*noblesse oblige*)	Act in solidarity with marginalized people and groups in pursuit of social justice; affirm critical hope	Disillusion and dis-enchantment with existing imaginaries, relationships, existence (including currents and counter-currents)
Educational aims	Develop human capital and competencies for innovation, leadership and entrepreneurship in the global markets	Develop values, skills for altruism, democracy, equality, inclusion, social cohesion, consensus on ends and means of progress globally	Transform oppressive structures and politics of knowledge through empowerment, voice, activism; framed by critical pedagogy	Political and existential questions and commitments kept in tension; interrupt enchantment with modernity; uncoercively rearrange desires; unlearn, work without guarantees

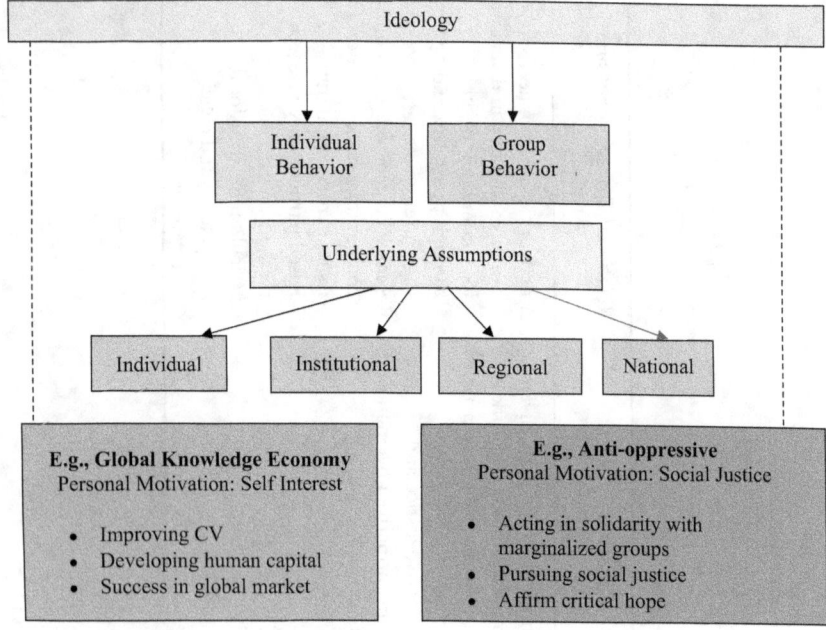

FIGURE 1.2   Example of Ideology Expressed Via Underlying Assumptions.

Organizational Culture

The second consideration in the CRI change model is organizational culture. When a set of beliefs and values become embodied in an ideology or organizational philosophy, it can guide the way individuals manage uncertainty of intrinsically difficult events (Schein, 2017). In discussions of internationalization as a response to persistent, and oftentimes powerful, external uncertain forces, then it becomes important to examine organizational culture (Bartell, 2003; Sporn, 1996). The concept of culture in higher education has traditionally been applied to disciplinary and structural issues with a focus on the analysis of the institution.

Culture can be thought of as having three distinct levels: 1) artifacts, 2) espoused values and beliefs, and 3) underlying assumptions (Bolman & Deal, 2021; Tierney, 2008; Eckel & Kezar, 2003; Schein, 2017). To illustrate, a simple cultural analysis outlining sample artifacts, beliefs, and underlying assumptions associated with each of Stein et al.'s (2016) four articulations are provided in Tables 1.3–1.5, respectively. While individuals and groups operate from multiple ideologies simultaneously, identifying which approaches are most dominant helps to understand underlying motivations and rationales to engage in this work.

TABLE 1.3 Sample Artifacts Across Four Articulations of Internationalization

	Global Knowledge Economy	Global Public Good	Anti-oppressive	Relational Transnationalism
Artifacts or symbols	International research collaboration center. Global innovation hub. Multilingual digital library. Global industry partnership office.	Community engagement centers. Public policy research centers. Sustainability initiatives and infrastructure.	Comprehensive equity, diversity, and inclusion framework. Critical scholarship and activism center. Restorative justice and transformative governance model.	A network of interconnected campuses situated in diverse local communities, linked through programs, and shared resources. Research centers that focus on comparative studies of local issues across community-based participatory research methods. Curriculum for translocal competence and civic engagement.

TABLE 1.4 Sample Values and Beliefs Across Four Articulations of Internationalization

Values and Beliefs	Global Knowledge Economy	Global Public Good	Anti-oppressive	Relational Transnationalism
	Universities' entrepreneurial capacity is key to addressing global issues. Access to global knowledge resources is fundamental to academic excellence. Strong industry partnerships are vital for relevant for education and research	Universities have a responsibility to their communities. Knowledge should be accessible and beneficial to all. Complex societal issues require collaboration across academic disciplines.	Oppression is embedded in societal structures, including educational institutions. Education can empower individuals and communities to create social change. Addressing oppression is a collective responsibility and institutions must be accountable.	Local knowledge is universally valuable. Interconnectedness of local and global. Engaged scholarship as a path to societal relevance.

TABLE 1.5 Sample Underlying Assumptions across Four Articulations of Internationalization

Underlying Assumptions	Global Knowledge Economy	Global Public Good	Anti-oppressive	Relational Transnationalism
	Western-centric models of knowledge and innovation are universally applicable. Market-driven solutions are the most effective for addressing global challenges. Economic progress should be the primary goal of higher education.	Education is a right, not a privilege. Higher education is beneficial for everyone. As long-standing institutions, universities have the capacity to address long-term systemic challenges.	Power dynamics are intrinsic to all social structures. Lived experience is a valid, relevant source of knowledge. Institutions have the capacity for transformative change.	Knowledge is contextual and pluralistic. Localities are simultaneously distinct and interconnected. Universities are embedded actors in social ecosystems.

The first level of culture, artifacts or symbols, includes visible products of the group such as the physical environment, artistic creations (clothing, manners of address), emotional displays, its observable rituals, and ceremonies. Symbols express an organization's culture that define who they are and how they do things (Bolman & Deal, 2021). The symbolic level of culture also includes structural elements, and for universities, this includes the executive authority and collegial governance as primary structures of work.

The structural dimension refers to the ways in which organizations accomplish program, fiscal and governance goals. "Artifacts include, among other things, insider language, myths and stories, mission statements and strategic plans, rituals and ceremonies (such as freshman convocation), reward structures and their implementation, and organizational hierarchies" (Eckel & Kezar, 2003, p. 28). Artifacts are difficult to decipher. "…observers can describe what they see and feel but cannot reconstruct from that alone what those things mean in the given group, or whether they even reflect important underlying assumptions" (Schein, 2017, p. 18). This ambiguity of symbols and images makes it difficult to infer deeper assumptions from artifacts alone. Group discussions among internal stakeholder groups (e.g., faculty, staff, administrators) can surface shared assumptions, helping explain why they either support and/or resist internationalization based on their values and beliefs.

The second layer of culture is concerned with espoused values, "which are the articulated beliefs about what is 'good,' what 'works,' and what is 'right.'" (Eckel & Kezar, 2003, p. 29). All group learning begins with an individual's original beliefs and values—their idea of how things should be. But "until the group has taken some joint action and together observed the outcome of that action, there is not yet a shared basis for determining whether what the leaders want will turn out to be valid" (Schein, 2017, p. 19).

Beliefs transform into assumptions through social validation—confirmed by shared social experience of a group—or when the group has empirically tested a belief or value to work reliably in solving the group's problem. As members reinforce each other's beliefs and values, the beliefs and values become transformed into shared assumptions. For example, faculty members who assume that internationalization perpetuates the commercialization of education and who then together test this assumption and find it to be true (or true enough), will have their shared assumption confirmed (i.e., that internationalization is commercially funded). Their shared assumption will then transform to a shared belief and patterned behaviors. In this example, the shared assumption will likely result in faculty members resisting an internationalization mission as a behavioral norm.

The third level of culture is concerned with deep underlying assumptions. To decipher patterns and predict future behavior, it is necessary to have a deeper understanding of basic assumptions (Eckel & Kezar, 2003; Schein, 2017). Assumptions guide actions and shape priorities and practices and because they are so deeply engrained, are rarely examined (Eckel & Kezar, 2003). Shared assumptions and understandings are expressed through stories, particular language, and norms and exist beneath the conscious level of individuals. Underlying assumptions surface in individual and organizational behavior and are most identifiable when they conflict with espoused values (Eckel & Kezar, 2003).

When basic assumptions are strongly held in a group, "members will find behavior based on any other premise inconceivable" (Schein, 2017, p. 21), and this is the challenge of change. In continuing the example of faculty, when internationalization as a commercial enterprise is engrained as a shared underlying assumption of faculty, any other behavior (such as developing global learning outcomes, co-curricular planning, and recruiting international students) will be considered inconceivable. Thus, working to make the invisible shared assumption visible so it can be deeply explored to allow alternative assumptions to emerge is an early step in the change process.

University Culture

The third consideration in the CRI change model is university culture. Higher education institutions are generally perceived as organizations that are slow to adapt to new threats and opportunities. Today, higher education institutions are interfaced with the fast-moving, market-driven dimensions of globalization creating uncertainty in how to adapt. The historical roots of shared governance and academic freedom have helped to create university culture that combines structure (collegial process) and power (executive authority) forms (Kivinen & Poikus, 2006) that enable institutions to function in unique ways. Operating within an increasingly competitive global market, emerging practices of knowledge production and dissemination are challenged by the rigidity of these historical structures; the collegial process and the executive authority, as university culture adapts to function as a responsive enterprise (Agnew & VanBalkom, 2009; Bartell, 2003; Sporn, 1996).

A shift from a stable to an unstable environment challenges the operation of these formalized structures. "Because organizations are perpetually in flux, undergoing shifts and changes, they must continually be aligned internally and with their external environment" (Tichy, 1982, p. 64). Institutions of higher education are challenged to adapt the power structures and culture amidst shifts within the environment. These very distinctive cultural characteristics inherent to institutions of higher education—executive authority, collegial governance, academic freedom, and academic disciplines—give university culture greater prominence in mediating the university environment (Bartell, 2003). Hence, university culture holds the capacity to influence transformative organizational culture change. Ongoing assessment of alignment within the institution, and between the institution and the environment, is critical to supporting the emerging functions of higher education in response to uncertainties in the environment when conflicts will surely arise. See Figure 1.3.

Understanding organizational culture is essential for minimizing conflict within institutions (Bolman & Deal, 2021; Tierney, 2008). Conflict frequently emerges where there's tension between established and new institutional elements—including priorities, structures, and processes. A classic example of this tension occurs in academic institutions when the hierarchical, efficiency-focused administrative structure often clashes with faculty governance systems that emphasize professional autonomy and collaborative decision-making.

Although the executive authority and the collegial governance process are essential to the livelihood of the institution (Sporn, 1996), this conflict

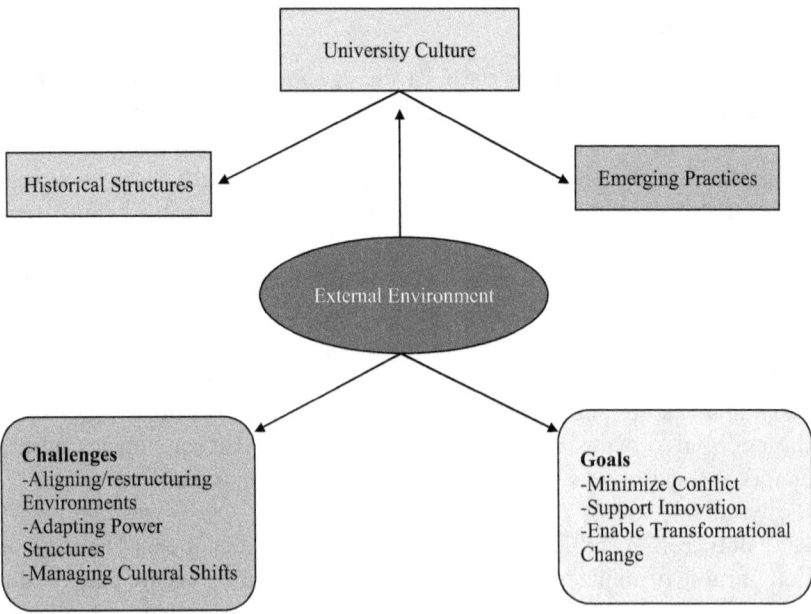

FIGURE 1.3 Navigating Change: University Culture and Organizational Adaptation.

slows the process of innovation and continuous transformational change. The complexity, high degree of differentiation, multiplicity of units and standards, autonomy of professors, control and management philosophies and mechanisms, which increasingly do not operate effectively, even in business organizations. In fact, "in the 2019 Harvard Business Review Analytic Services survey, 69% of the respondents listed overcoming hierarchical decision making as their biggest challenge to adapting to continuous change. The second most-cited challenge was aligning transformation efforts with exiting business models (50%)" (Harvard Business School Publishing, 2020, p. 4). There are likely to be complicating and inhibiting factors vis-á-vis pressures for institutional change, particularly, for internationalization of the university as an identified strategic high priority.

Underlying Assumptions and Sense-Making

Conflict among the academic community frequently surfaces as higher education responds to uncertainty. Conflict is indicative of an incongruence of underlying assumptions, values, and beliefs. Thus, to manage the conflict, it is important to understand the underlying assumptions that fuel the conflict. Assumptions concerning how higher education should respond to global forces (uncertain environment) will likely challenge or disrupt assumptions concerning how things ought to be.

This disruption is what Argyris (1999) calls frame breaking. Basic assumptions are difficult to alter because changing the assumption requires a reexamination of cognitive structures in a process called double-loop learning or frame breaking (Argyris, 1999; Schein, 2017). "Such learning is intrinsically difficult because the reexamination of basic assumptions temporarily destabilizes our cognitive and interpersonal world, releasing large quantities of basic anxiety" (Schein, 2017, p. 22). As an alternative to anxiety, individuals perceive events as congruent with assumptions by distorting, denying, projecting, or by other false pretenses. Because individuals rationalize congruence of assumptions to values and beliefs, and because an incongruence between and among the three levels of culture often does exist to maintain the status quo, or resist change, it is important to examine each of the three levels to determine CRI.

Change can occur more readily when individuals and groups understand the unspoken values and beliefs they share as a group. As illustrated in Figure 1.4, by bringing the underlying assumptions (invisible) into the open (visible), individuals can develop new insights that lead to different behaviors and actions. This process of revealing thought processes and deriving meaning is ultimately aimed at getting individuals to think (and act) differently (Kegan & Lahey, 2009; Schein, 2017; Senge, 1990;).

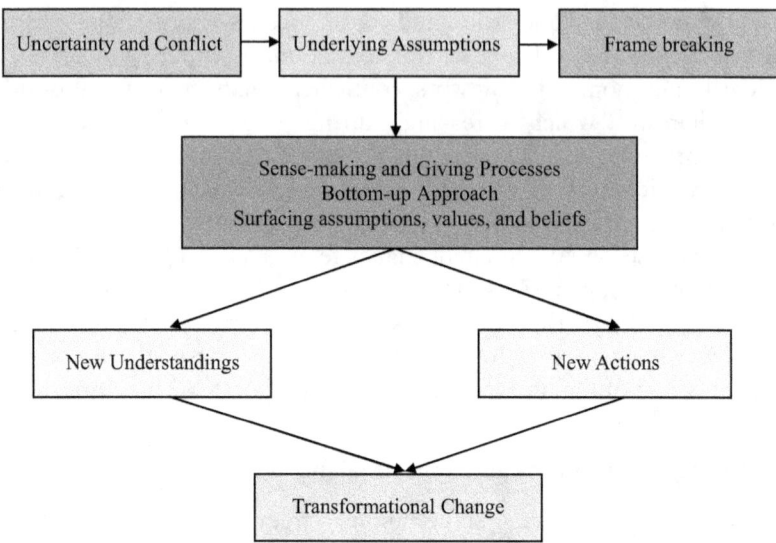

FIGURE 1.4 Underlying Assumptions and Sense-Making.

Targeting deeply embedded and rarely examined assumptions is necessary to transform an institutional culture. That is, to get members of the academic community to think differently (new understandings) about their work in a modern university such that internationalization is supported (new action).

Describes case study research of 28 institutions attempting transformational change. She examined two gaps in understanding how sense-making/giving works: 1) that sense-making works from the bottom up (e.g., faculty), rather than top-down (senior administration) and 2) how it occurs over time. Sense-making/giving is a way to reveal assumptions, values, and beliefs in a process of surfacing individuals' socially constructed realities. For example, individual or group actions that resist internationalization (or some aspects of it) may be rooted in assumptions about the meanings, motivations, and rationales of internationalization. Therefore, it is important to create sense-making/giving opportunities for individuals to think deeply both individually and collectively about their assumptions such that new understandings may lead to support for internationalization. In this way, the organization becomes deliberately developmental in their approach to change (Kegan & Lahey, 2016).

Building on this understanding of how underlying assumptions and sense-making processes shape organizational change, it becomes critical to examine the conditions that foster or inhibit transformation within higher education institutions. The enabling environment—comprising both internal and external factors—creates the context in which cultural change and internationalization efforts either flourish or fail. This next section explores how institutions can cultivate an environment that supports meaningful transformation while navigating the complex interplay of structural, cultural, and individual factors discussed above.

The Enabling Environment

The CRI model extends beyond an institution's internal dynamics to analyze the external "enabling environment" in strategic planning for internationalization. This environment encompasses forces in four major areas: 1) the global knowledge economy, 2) technological advancements, 3) demographic patterns, and 4) geopolitical shifts, all of which have implications for higher education. As outlined in Table 1.6, and within the chapters in this book, these forces converge to create global inequities in higher education. The global knowledge economy influences universities to prepare for 21st-century challenges through global competencies, international recruitment, and globally relevant curricula. However, this force faces significant criticism for potentially commercializing education, treating students as consumers rather than learners, creating disparities between different socioeconomic groups, promoting cultural homogenization, contributing to brain drain from developing countries, and potentially compromising academic freedom due to geopolitical pressures.

Technological forces emphasize increased accessibility to education through digital tools like massive open online courses, blended learning, and educational video games. Technology enables new student markets, provides flexible learning options, and promotes digital literacy. While there is increased accessibility for some students, others without technology or its infrastructure are excluded from these learning tools and platforms.

Demographic patterns highlight global population changes including aging populations and migration patterns. This creates increased demand for international education and necessitates universities to develop diverse programming and support systems. Universities must adapt their curricula and practices to serve an increasingly diverse student body and foster cross-cultural learning.

Finally, geopolitical shifts emphasize how government policies and international relations affect higher education. These shifts can either support or impede student and scholar mobility across borders, while political tensions can disrupt academic collaborations and knowledge flow.

Viewing global forces as interdependent and converging helps to understand both the opportunities and challenges facing higher education in an increasingly interconnected world.

TABLE 1.6 Global Forces: Implications and Critique of Higher Education Internationalization

External Enabling Environment

Global Forces	Implications for Higher Education	Critique of Global Forces Impacting Higher Education
Global Knowledge Economy & Interdependence	Prepare students for diverse social, political, and economic pressures of the 21st century (i.e., global competencies). Growth of intellectual capital. Recruitment of international talent. Develop globally relevant curricula, student mobility programs, international research networks and opportunities, and policies supporting the internal transformation of the university. Develop global citizens,Interdisciplinarity. Transnationalism. Entrepreneurialism. Adapt to evolving demands of the global job market.	*Commercialization & Commodification of Education*: Increased focus on international student recruitment and tuition revenues can lead to a commercialized approach to higher education, where students are seen as consumers rather than learners. Impact quality of education, undermine academic integrity and quality and prioritize financial gain over educational values. *Inequities & Access Disparities*: Global forces in higher education internationalization can exacerbate existing inequities and access disparities. Not all students have equal opportunities to study abroad or access to international programs due to financial constraints, visa restrictions, language barriers, or limited institutional resources. This can perpetuate social and economic inequalities, contributing to the growing digital divide. *Cultural Hegemony & Homogenization*: Dominance of certain cultural and educational norms, potentially eroding local traditions and knowledge systems. Risk of homogenization in teaching methods, curricula, and research agendas, overlooking diverse perspectives and local context. *Brain Drain*: Higher education internationalization can contribute to brain drain, where talented individuals from developing countries seek educational and career opportunities abroad and may not return to their home countries. This can result in a loss of skilled workforce and hinder local development. *Academic Freedom*: Geopolitical shifts and government policies can pose challenges to academic freedom and institutional autonomy in higher education. Restrictions on research topics, limitations on collaborations with certain countries, or censorship can impede intellectual growth and hinder internationalization efforts.

Technological Advancements	Increased accessibility to education and increased connections worldwide.
Focus on digital literacy.
Integration of technology through teaching, research, service.
Digital learning tools such as MOOCs, blended learning, collaboration labs, educational video games, etc.
New student markets. Access for those who might not otherwise have access.
Access to low-cost different knowledge sources.
Increased flexibility in where and when knowledge is accessed.
Changes in design learning in curricula.
Unbundling. Personal learning.
New forms in digital learning in curricula.

(Continued)

TABLE 1.6 (Continued)

External Enabling Environment

Global Forces	Implications for Higher Education	Critique of Global Forces Impacting Higher Education
Demographic Patterns	Population growth, aging populations, changing migration patterns. Demand for higher education is increasing globally, with more students seeking educational opportunities abroad. New migration and immigration patterns. Growing diversity across all areas of social, political, and economic identity. Increased demand for individuals who can work in different cultural contexts. Universities attract international students and foster cultural diversity on campuses. Develop curricular and co-curricular programming and strong academic and social support. Develop policy and practices that ensure education is available to all students. Opportunities to increase diversity of student and faculty populations and to incorporate diverse ideas and perspectives into the curriculum. Importance of catering to the needs and preferences of a diverse student body.	
Geopolitical Shifts	Changes in government policies, international relations, and regional conflicts. Government policies that support and/or impede mobility of students/scholars across borders. Political tension and conflicts disrupt academic collaborations and restrict flow of knowledge.	

The CRI model assumes that a receptive culture will be more successful in the change process, that conditions can be created to strengthen this culture, and that cultural readiness increases the likelihood of quality in internationalization policies and practices. By employing cultural analysis, leaders can build capacity for innovative strategies and evidence-based practices of global engagement, avoiding the pitfall of focusing solely on internal organizational functioning without considering external feedback essential for institutional survival.

Conclusion: The CRI Model Strategic Contribution

The CRI model makes significant contributions to advancing higher education internationalization through its holistic approach that goes beyond simply listing activities. By emphasizing the creation of conditions that foster institutional cultural readiness, the model considers both internal and external factors influencing internationalization. A key strength of the CRI model is its operationalization of Sporn's typology of cultural strength and orientation, which allows for measuring internationalization progress and ensuring coordinated implementation. The model's consideration of institutional context, drawing on ideology, organizational culture and its subset university culture, and systems theory, makes it widely applicable across various types and sizes of institutions.

Central to the CRI model is its focus on cultural analysis, assuming that a culture receptive to internationalization is more likely to succeed in the change process. By integrating multiple theoretical frameworks, including concepts from ideology, organizational culture, and university culture, the model provides a comprehensive framework for understanding and planning internationalization efforts. The CRI model also emphasizes examining underlying assumptions and the importance of sense-making as foundational steps in the change process, encouraging new thinking and actions to support internationalization. Furthermore, the model's recognition of the external environment, considering a wide range of influences from history and geopolitics to market forces and the international community, provides a framework for navigating the complex landscape of internationalization.

The CRI model acknowledges the need for universities to balance multiple roles and engage with diverse stakeholders within the local, national, and global contexts. Ultimately, the CRI model supports the development of innovative strategies, policies, and plans that foster evidence-based practices of global engagement, providing a comprehensive and nuanced approach to advancing higher education internationalization that considers the complex interplay of internal and external factors influencing this process.

Implications for Ethical Policies and Practices

1 *Multiple Ideologies*: Researchers and practitioners need to navigate the different ideologies that drive internationalization (e.g., knowledge economy; public good) understanding that these multiple approaches operate simultaneously at various levels (e.g., personal; institutional, national), considering the far-reaching implications of each.
2 *Power Imbalances*: Global engagement efforts should be mindful of and work to mitigate historical and current power imbalances between and among countries, institutions, schools/faculty, and individuals, particularly in decision-making processes.
3 *Critical Self-, Institution-, and National-reflection*: Researchers and practitioners have an ethical responsibility to critically examine their own assumptions, biases, and ideologies, and that of their institution and country, that may influence the direction and purpose of internationalization efforts.
4 *Respect Local Contexts*: When engaging in internationalization, there is an ethical duty to respect and adapt to local cultural, social, and academic contexts rather than imposing external, unwanted models.
5 *Cultural Sensitivity and Respect*: Internationalization strategies can be developed, implemented, and evaluated with deep cultural understanding and respect for diverse perspectives and values.
6 *Inclusion*: Global engagement initiatives should actively work to address social and economic inequalities, ensuring equitable access and benefits for all participants.
7 *Academic Freedom and Integrity*: Maintaining academic freedom and research integrity in the face of internal and external market influences is essential for ethical global engagement.

Notes

1 See Chapter 11 for a detail discussion of university macro missions and their dominant philosophies as they related to contemporary internationalization of higher education.
2 See Chapter 11 for a detailed discussion of internationalization drift.

References

Agnew, M., & VanBalkom, W. D. (2009). Internationalization of the university: Factors impacting cultural readiness for organizational change. *Intercultural Education*, 20(5), 451–462.
Argyris, C. (1999). *On organizational learning* (2nd ed.). Blackwell.
Bartell, M. (2003). Internationalization of universities: A university culture-based framework. *Higher Education*, 45, 43–70.

Bolman, L, & Deal, T. (2021). *Reframing organizations: Artistry, choice, and leadership* (7th ed.). Jossey-Bass.
Chen, G. M., & Starosta, W. J. (Eds.). (1996). *Foundations of intercultural communication*. Routledge.
Eckel, P., & Kezar, A. (2003). *Taking the reins: Institutional transformation in higher education*. Praeger Publishers.
Harvard Business Review (2020). *Continuous transformation starts with culture*. Harvard Business Review Analytics Servies, Briefing Paper.
Johnson, D. W., & Johnson, F. P. (2009). *Joining together: Group theory and group skills* (10th ed.). Pearson.
Kegan, R., & Lahey, L. L. (2009). *Immunity to change: How to overcome it and unlock potential in yourself and your organization*. Harvard Business Press.
Kegan, R., & Lahey, L. L. (2016). *An everyone culture: Becoming a deliberately developmental organization*. Harvard Business Review Press.
Kivinen, O., & Poikus, P. (2006). Privileges of Universitas Magistrorum et Scolarium and their justification in charters of foundation from the 13th to the 21st centuries. *Higher Education, 52*, 185–213.
Knight, J. (2004). Internationalization remodeled: Definition, approaches, and rationales. *Journal of Studies in International Education, 8*(1), 5–31.
Marginson, S. (2023). Limitations of the leading definition of 'internationalisation' of higher education: Is the idea wrong or is the fault in reality. *Globalisation, Societies and Education*. https://doi.org/10.1080/14767724.2023.2264223
Schein, E. H. (2017). *Organizational culture and leadership* (5th ed.). John Wiley & Sons.
Senge, P. (1990). The leader's New Work: Building learning organizations. *Sloan Management Review*, Fall, 32(1), 7–23 7–23.
Sporn, B. (1996). Managing university culture: An analysis of the relationship between Institutional culture and management approaches. *Higher Education, 32*, 41–61.
Stein, S., Andreotti, V., Bruce, J., & Suša, R. (2016). Towards different conversations about the internationalization of higher education. *Comparative and International Education, 45*(1), 1–18.
Stier, J. (2004). Taking a critical stance toward internationalization ideologies in higher education: Idealism, instrumentalism and educationalism. *Globalisation, Societies and Education, 2*(1), 83–97.
Tajfel, H., & Turner, J. C. (1979). An integrative theory of inter-group conflict. In W. G. Austin, & S. Worchel (Eds.), *The social psychology of intergroup relations* (pp. 33–47). Brooks/Cole.
Tichy, N. (1982). Managing change strategically: The technical, political, and cultural keys. *Organizational Dynamics*, Autumn, 11(2) 59–80.
Tierney, W. (2008). *The impact of culture on organizational decision-making*. Routledge.
Triandis, H. C. (1995). *Individualism and collectivism*. Westview Press.

2
CRITICAL APPROACHES TO INTERNATIONALIZATION OF HIGHER EDUCATION

Jos Beelen

Introduction

In one of his blogs for *University World News*, De Wit (2018) noted that critical thinking about internationalization of higher education is heightening. He mentions the global political climate, which has significantly worsened since 2018. But also "a growing concern about the elitism and lack of inclusiveness of internationalisation in practice".

Internationalization of higher education has been approached critically for a considerable period. Over time, we have started to identify processes of inequality, unintended consequences (see Kamyab and Raby, 2023), and even negative effects of internationalization practices.

While the internationalization of higher education is generally believed to be positive, there are many reasons to challenge the 'inherent goodness' of internationalization (see Marginson, 2023).

Some of these unintended consequences of internationalization have even led to a process of 'de-internationalization', for example in the Netherlands, where internationalization is shrinking for a range of reasons, discussed in the case study at the end of this chapter.

In the discourse on the consequences, a considerable obstacle has been the 'fuzziness' of the term 'internationalization' and the prolific misconceptions being discussed. The discourse is further complicated by the continued invention of new terms, such as Comprehensive Internationalization, intelligent internationalization and virtual internationalization.

DOI: 10.4324/9781315623337-3

Therefore, De Wit (2024, p. 10) advocates ending to use the term 'internationalization' "in a sloppy way" which means deconstructing the term and saying precisely which component of internationalization we mean

Internationalization: more definitions

Internationalization has long been a contested term. Critiques of the traditional Anglo-Saxon forms of internationalization, mainly focusing on student recruitment for profit, are well known. This has led to the coining of new definitions that suit a specific context better.

These critiques have resulted in highlighting emerging forms of internationalization outside the Euro-American context or 'globalization of internationalization' (see De Wit et al., 2017). Not long after the introduction of this term, several alternative—and greatly varying—alternative definitions of internationalization started appearing. Below, we discuss two, one from China and one from South Africa:

Higher education internationalization in the Chinese context can be defined as a nationally coordinated, institutionally integrated and comprehensive effort to import the Western-led world standards in teaching, research, management and facility development through the exposure of academic staff, students and administrators to Western practices, and to export the Chinese discourse, voice and cultural understanding in the international community through international student education in China and Chinese language/culture promotion overseas. (Liu, 2020, p. 241)

Liu's definition suggests that internationalization is synonymous with the adoption of Western practices, particularly in areas like teaching, research and administration. This could imply that non-Western forms of knowledge, teaching and governance are inferior or irrelevant in the internationalization process, which risks marginalizing local educational innovations and values. A more balanced view would consider not only Western standards but also the rising influence of Asian, African and Latin American educational models. In its current form, Liu's definition is a combination of re-westernization and de-westernization.

The South African definition is entirely different:

Internationalisation of higher education is a critical and comparative process of the study of the world and its complexities, past and present inequalities and injustices, and possibilities for a more equitable and just future for all. Through teaching, learning, research and engagement, internationalisation fosters epistemic plurality and integrates critical, antiracist and anti-hegemonic learning about the world from diverse global perspectives to enhance the quality and relevance of education.

(Heleta & Chasi, 2022, pp. 9–10)

This definition takes the local situation and local needs as a starting point. It is therefore logical that Heleta (2023) objects to the inclusion of "institutional and educational models and curriculum from the Netherlands and Britain" in the South African Policy Framework for Internationalisation of Higher Education in South Africa Heleta, 2023, p. 826). That framework includes both the definition of internationalization of the curriculum and internationalization at home, but without reference to the original authors. The definition by Heleta & Chasi contains elements of 'anti-oppressive internationalization' and 'relational translocalism', articulated by Stein et al. (2016), and discussed below. The definition will also be discussed, from a Global South perspective, in Chapter 6.

Critiquing the existing definition of internationalization

Marginson (2023) explores the most cited definition of internationalization, that by Knight, from 1994, revised in 2004 (Knight, 2004) and concludes that this definition proliferates Euro-American domination in international higher education. He also critiques the extension of the revised definition of internationalization that was coined in 2015 through a study on internationalization for the European Parliament (De Wit et al., 2015). That extended definition includes the contribution of internationalization to the quality of higher education and a meaningful contribution to society. Marginson points at the ambiguity of 'quality' and 'meaningful contribution' and maintains that the revised definition is still "privileging the national/international above the global" and comments on "its ambiguous universalism, and its Euro-American-centrism" (p. 8).

In an opinion piece and partly in response to Marginson, De Wit (2024) points out that rationales for and contexts of internationalization are changing over time and that definitions should be seen in relation to the development of internationalization of higher education at the time that they were coined. He advocates describing new directions for internationalization, rather than continuing to redefine. He then continues to give the characteristics of international higher education, without calling this a definition:

> Internationalisation of higher education is a critical and comparative process of the study of the world and its complexities, past and present inequalities and injustices, and possibilities for a more equitable and just future for all. Through teaching, learning, research and engagement, internationalization fosters epistemic plurality and integrates critical, antiracist and anti-hegemonic learning about the world from diverse global perspectives to enhance the quality and relevance of education.
>
> *(De Wit, 2024, pp. 9–10)*

This incorporates some of the components of the South African definition discussed above.

Affirming academic values in internationalization

Some of internationalization's most ardent supporters have also been its strongest critics, shining a light on understandings and practices that limit inclusion and societal impact.

Since circa 2010 some have cautioned against the focus on revenue generation, the Global Knowledge Economy and on rankings. Particularly in the United Kingdom, the US and Australia this focus would come at the expense of the traditional values, meaning the 'end of internationalization' (Brandenburg & De Wit, 2010).

Overreliance on internationalization's non-academic aims has long been observed to generate significant negative consequences at a national or regional level, such as brain drain, cultural and educational homogenization and English-language dominance (International Association of Universities, 2012).

In 2014 the International Education Association of South Africa (IEASA) hosted a global dialogue on the future of higher education internationalization within the context of globalization and uneven global power structures, attended by representatives of 24 national, regional, transnational and private higher education networks and organizations. The event produced a common declaration that called for three integrated areas for increased development: enhanced "quality and diversity" of mobility programs, increased "focus on internationalization of the curriculum and related learning outcomes" and a global commitment to "equal and ethical higher education partnerships" (International Education Association of South Africa, 2014, p. 2). They affirmed all institutions' responsibility to enable "all students to develop global perspectives and intercultural communication competencies" (Whitsed & Green, 2013, n.p.).

Critiques of internationalization

Vavrus and Pekol (2015) highlight the growing recognition of the limitations and inequalities inherent in traditional models of internationalization, which often focus on economic benefits, institutional prestige and student mobility without critically examining the broader social, cultural and political implications. The authors argue for a shift toward a "critical" approach to internationalization, one that is informed by principles of equity, social justice and decolonization. This approach challenges dominant power structures in global education, which often marginalize certain regions, knowledge systems and cultures.

Vavrus and Pekol (p. 9) also discuss representation: how "language and visual images serve as ideological systems of representation". They draw upon Hall, who wrote that a privileged English identity has led to a marginalized identity for the rest of the world.

A range of recent publications engage with critical approaches to internationalization.

Hartman et al. (2020) in their article 'Coloniality-decoloniality and critical global citizenship: Identity, belonging, and education abroad' explore how the concepts of coloniality and decoloniality intersect with the growing field of study abroad and global citizenship education. Using the term 'hegemonic internationalization' they critically examine the ways in which traditional study abroad programs often reproduce colonial structures, reinforcing power imbalances and creating a narrow, Eurocentric understanding of global citizenship.

The article argues that international education programs, particularly those from the Global North, have historically been shaped by colonial legacies. These programs frequently position students from wealthy, Western countries as "global citizens" with a sense of entitlement to explore, learn and engage with the 'other', while overlooking the diverse experiences and voices of students from the Global South.

Bamberger and Morris (2023) conclude that while internationalization can be a force for positive change, it must be critically examined and carefully managed to avoid reinforcing existing inequalities. Universities should move beyond commercial interests and global citizenship rhetoric to embrace a more inclusive, equitable and socially responsible model of internationalization that reflects diverse perspectives and challenges postcolonial power structures in higher education.

Like Bamberger and Morris (2023), Bailey (2024) critiques the idea of global citizenship often promoted in internationalized educational settings. While the concept is framed as fostering global awareness, cross-cultural understanding and social responsibility, Bailey argues that in practice, it can sometimes function as a shallow, neoliberal concept that fails to challenge existing power structures.

From the Critical Internationalization Studies Network, Pashby draws on critical theory, postcolonialism and intercultural education to analyze and improve the ways in which global citizenship is conceptualized and taught (see e.g. Pashby, 2015).

In the framework of International Higher Education for Society (IHES), Cai and Leask (2024) critique traditional approaches to internationalization, which focus mainly on institutional benefits (such as enhancing rankings or attracting international students) and have overlooked the broader societal and global contexts in which higher education operates.

By adopting an "outside-in" approach, which considers external societal needs and challenges, the paper calls for a more inclusive, socially responsible model of internationalization. This would involve universities engaging more deeply with global issues, providing students with opportunities to contribute to solving global challenges, and ensuring that internationalization benefits both sending and receiving societies in meaningful ways.

The observation made by De Wit (2018), that critical thinking about internationalization of higher education is heightening, seems justified, considering the range of recent papers and books on the subject.

Critiquing mobility as an exclusive practice

It has long been clear that student mobility would continue to remain an option only for a small 'cultural elite" of students (Saarikallio-Torp & Wiers-Jenssen, 2010). Focusing on student mobility for a minority of students and leads to "reproduction of social privilege and class divides across generations" (King et al., 2010. p. 2). Nevertheless, attempts to increase student participation in mobility have continued. The Norwegian government currently aims to send all students abroad, but has set an intermediate target of 50% which universities struggle to attain. It can be doubted, looking back at the past thirty years, that setting high targets will have much effect. Still, it is important to understand the factors that influence participation in mobility.

In higher education, the term 'internationalization' is frequently used as a synonym for mobility. This mobility can range from incoming degree mobility (students studying for a degree abroad) to facilitating outgoing credit mobility in the framework of student exchange.

With the term 'internationalization abroad', Knight (2008) has tried to capture these mobility-related aspects of internationalization. She also distinguishes 'internationalization at home', which quickly gained recognition as one of the two main streams in international higher education. Knight considers both modalities of internationalization as connected and not as opposites.

The exclusive character of study and internships abroad remains one of the most persistent issues in the internationalization of higher education in many contexts (see Kommers & Bista, 2021).

Internationalization, understood as mobility of staff and students has also been critiqued for its negative impact on the environment (see Nikula et al., 2024, pp. 47–48). To mitigate these circumstances, the Climate Action Network for International Educators (CANIE) brings practitioners in higher education together.[1]

Being included in and excluded from internationalization

The introduction of internationalization at home around 2000 can be considered a critical approach to the then—and now—dominant mode of internationalization: mobility of staff and students. The original definition of internationalization at home (Crowther et al., 2001) did not contain a reference to all students, or the purpose of internationalization at home, but the redefinition (Beelen & Jones, 2015) did include this. The year 2015 also saw also a new definition of internationalization of the curriculum (Leask, 2015). Both internationalization at home and internationalization of the curriculum have generally been positively received, but there have also been critiques, depending on the context. Chapter 4 consists of an in-depth exploration of critical approaches to internationalized teaching and learning.

The Critical Internationalization Studies Network

The discussion on critiques of internationalization took a new turn with the emergence of this network.[2] Stein et al. (2016) date the historical dominant global imaginary to the beginnings of modernity, colonialism and the trans-Atlantic slave trade. Europe asserted a vision for the world, aiming for security, prosperity, individualism, progress, democracy, meritocracy and universal knowledge, but at a cost. Harmful societal relations and processes were reproduced, and continue to reproduce, through modernity, colonialism, causing insecurity, exploitation, expropriation, poverty and onto-epistemological dominance.

Stein and the critical internationalization network summarized their views in four articulations of internationalization which they connected to main goals, secondary goals, institutional driver, personal motivation and educational aims. (Stein et al., 2016, p. 13). These articulations are shown in Table 2.1 and figure prominently throughout this book. They can even be considered its raison d'être.

Critiquing critical internationalization

Critical internationalization itself is also receiving criticism. Marginson (2023) critiques the critical internationalization movement for -at the same time- being critical while continuing to recruit international students for profit. This practice is confirmed by a case study (Heath & Johnstone, 2024) of a Canadian university where imaginaries of internationalization, interculturalization and indigenization go hand in hand with a focus on generating revenue through international student recruitment. Currently,

TABLE 2.1 Stein et al.'s Four Articulations of Internationalization

	Internationalization for the Global Knowledge Economy	Internationalization for the Global Public Good	Anti-Oppressive Internationalization	Relational Translocalism
Main goal	Improve individual and national economic advantage within global "knowledge society"	Democratize access to modern institutions; expand opportunities for social mobility	Work in partnership for systemic change toward global justice, anti-colonial and anti-racist approach	Center interdependence, expand imaginaries of existence beyond what is currently possible, but cautious of escapism
Secondary goals	Income generation (particularly to address deficits generated by public defunding)	Make the dominant/existing system fairer and more inclusive	Theorize links between different systemic oppressions; problematize and contest "inclusion"	Decenter and disarm; contextualize and deprioritize the logic of modernity and global capitalism; pluriversality
Institutional driver	Branding and prestige; novel resource streams; performance and productivity	Equitable balance between international/local students; advancing liberal democratic ideals	University as critic and conscience of society; enactment and protection of academic freedom	Protect spaces of dissent; revitalize marginalized knowledge; experiment with alternatives; trace existing patterns of violence
Main personal motivation	Improve CVs; develop differential human capital for success in global labor market	Self-betterment; benevolent social entrepreneurship and public responsibility (*noblesse oblige*)	Act in solidarity with marginalized people and groups in pursuit of social justice; affirm critical hope	Disillusion and disenchantment with existing imaginaries, relationships, existence (including currents and counter-currents)

(*Continued*)

TABLE 2.1 (Continued)

	Internationalization for the Global Knowledge Economy	Internationalization for the Global Public Good	Anti-Oppressive Internationalization	Relational Translocalism
Educational aims	Develop human capital and competencies for innovation, leadership and entrepreneurship in the global markets	Develop values, skills for altruism, democracy, equality, inclusion, social cohesion, consensus on ends and means of progress globally	Transform oppressive structures and politics of knowledge through empowerment, voice, activism; framed by critical pedagogy	Political and existential questions and commitments kept in tension; interrupt enchantment with modernity; uncoercively rearrange desires; unlearn, work without guarantees

Table 1: Summary of the four articulations of critical internationalization (Stein et al., 2016, p. 13.)

the number of international students in Canada is dropping rapidly, but mainly because of Canadian and visa policies and the housing crisis (Greenfields, 2024).

Indeed, critical internationalization scholars themselves have argued that critical approaches to internationalization, for example to its ongoing coloniality, must also be subjected to critical scrutiny, raising the question of "the limits of critique itself" (Stein & McCartney, 2021, p. 3).

Critical internationalization in the Netherlands

The Netherlands has a prominent presence in the world of non-Anglophone higher education.

In 2018, Altbach and De Wit, noted: "In the Netherlands, arguably one of the most internationally minded countries in the world, an intense debate about the limits of internationalization has started, in the media, in politics and in the higher education sector itself." Indeed, the Netherlands has a long tradition of international trade connected to a long colonial history from its 'Golden Age' in the 17th century. The deep-seated interest in all matters international is manifest, for example, in the fact that the Netherlands has supplied three NATO Secretaries General since 1971, with the current one taking office in 2024. In international higher education, the Dutch presence becomes manifest in its strong representation in organizations such as the European Association for International Education (EAIE), which is based in Amsterdam. The highest number of respondents to the EAIE Barometers came from Dutch HEIs (Rumbley & Sandström, 2019, p. 27).

Traditionally, internationalization in the Netherlands has focused on enrolling international students into master programs delivered by research universities in English to drive up their quality. 75% of master programs are now taught in English. In its Barometer, the European Association for International Education found that financial considerations are relevant for 42% of universities in the United Kingdom but only for 6% in the Netherlands. (Rumbley & Sandström, 2019, p. 7). Although Dutch HEIs responded that financial considerations had a low priority, Wingrove et al. (2024) note that Dutch HEIs have led the way in EMI and attributes this to university autonomy.

From 2006 to 2023, the number of international students in the Netherlands rose sharply, from 31,492 to 128,004, mostly through the increase of international students in English medium bachelor programs at research universities. In universities of applied sciences currently, 92% of programs are delivered in Dutch.[3]

In 2023, the top ten countries of origin of international students included only one non-European country: China, with 6,207 students.[4] The rapidly rising number of international students was also influenced by Brexit, which made studying in the United Kingdom less attractive. This left the government with few options, since the great majority of international students stem from within the European Union with its free flow of persons. EU students are therefore considered equal to Dutch students. By offering English medium education to recruit fee-paying extra-European students, the doors were opened to European students that do not bring extra revenue.

Reactions: we have too many international students

The increasing number of international students led to reactions in the Netherlands, in universities, public opinion and within parliament. The debates were characterized by a 'sloppy' use of the term 'internationalization' (see De Wit, 2024, p. 10). In the debate, frequently no distinction is made between degree or credit mobility or between research universities and universities of applied sciences. 'Internationalization' is also frequently interpreted as teaching in English.

Universities worried about capacity to have so many students and about their ability to deliver quality education in English. Because of the housing crisis, they started advising incoming degree-seeking students to not make travel arrangements or enroll in an academic program until they have secured accommodation. Unless the receiving university provides sufficient affordable accommodation, students without resources may be forced to cancel their plans for study abroad in some cities. That makes student mobility an even more exclusive practice, affordable only to students with extra resources at their disposal.

With right-wing political sentiments on the rise, questions were being raised about the displacement of Dutch students by internationals. There were also concerns about the loss of Dutch as an academic language and the accessibility of education in a foreign language.

The Dutch Ministry of Education and Culture described the positive economic value of international students and stressed the importance of brain gain for the knowledge economy. By doing this they reduced internationalization to its economic dimension, intending to convince right-wing critics, who would not be sensitive to the other, positive dimensions of internationalization.

In 2023 the Ministry of Education proposed the law 'Internationalization in balance' which includes several instruments to regulate the flow of international students in bachelor programs. Among the measures proposed are reducing the number of bachelor programs taught in English. Universities must demonstrate that they meet the criteria to deliver education in other languages than Dutch, for example, because of shortages in the labor market or international positioning. They must also develop language policies that support the development of the Dutch language. Universities can apply a cap on the number of non-EU students and adjust their tuition fees.

Universities have reacted that these measures will have negative consequences for their autonomy, which Wingrove et al., 2024) argue caused the current situation in the first place. Another issue is that they may not have Dutch-speaking staff. These strategies will lead to fewer EU students coming to the Netherlands thus reducing the cost of higher education. The developments in the Netherlands do not stem from a critical approach to internationalization and its purposes but rather from the consequences of neoliberal actions that have now led to what can be termed anti-internationalization or de-internationalization. However, there are also actions that fit in the framework of critical internationalization's articulations beyond the global knowledge economy (see Stein et al., 2016, p. 13).

Actions for critical internationalization in the Netherlands

While the term 'critical internationalization' is little used in the internationalization discourse in the Netherlands, there are actions that HEIs and organizations undertake that constitute critical internationalization.

Inclusivity in study abroad

A study by Nuffic (Favier et al., 2022) identified which Dutch students were least likely to study abroad and why. The study showed that students who represent the first generation in their families to enroll in higher education were the least likely to go abroad. Students from high-income families were more likely to go abroad. This correlation was clear for students in research universities, but less for students in universities of applied sciences, who more frequently go abroad for (paid) internships.

Another study (Ovchinnikova et al., 2024) among Dutch and Belgian students demonstrated that students who perceive their foreign language proficiency as 'advanced' rather than 'intermediate' are more likely to study abroad. In Education First's English Proficiency Index, the Netherlands consistently scores the highest (see Education First, 2024). However, having a high proficiency in general English does not mean that this suffices for academic purposes.

Nuffic has established a 'National Taskforce Inclusive Internationalisation' to stimulate students to gain international competences through a mobility experience.

These competences should help students with their personal development and increase their chances in the labor market. Every student therefore should have the opportunity to develop international competences.

Nuffic also developed the interactive game Go!ForAll, aimed at lecturers in higher education and in vocational education and training schools, This makes the game an inclusive effort to bring internationalization also to that sector of education.[5] Nuffic has also dedicated programs for internationalization in primary and secondary education. While it is positive that the importance of internationalization outside higher education is acknowledged, a significant increase in study abroad cannot be expected because of these actions.

For travel to European destinations 63% of mobile Dutch students choose to travel by plane, 14 % by plane and 12 % by bus. Reasons that students give for choosing plane travel are speed and ease of reaching their destination. In this survey of 109 students, 75 indicated that they would choose a sustainable alternative if they would be compensated for the higher cost (Peeters & Slappendel-Henschen, 2022).

Internationalization at home

Since its introduction in 2001, internationalization at home (Crowther et al., 2001; Beelen & Jones, 2015) has been embraced by the majority of HEIs in the Netherlands and Flanders. A study from 2014 found that 76% of Dutch HEIs had internationalization at home in their institutional policies (Van Gaalen et al., 2014). However, the study also found that activities lag behind institutional ambitions (p. 7), while at the same time, activities are taking place that are not connected to institutional policies. A later study (Van Gaalen & Gielesen, 2016, p. 154) therefore concluded that Dutch higher education institutions include internationalization at home in their policies but do not generally have established implementation strategies. Nor do they use monitoring tools to determine the extent to which policies are being implemented. In a study of the University of Groningen, Van den Hende (2024, p. 127) called curriculum internationalization "a dynamic organizational change process" and concluded that "institutional strategies for curriculum internationalization are largely inadequate for academic staff and their specific disciplinary contexts".

To stimulate international learning opportunities for non-mobile students, the Dutch Ministry of Education has made a total of € 4.950.000 available in scholarships for academics who develop Virtual Exchange or Collaborative Online International Learning (COIL) as component of internationalization at home.

A survey after 454 projects had been funded, shows that most online practices were with partners in the Global North: such as the USA (60 projects) and with neighboring countries Germany (57), Belgium (45) and the United Kingdom (44) (Kemman et al., 2024, p. 23).

With 34 projects, South Africa was the most frequently chosen country in the Global South.

Online collaboration was most frequently practiced in business programs.

In 66% of the practices, the Dutch partner had the largest share in design and development of the collaboration. Only in 31% of cases the partners had an equal share (p. 23).

While online collaboration allows for working with partners across the world, Dutch HEIs choose predominantly to work with partners in the Global North, and particularly with neighboring countries and in business programs. Many online collaborations therefore fall in the articulation of Global Knowledge Economy (Stein et al., 2016, p. 13. While COIL has the potential for practicing critical internationalization, for example with partners from the Global South, this potential is not yet used.

Another critical note is that vocational education and training schools are excluded from these scholarships, although it can be argued that Virtual Exchange and COIL are equally relevant for student and staff in those schools.[6]

In a study about outgoing student mobility (Favier et al., 2022), 45% of the respondents do not consider internationalization at home an option that can replace an experience abroad. According to the authors, this may be because many curricula already include learning foreign languages and online collaboration and that the respondents therefore expect little additional benefits from internationalization at home.

Nuffic has a dedicated community for internationalization at home, which includes a focus on vocational education and training schools, thereby including an education sector that is often forgotten.[7]

Research into internationalization at home is being conducted by the research group Global Learning at The Hague University of Applied Sciences and at the Centre for Transformational Education at the University of Groningen. In The Hague, the focus is on the implementation of internationalization at home, the competences of lecturers and the role of COIL in an internationalized curriculum. In Groningen, research explores the role of the disciplines and transformational learning within internationalization at home.

While internationalization at home has had a strong presence in the Netherlands for almost 25 years in institutional policies, practice in teaching and learning is far from reaching its potential.

Critiquing rankings and competition

In 2023 Utrecht University took the unusual step to exclude itself from the Times Higher Education ranking. The university pointed out that it wants to focus on collaboration rather than competition, that it considers it impossible to capture the variety of the institution in one number and the data and methods of the rankings "highly questionable" (Universities of the Netherlands, 2023).[8]

This fits in a development that can be found in the *Barometer* of EAIE, based in Amsterdam (Rumbley & Hoekstra-Selten, 2024, p. 86). In Western Europe 'reputation or rankings' were not the most frequently selected consideration for delivering impact through internationalization. Instead, that was 'student learning outcomes. The *Barometer* notes that there are considerable differences between European countries in delivering impact of internationalization on rankings, ranging from Hungary (65%), Czechia (66%) and Italy (68%) to the Netherlands with just 19%. This may be because 11 out of 12 research universities in the Netherlands are already in the top 200 of THE.[9]

Acting on awareness of unintended consequences

There are indications that Dutch HEIs are aware of the unintended consequences of outbound mobility and are prepared to act on this. In 2017, the first Dutch higher education institution signed the Stop Orphanage Volunteering University Pledge to not support students volunteering or doing internships in orphanages in Africa, since many of the children are not orphans in the first place and because the coming and going of interns and volunteers is detrimental to children's affective development.[10]

Decolonization in Dutch higher education

The discourse on decolonization is vibrant, particularly in relation to the long colonial history of the Netherlands and Indonesia. The discussion is kept alive by the fact that former Dutch colonies in the Caribbean still constitute components of the Kingdom of the Netherlands. Students from Surinam (independent since 1975) can study in the Netherlands for the same tuition fees as students from the Netherlands, the rest of the European Union plus Liechtenstein, Iceland, Norway and Switzerland.

While the discussion on decolonization is alive, there is no systematic approach to or consensus about decolonization of higher education. Decolonization as a topic is not included in mandatory professional development for academics. Depending on academic discipline, diversity of students and staff, decolonization may be included in teaching and learning. Some universities or departments have a high profile on decolonization, such as the Africa Centre at the University of Leiden.

Scienceguide, an online journal about research in Dutch universities of applied sciences, has published only six articles about decolonization of higher education in the Netherlands since 2020.[11] One of these is about a paper on decolonizing the academic self, written by authors from the United Kingdom, Belgium and the Netherlands (Wimpenny et al., 2021). In this autoethnographic study on curriculum internationalization and the 'decolonizing academic', they reflected on the mindsets of academics and their role in decolonizing teaching and learning. The Africa Knows! Conference, organized by the Africa Studies Centre at Leiden University in 2020–2021 had the theme 'decolonising minds',[12] The conference pushed the topic of decolonization temporarily to the forefront but with little lasting impact on the Dutch higher education sector. Therefore, it is all the more worrying that the Africa Studies Centre may have to close because of a round of budget cuts that hit Dutch higher education in 2024.

On balance: critical internationalization in the Netherlands

In the discourse on internationalization of higher education in the Netherlands, critical internationalization does not figure prominently. However, critical approaches and practices have emerged, such as stepping out of the rankings, limiting harmful mobility, making mobility more inclusive and attempts to making the benefits available to all students through a consistent focus on internationalization at home. On the other hand, university autonomy, public underfunding and demographics, leading to dwindling enrollment, have led Dutch research universities to adopt neoliberal strategies that are now being corrected by the government, itself acting on the basis of neoliberal motives.

Conclusions

This chapter aimed to give an overview of approaches to critical internationalization. These include calls to return to lost values of internationalization. In the process, new definitions of internationalization in different regions of the world emerge and are critiqued. The conceptual fog remains. The paradox of lofty motives versus neoliberal practices has become manifest, including in the Netherlands. Yet, critical approaches to internationalization are on the rise which is promising for institutions, academics and students alike. Recruiting international students and study abroad remain the main modalities of internationalization, leading to paradoxes about stimulating mobilities while attempting to address climate change. Inclusive alternatives to mobilities are available and may be gaining traction, although (geo)political circumstances are not favorable. Internationalization for the global knowledge economy will therefore continue to exist next to more idealistic articulations of internationalization, often within the same university.

Implications for ethical policies and practices

Discuss internationalization in a less 'sloppy' way

The discourse on internationalization should be precise what we actually mean to say and distinguish between the different enactments of the components of internationalization.

University leadership understanding critical approaches to internationalization

Institutional leadership should be aware of the unintended consequences of their internationalization policies and act upon them.

Focus on inclusive internationalization beyond inclusive mobilities

Academics, staff and students should be aware that inclusivity in internationalization starts at home.

Higher education building on internationalization learnings from secondary education

Research into what extent internationalization processes in higher education differ from those in secondary, primary and vocational education and how HEIs can build on these experiences.

Emancipation of internationalization in TVET

From elitist research universities, internationalization has 'descended' to universities of applied sciences and Technical and Vocational Education and Training (TVET), whose students are now included in the Erasmus program in Europe. How to stimulate the development of internationalization in the TVET sector and to avoid mistakes from higher education is a question for leadership in both higher education and the TVET sector.

Notes

1 https://canie.org.
2 https://criticalinternationalization.net.

3 https://nltimes.nl/2024/10/15/rules-english-lectures-dutch-universities-soon-become-even-stricter.
4 https://www.nuffic.nl/en/subjects/facts-and-figures/top-10-countries-of-origin-over-time.
5 https://www.nuffic.nl/en/goforall-the-experience-game-about-inclusive-internationalisation.
6 https://www.dus-i.nl/subsidies/virtuele-internati.nale-samenwerkingsprojecten (website in Dutch).
7 https://www.nuffic.nl/onderwerpen/internationalisation-at-home (website in Dutch).
8 https://www.uu.nl/en/news/why-uu-is-missing-in-the-the-ranking.
9 https://www.timeshighereducation.com/world-university-rankings/latest/world-ranking#!/length/50/locations/NLD/sort_by/rank/sort_order/asc/cols/stats.
10 https://bettercarenetwork.org.
11 https://www.scienceguide.nl.
12 https://www.africaknows.eu.

References

Altbach, P., & de Wit, H (2018, 23 February). The challenge to higher education internationalisation. *University World News.* https://www.universityworldnews.com/post.php?story=20180220091648602

Bailey, L. (2024). *Challenging the internationalisation of education: A critique of the global gaze.* Routledge.

Bamberger, A., & Morris, P. (2023). Critical perspectives on internationalization in higher education: Commercialization, global citizenship, or postcolonial imperialism? *Critical Studies in Education, 65*(2), 128–146. https://doi.org/10.1080/17508487.2023.2233572

Beelen, J., & Jones, E. (2015). Redefining internationalization at home. In A. Curai, L. Matei, R. Pricopie, J. Salmi & P. Scott (Eds.), *The European higher education area: Between critical reflections and future policies* (pp. 67–80). Springer. Retrieved from http://link.springer.com/book/10.1007/978-3-319-20877-0

Brandenburg, U., & De Wit, H. (2010, winter edition): The end of internationalization. *Boston College Newsletter, 62,* 15–17.

Cai, Y., & Leask, B. (2024). Rethinking internationalization of higher education for society from an outside-in perspective. *Journal of Asian Public Policy,* 1–19. https://doi.org/10.1080/17516234.2024.2406093

Crowther, P., Joris, M., Otten, M., Nilsson, B., Teekens, H., & Wächter, B. (2001). *Internationalisation at home; A position paper.* European Association for International Education.

De Wit, H. (2018, 31 August). Internationalisation of HE – Successes and failures. https://www.universityworldnews.com/post.php?story=20180828132002280

De Wit, H. (2024). 'Everything that quacks is internationalization' – Critical reflections on the evolution of higher education internationalization. *Journal of Studies in International Education, 28*(1), 3–14. https://doi.org/10.1177/10283153231221655

De Wit, H., Gacel-Avila, J., Jones, E., & Jooste, N. (Eds.). (2017). *The globalization of internationalisation; Emerging voices and perspectives.* Routledge.

De Wit, H., Hunter, F., Howard, L., & Egron-Polak, E. (Eds.). (2015). *Internationalisation of Higher Education.* European Parliament, Directorate-General for Internal Policies.

Education First (2024). *English proficiency index.* https://www.ef.com/assetscdn/WIBIwq6RdJvcD9bc8RMd/cefcom-epi-site/reports/2024/ef-epi-2024-english.pdf

Favier, F., Thravalou, E., & Peeters, L. (2022). *Inclusie in uitgaande mobiliteit. Welke groepen studenten zijn het minst geneigd om naar het buitenland te gaan en waarom?* [Inclusion in outbound mobility: Which groups of students are least likely to go abroad what are their reasons?]. Nuffic.

Greenfield, M. (2024, 26 September). Data shows 35% drop in interest in studying in Canada. *University World News.* www.universityworldnews.com/post.php?story=20240926140444361

Hartman, E., Pillard, N., Ferrarini, C., Messmore, N. Sabea, E., Al-Ebahim, B., & Brown, J. M. (2020). Coloniality-decoloniality and critical global citizenship: Identity, belonging, and education abroad. *Frontiers: The Interdisciplinary Journal of Study Abroad,* 32(1), 33–59.

Heath, T., & Johnstone, C. (2024). Imaginaries, integration, and resistance: The case of initiatives in internationalization, interculturalization and indigenization in a Canadian University. *Journal of Studies in International Education,* 28(2), 278–295. https://doi.org/10.1177/10283153221137652

Heleta, S. (2023). Critical review of the policy framework for internationalisation of higher education in South Africa. *Journal of Studies in International Education,* 27(5), 817–833.

Heleta, S., & Chasi, S. (2022), Rethinking and redefining internationalisation of higher education in South Africa using a decolonial lens. *Journal of Higher Education Policy and Management.* https://doi.org/10.1080/1360080X.2022.2146566

International Association of Universities (2012). *Affirming academic values in internationalization of higher education: A call for action.* Author. International Association of Universities (IAU).

International Education Association of South Africa (2014). *Nelson Mandela bay global dialogue declaration on the future of internationalisation of higher education.* Author. International Education Association of South Africa (IEASA).

Kamyab, S., & Raby, R. (2023). *Unintended consequences of internationalization in higher education.* Routledge.

Kemman, M., Kleter, S., Van Wijk, F., Tossaint, E., & O'Dowd, R. (2024). *Onderzoek VIS-projecten, Tussenrapport 2024* [Research Virtual International Collaboration projects, Interim report, 2024] Dialogic. https://dialogic.nl/wp-content/uploads/2022/01/Dialogic-Tussenrapport-VIS-onderzoek-2024.pdf

King, R., Findlay, A., & Arens, J. (2010). *International student mobility literature review; Report to HEFCE, and co-funded by the British Council, UK National Agency for Erasmus.* Higher Education Funding Council for England.

Knight, J. (2004). Internationalization remodeled: Definition, approaches, and rationales. *Journal of Studies in International Education,* 8(1), 5–31. https://doi.org/10.1177/1028315303260832

Knight, J. (2008). *Higher education in turmoil; the changing world of internationalization.* Sense Publishers.

Kommers, S., & Bista, K. (Eds.). (2021). *Inequalities in study abroad and student mobility; Navigating challenges and future directions.* Routledge.

Leask, B. (2015). *Internationalization of the curriculum.* Routledge.

Liu, W. (2020). The Chinese definition of internationalisation in higher education. *Journal of Higher Education Policy and Management.* https://doi.org/10.1080/1360080X.2020.1777500

Marginson, S. (2023). Limitations of the leading definition of 'internationalisation' of higher education: Is the idea wrong or is the fault in reality? *Globalisation, Societies and Education.* https://doi.org/10.1080/14767724.2023.2264223

Nikula, P.-T., Lamont, A., & Renders, E. (2024). Digital approaches to sustainability. In C. Woodman, M. Whatley, & C. Glass, *Digital internationalization in higher education* (pp. 45–56). Routledge.

Ovchinnikova, E., Van Mol, C., & Jones, E. (2024). Foreign language skills in the study abroad decision-making process and destination choices. *Journal of Studies in International Education*. https://doi.org/10.1177/10283153241251925

Pashby, K. (2015). Reimagining global citizenship education in an era of neoliberalism. *Globalisation, Societies and Education, 13*(3), 329–350.

Peeters, L., & Slappendel-Henschen, A. (2022). *Trein of vliegtuig? Een studie naar de kansen en mogelijkheden voor duurzaam internationaliseren* [Train or plane? A study into opportunities and possibilities for sustainable internationalisation]. Nuffic.

Rumbley, L., & Hoekstra-Selten, J. (2024). *The EAIE barometer; Internationalisation in Europe* (3rd ed.). EAIE.

Rumbley, L., & Sandström, A.-M. (2019). *The EAIE barometer; Money matters*. EAIE.

Saarikallio-Torp, M., & Wiers-Jenssen, J. (Eds.). (2010). *Nordic students abroad. Student mobility patterns, student support systems and labour market outcomes*. Helsinki: The Social Insurance Institution of Finland.

Stein, S. (2021). Critical internationalisation studies at an impasse: Making space for complexity, uncertainty, and complicity in a time of global challenges. *Studies in Higher Education, 46*(9), 1771–1784. https://doi.org/10.1080/03075079.2019.1704722

Stein, S., Andreotti, V., Bruce, J., & Suša, R. (2016). Towards different conversations about the internationalization of higher education. *Comparative and International Education/Éducation Comparée et Internationale, 45*(1), Article 2.

Universities of the Netherlands (2023). Ranking the university & Administrative response from Universities of The Netherlands (UNL). www.universiteitenvannederland.nl/files/publications/Ranking_the_university_ENG.pdf

Van den Hende, F. (2024). *Curriculum internationalisation: A dynamic organisational change process*. Doctoral dissertation University of Groningen.

Van Gaalen, A., & Gielesen, R. (2016). Internationalisation at home: Dutch higher education policies. In E. Jones, R. Coelen, J. Beelen, & H. de Wit (Eds.), *Global and local internationalization* (pp. 149–154). Sense Publishers.

Van Gaalen, A., Hobbes, H. J., Roodenburg, S., & Gielesen, R. (2014). *Studenten internationaliseren in eigen land; Nederlands instellingsbeleid* [Students internationalise in their own country; Policies of Dutch HEIs]. EP-Nuffic.

Vavrus, F., & Pekol, A. (2015). Critical internationalization: Moving from theory to practice. *FIRE: Forum for International Research in Education, 2*(2). Retrieved from http://preserve.lehigh.edu/fire/vol2/iss2/2

Wimpenny, K., Beelen, J., Hindrix, K., King, V., & Sjoer, E. (2021) Curriculum internationalization and the 'decolonizing academic'. *Higher Education Research & Development*. 10.1080/07294360.2021.2014406

Wingrove, P., Zuaro, B., Nao, M., Yuksel, D., Littvay, L., & Hultgren, A. (2024). University autonomy is a predictor of English medium instruction in European higher education. *Higher Education*. https://doi.org/10.1007/s10734-024-01333-8

Whitsed, C., & Green, W. (2013, 26 January). Internationalisation begins with the curriculum. *University World News*, issue 311. Retrieved from www.universityworldnews.com

3

UNIVERSITY GOVERNANCE AND INTERNATIONALIZATION

Navigating Disciplinary Cultures and Power Dynamics

Melanie Agnew

Introduction

Internationalization is increasingly driven by economic rationales (Buckner & Stein, 2020; De Wit & Altbach, 2021; Jiang, 2010; Stein et al., 2016; Stier, 2004). This economic focus necessitates taking a critical stance to internationalization. Critical internationalization is defined here as an approach to higher education that challenges traditional market-driven and Western-centric models of internationalization. The approach relies on the analysis of power dynamics and inequities, the questioning of whose knowledge is valued, and the shift of attention beyond economic rationales for internationalization.

To successfully implement a critical approach to internationalization of higher education, institutions must first understand the complex cultural dynamics that shape their operations, particularly as autonomy and academic freedom are deeply embedded in governance structures (Bartell, 2003; Kezar & Eckel, 2002; Kivinen & Poikus, 2006; Sporn, 1996, 1999). Therefore, understanding how a university is governed relative to its mission, leadership, governance, and academic disciplines is necessary for determining effective strategies to support critical internationalization.

The examination of governance in higher education's critical internationalization must begin by confronting the historical power structures that have shaped—and continue to shape—academic institutions worldwide. Colonial legacies and their ongoing influence on knowledge production and dissemination provide essential context for understanding how governance structures either perpetuate or challenge existing power dynamics.

This chapter examines the complex interplay between governance structures and internationalization in higher education through several key lenses. It begins by exploring how external forces and historical power dynamics shape institutional autonomy and academic freedom. The chapter then analyzes various models of university governance—hierarchy, anarchy, monarchy, and oligarchy—to demystify the internal working of governance subcultures. Following this, it examines how different academic disciplines approach internationalization, providing frameworks for understanding and engaging faculty across disciplinary boundaries. Throughout, the chapter maintains a critical perspective on how governance structures can either perpetuate or challenge existing power dynamics in global higher education.

External Environment and its Impact on University Governance

Academic Freedom and Institutional Autonomy

Self-governance is a central tenant of university culture thatprofoundly shaping academic work. Effective governance structures promote accountability, fairness, and inclusivity. These principles are essential in how the academic community expresses its values and pursues its mission. Among the various functions of governance, two stand out as particularly vital—maintaining institutional autonomy and protecting academic freedom. These elements are essential for universities to fulfill their roles as centers of *independent* thought and inquiry.

Contemporary Challenges

The earliest version of the academic freedom statement of the American Association of University Professors (AAUP) is the 1915 Declaration of Principles on Academic Freedom and Academic Tenure, which was updated in 1940 (AAUP). It protects faculty members' rights to research and teach in their respective content areas, regardless of its controversial nature. However, the Academic Freedom Index[1] (2024) reports that academic freedom continues to be under severe threat around the world. The report indicates that 23 countries are experiencing various degrees of erosion of academic freedom and only increasing in 10 countries. Of particular interest, the report draws a correlation between those countries that are highly polarized and have declining academic freedom. This may demonstrate the fragility of polarized countries and the risk to democratic ideals like liberty, equality, justice, and participation, which can act as political drivers to maintain the status quo and promote the commercialization of education.

The recent conflict in Gaza has firmly tested the strength and durability of institutional autonomy and academic freedom in higher education around the world. In the United States, for example, one only needs to Google news broadcasts highlighting the intense pressure from legislators investigating three presidents of prestigious universities (Carillo, 2023). The primary inquiry from lawmakers during the hearings was whether calling for the genocide of Jewish people violated their respective universities' codes of conduct. When excessive government control infiltrates the decision-making process of higher education institutions, it can lead to a stifling of academic freedom, reduced institutional autonomy, and potentially biased or politically motivated curriculum choices. According to Reich (2023), this controversy was additionally called into question when university donors wanted the presidents ousted for their lack of response: "But to use [the] power [of] major donors to force or seek the ouster of these presidents is almost as repugnant as the failures of these presidents to unambiguously condemn calls for genocide" (Reich, 2023). The challenge to preserving institutional autonomy and academic freedom was demonstrated in the case of Gaza at many universities, signaling the strength and persistence of the triple helix in negotiating the mission of higher education worldwide.

The Triple Helix of Control

The congressional hearings and the presidents' responses emphasize the complexity of how higher education is coordinated and controlled in the triple helix of market (donors), state (politicians) and education (presidents). In the case of Gaza, the following was demonstrated: 1) the heavy-handedness of government supported by formal authority and political ideology in university affairs as it relates to the fragility of academic freedom; 2) the ways in which the external environment influences internal decision-making; 3) the dynamic reciprocity of influence between universities, market, and state (triple helix); and 4) what can occur when too much government control penetrates higher education institutions decision-making processes. The pressure from government and major donors on three prestigious institutions demonstrates the fragility of organizations where autonomy is crucial for pursuing freedom of speech and action.

These contemporary pressures on higher education institutions reflect longstanding patterns of power and control that trace back to colonial influences. Understanding these historical power dynamics provides crucial context for how modern governance structures evolved and continue to operate.

Appropriation, Occupation, and Control

As we consider the role of governance in higher education, it is necessary to examine the complex historical and power dynamics that have shaped—and continue to influence—higher education, particularly through the lenses of colonialism and decolonialism. Colonialism deeply embeds itself in university policies, structures, funding streams, and culture, often prioritizing the history, literature, and scientific knowledge of colonizers while minimizing contributions from indigenous cultures. At the 2011 International Conference on *Decolonising Our Universities* at Universiti Sains Malaysia, participants wrote this statement published in Global Higher Education:

> We agreed that for far too long have we lived under the Eurocentric assumption – drilled into our heads by educational systems inherited from colonial regimes – that our local knowledges, our ancient and contemporary scholars, our cultural practice, our indigenous intellectual traditions, our stories, our histories and our languages portray hopeless, defeated visions no longer fit to guide our universities – therefore, better given up entirely.
>
> *(GlobalHigherEd, 2011)*

Colonial policies have led to epistemic injustice, where knowledge systems of marginalized communities are devalued and erased by dominant knowledge cultures (Fricker, 2007; Gonzales, et al. 2023; Stein, 2017; Tuck & Yang, 2012). The aim of epistemic justice is to ensure equal access to knowledge, recognizing and valuing different ways of knowing. This concept highlights the need to address systemic biases and inequities in knowledge production and dissemination. In higher education, epistemic injustice reinforces power dynamics and affects which knowledge systems are prioritized within the teaching and learning environment, delimiting the knowledge students acquire. This reality restricts students' ability to be self-reflexive and diminishes the opportunities to evaluate different sources of knowledge.

Decolonialism, on the other hand, is a movement that seeks to challenge the legacies of colonialism. It aims to deconstruct dominant narratives while amplifying marginalized perspectives, particularly those of non-Western and Indigenous peoples (Stein & De Andreotti, 2016). However, decolonialism can sometimes lead to cultural relativism, where all cultural practices and beliefs are considered equally valid, potentially disregarding human rights or perpetuating harmful practices (Kanarek, 2014). In other words, cultural relativism may jeopardize human rights in that cultural traditions can justify actions that violate those rights.

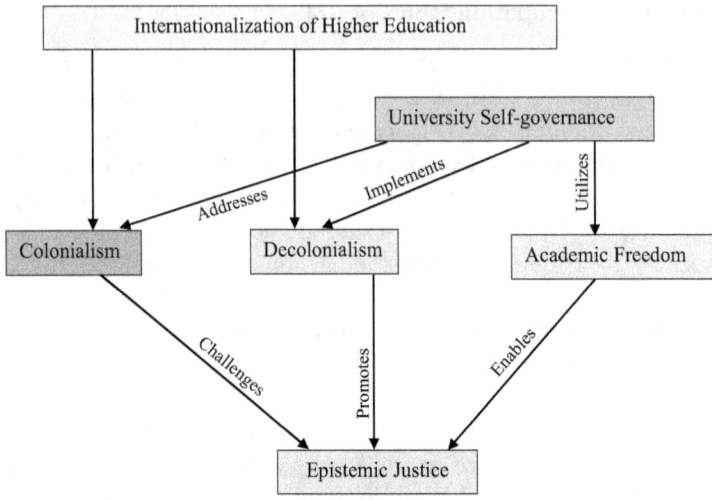

FIGURE 3.1 Academic Freedom: Path to Epistemic Justice.

The relationship between cultural relativism and human rights presents a fundamental tension in decolonial contexts. While cultural relativism advocates for respecting traditional practices and resisting Western impositions, this stance can conflict with universal human rights principles that prioritize individual protections. Successfully navigating this tension requires a nuanced approach that both honors cultural diversity and upholds fundamental human rights.

University governance offers many opportunities to critically address the impacts of colonialism and decolonialism. Specifically, it has the capacity to address systemic inequities through discourse and action drawing upon institutional autonomy and academic freedom (Figure 3.1). On the other hand, the formal governance structure operating within higher education is created and occupied by the dominant majority that perpetuates systemic inequities. While the challenges of addressing colonialism and decolonialism in higher education are complex, the structure and practices of university self-governance provide a potential framework for navigating these issues and promoting equity in academia.

University Governance

Models of Bi-Cameral Governance

Models of university governance have evolved over time. The bi-cameral governance structure, which is the focus here, consists of two interrelated but separate bodies—the faculty and senior administrators, including boards of governance (Greenfield, 2022). It is intended to support inclusive and transparent decision-making, directly impacting academic freedom by safeguarding the roles of both administrators and faculty. Effective governance structures that ensure faculty participation in decision-making and protect against external pressures are essential for maintaining an environment where academic freedom thrives, and educational aims are preserved.

However, when faculty and administrators of an institution operate from dominant views and do not understand and/or support inclusion practices, they run the risk of creating conditions that breed and or perpetuate systemic inequities. Further, faculty in some disciplines may have more power and influence due to commercial relevance (e.g., engineering and technology, biotechnology, and business and economics) in times of severe budget cuts and weak public support for education. Faculty in commercially relevant fields may have more support for their research interests due to the economic benefits to the institution and can therefore have stronger voices in decision-making processes at the campus level.

One central and well-established aspect of university governance is the tenure and promotion system. This system operates as a peer-review evaluation system rewarding faculty for teaching, research, and service. It provides peer support for sustained or improved performance expectations in research, teaching, and service, and is typically weighted in most universities according to institutional type—research or teaching. This faculty-developed self-governing policy differentiates at the department level (disciplinary) rendering variation among standards for tenure and promotion across academic departments and schools/colleges. Because it is a system used to measure faculty performance for promotion and tenure, it can be a highly motivating and often-feared accountability measure for promoting faculty and, at the same time, advancing campus priorities, like internationalization.

However, it too can reinforce existing systemic inequities when dominant voices prevail, and underlying assumptions therein go unexamined. This occurs when dominant voices within the institution, who often represent the majority, be it disciplinary, rank, or social group, set and influence standards and criteria for tenure and promotion. Whether inadvertent or intentional, those with dominant voices can exercise bias that favors curricula, disciplines, funding, types of service, teaching methodologies, program philosophy, and institutional values, to name several aspects of university culture. As a result, faculty members who may already be marginalized by race, class, gender, sexual orientation, discipline, language, research methodologies, etcetera, may find they are being measured against standards that may not align with their teaching, research, and service interests.

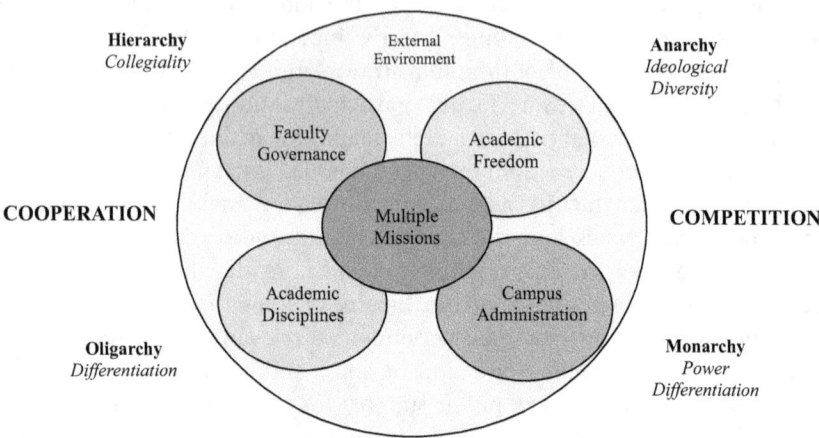

FIGURE 3.2 Higher Education Organizational Culture.

Subcultures of the Bi-Cameral Governance Structure[2]

Within the bi-cameral governance system, sub-cultures also emerge, influencing decision-making and power dynamics. Understanding these subcultures is vital to grasp how governance plays out to support and/or impede internationalization efforts and other campus priorities.

Within the institutional governance framework, various formal governance models exist among the sub-cultures (such as administration, faculty, departments, and unit heads) as illustrated in Figure 3.2. These models foster collaboration and competition and operate to maintain the status quo or work to address inequities and oftentimes are done simultaneously.

Hierarchical Governance

Academic institutions typically feature a *hierarchical* governance structure within the faculty sub-culture, comprising of full, associate, and assistant professors, and non-tenured or adjunct faculty. Decision-making authority is generally concentrated among those in higher positions, particularly full professors who have successfully navigated the tenure and promotion process. Their authority extends to various academic matters, including tenure and promotion of colleagues, research priorities, curriculum development, hiring decisions, community service initiatives, and resource allocation. This hierarchical structure can create tension between academic independence and the cooperation required for effective academic work, potentially creating collegial challenges. It's important to note that this analysis focuses on *formal governance* structures and does not account for social attributes, such as popularity or personality traits, that may increase an individual's influence regardless of their rank.

Academic work often requires a high degree of independence, as faculty members pursue their individual research interests, develop their courses, engage with community, and most do so with the aim of earning tenure. At the same time, successful academic work also relies on collaboration, whether through department or interdepartmental governance, joint research projects, or curriculum development. The centralized decision-making of higher-ranking individuals can sometimes suppress the independence, innovation, creativity, and contributions of lower-ranking or non-tenured faculty, which may quickly lead to feelings of disenfranchisement and a lack of collegiality and support needed to meet or exceed formal performance standards.

Anarchical Governance

An *anarchical* governance structure in higher education is characterized by a lack of formal authority and a decentralized decision-making process. Power is most dispersed with "committees of the whole" in that all faculty members can participate. This structure can exist at the department, unit, or institutional levels and can operate in tandem with and independent from representative structures like faculty senates. In the United States, for example, the faculty senate operates as a horizontal structure, where each member has an equal say in decisions related to curriculum, hiring, tenure, mission, values, and other academic matters. While ideological diversity among faculty members can lead to a more participatory decision-making process and a broader range of perspectives and ideas, it can also result in a lack of accountability and efficiency without a central authority. Ideological differentiation can be challenging in an anarchical structure due to the competing expectations of academic independence and competition. The most problematic challenge for leadership in this arrangement, however, may be the ambiguous or contested decision-making authority.

For example, consider a university department where decisions about curriculum changes are made by committee. Every faculty member has an equal vote, and decisions are made collectively. This formal arrangement ensures that diverse viewpoints are considered and that all faculty members have a voice. However, without a central authority to guide or expedite the decision-making process, reaching a consensus can become time-consuming, inefficient, and difficult. If there is a significant ideological diversity within the department, debates can become prolonged and highly contentious, leading to delays in academic work. Additionally, if some faculty members are more vocal or persuasive than others, their viewpoints might dominate the process, potentially skewing decisions in their favor (whether right or wrong) and causing resentment among other faculty members who feel their opinions are not adequately considered. This lack of clear decision-making authority can create an environment where it is difficult to hold anyone accountable for the outcomes. Consequently, this can negatively impact the department's efficiency, effectiveness, and work climate in responding to academic needs.

Monarchical Governance

A *monarchical* governance structure in higher education is characterized by a hierarchical decision-making process with power concentrated in a single leader or a small group of leaders. This includes positions such as the president, provost, deans, or other unit heads who hold significant decision-making authority. In this structure, the president or another leader has ultimate decision-making power and can make decisions with minimal input or feedback from stakeholders. While this can lead to a streamlined decision-making process, allowing decisions to be made quickly and efficiently, it can also result in a lack of transparency, accountability, and input from other stakeholders. Decisions made without broad input will likely fail to address the wider political, economic, and educational needs of the institution, leading to considerable conflict and disgruntlements among those who will experience the impact of such a decision. Power differentiation in a monarchical structure faces challenges due to the conflicting expectations of competition and interdependence.

Consider how a university president might implement an international initiative under monarchical governance. In this structure, the president typically makes decisions independently. They may not consult faculty, staff, students, the local community, or international partners. This approach has both advantages and drawbacks. On the positive side, it enables swift implementation and rapid responses to external pressures. However, the lack of stakeholder input often creates problems. Faculty and staff may feel excluded and resist the initiative. Critical concerns about academic programs and resource allocation might be overlooked. When significant funding is required, it can divert resources from existing programs. This reallocation often breeds resentment among faculty and deans.

Despite these challenges, a monarchical governance structure can be effective in situations requiring decisive and rapid action, like responding to a global pandemic. Balancing the need for efficient decision-making with the importance of inclusivity, transparency, and accountability is crucial to addressing the broader needs and concerns of the institution. For example, even in a monarchical structure, the president could establish advisory committees or hold town hall meetings to gather input before making significant decisions, thereby fostering a sense of involvement, and mitigating some of the potential downsides of a top-down approach.

Oligarchic Governance

In a sub-culture with *oligarchic* governance, decision-making is concentrated within a small group of people who hold most of the power and authority. These individuals often possess specific areas of expertise and are responsible for decisions related to those areas. This can be seen in academic disciplines whereby faculty members exercise authority based on their expertise. They design coursework and curriculum and make decisions about hiring new colleagues or adjunct instructors. One significant challenge in this system is structural differentiation, which juxtaposes expectations of competition and academic interdependence. On the one hand, faculty members and departments may compete for resources, recognition, and influence which can drive innovation, creativity, and excellence, but it can also create tensions and fierce rivalries. On the other hand, academic interdependence demands collaboration, effective shared governance, and a collective effort to enact the institution's values, achieve its common goals, and work professionally to realize its mission.

For example, in a university governed by a small group of senior faculty members, decisions about curriculum changes, research priorities, and faculty hiring are formally made by this select few. While these faculty members may have deep expertise and a broad perspective on the institution's needs, their concentrated power can easily lead to mistrust and retribution among the broader faculty. Assistant faculty members and other stakeholders, for example, might feel excluded from the decision-making process, leading to perceptions of bias, perception confirmation, favoritism, and/or resistance to new ideas. This can hinder innovation and collaboration, maintain the status quo, and create a fragmented academic community in which nobody wins.

To address these challenges, institutions can implement more inclusive governance structures, such as involving a broader range of faculty, staff, and external stakeholders in decision-making committees, increasing transparency in how decisions are made, and creating multiple communication channels that will increase broad involvement in the process. By balancing faculty expertise with broader participation from existing stakeholders, universities can enhance trust, encourage cooperation, and ensure that decisions reflect the perspectives and expertise to realize their mission.

Understanding how various governance models and related tensions manifest in higher education is crucial for leadership in achieving institutional missions and strategic goals, such as internationalization. The reciprocity of influence between governance structures and institutional goals significantly impacts leadership effectiveness in higher education. Organizational behavior impacts how culture is simultaneously created and shared among its members. That is, it establishes "how we do things around here". While governance models, whether informal or formal, exist in all universities, it is not always expressed in similar ways across a university or a system of universities.

The Academic Disciplines

Disciplinary Categories and Knowledge Production

While governance structures frame university decision-making, academic disciplines are central to higher education to curriculum development and, hence, knowledge creation and dissemination. The disciplines influence teaching, research, methods, and assessments, significantly shaping how internationalization is perceived and implemented. Shifting focus from broad governance structures to specific disciplines highlights unique challenges and opportunities to the internationalization process.

One major challenge to realizing an internationalization mission is faculty engagement (Agnew, 2012; Bulnes & De Louw, 2022; Clifford, 2009; Eftekhari, et al. 2025; Leask, 2015). Internationalization of the curriculum, which directly informs global learning and is a root-level, fundamental, and necessary strategy for campus-wide internationalization. Global learning is defined as "…a critical analysis of and an engagement with complex, interdependent global systems and legacies (such as natural, physical, cultural, economic, and political) and their implications for people's lives and earth's sustainability" (AAC&U, n.d.). To this end, campus-wide faculty participation is central to internationalization. Engaging faculty through professional development focused on curriculum internationalization can boost faculty involvement (Bulnes & De Louw, 2022; Clifford, 2009; Eftekhari, Yousefzadeh, & Coelen, 2025). Eftekari et al. (2025) further suggests that equipping leaders with specific strategies and resources can help them effectively engage faculty (i.e., academics) in initiatives like the internationalization of the curriculum, which is central to internationalization. This includes incorporating international content, methodologies, and assessments. Faculty who are equipped to internationalize curriculum can better adopt effective teaching strategies and prepare graduates for the joys and demands of the 21st century.

Researchers have examined differences in disciplinary approaches to knowledge acquisition, production, and dissemination (Becher & Trowler, 2001) and in how faculty members think about internationalization within the context of their discipline (Agnew, 2012; Bulnes & de Louw, 2022; Clifford, 2009; Eftekhari, et al. 2025; Green & Whitsed, 2015; Jones & Killick, 2013; Landorf et al., 2018; Leask, 2015).

In interviewing 37 faculty members across three institutions in the United States, Agnew (2012) identified specific disciplinary attributes arranged by Becher and Trowler's four disciplinary categories (Table 3.2). While it can be difficult to discern disciplinary boundaries between the categories, faculty members in this study self-selected into one category based on Becher and Trowler's description. Only one of the 37 faculty members articulated that he has worked hard to think in interdisciplinarity terms and, as such, self-selecting into one disciplinary domain was difficult to do. This spotlights the idea that faculty members live very deeply in their respective disciplines, or "tribes and territories" (Becher & Trowler, 2001). This siloed effect can be problematic for interdisciplinary and transdisciplinary teaching, research, and service needed to address global issues.

This discussion explores the research-based attributes identified by Agnew (2012) and connects them to the global learning approaches outlined by Landorf et al. (2018). Suggestions are provided on how to engage discipline-specific faculty members in the process of internationalizing their curriculum. Understanding the academic disciplines relative to critical internationalization helps to distinguish distinct norms, values, power structures, and decision-making processes that shape each field. This means leaders will better navigate and challenge entrenched dynamics that often maintain the status quo and perpetuate systemic inequities.

Disciplinary Categories and Their Approaches to Internationalization

Epistemological orientations were identified using Becher and Trowler's four disciplinary categories—hard applied/pure and soft applied/pure (Agnew, 2012) in the US context. Table 3.2 provides a comprehensive summary of how internationalization manifests across these four disciplinary categories. This table synthesizes key findings from Agnew's (2012) study, highlighting the distinct attributes and approaches to internationalization for each category. Findings indicate that internationalization manifests in different ways relative to subjective-objective and the applied or pure qualities of the discipline categories.

Table 3.1, 3.2 and 3.3 present a progressive analysis of how academic disciplines approach and engage with internationalization Table 3.1 begins by mapping the fundamental characteristics of each disciplinary category

TABLE 3.1 Summary of Internationalization in the Context of Disciplinary Categories

	Applied	Pure
Hard	Competitive; purposive; functional Economic imperative Technology and product-driven International governing regulations International faculty/little technology transfer Relevance of language ability	Discipline is borderless Universal language Transcends cultural context Value-free; impersonal Relevance of the scientific process (data) Standardized curricula/governing regulation English as the global language Prone to homogenization
Soft	Value of reflective practice Relevance of local culture Challenge beliefs, values, assumptions Value human experience Application of learning Multiple ways of knowing	Inherently international Inherently interdisciplinary Highly interpretative Value of human experience Relevance of local culture Multiple ways of knowing

TABLE 3.2 Discipline-based Attributes (Agnew, 2012) and Approaches to Global Learning (Landorf et al., 2018).

Disciplinary Group	Attributes	Approaches to Global Learning
Hard-pure (pure math and sciences)	Discipline is borderless Universal language Transcends cultural context Value-free; impersonal Relevance of the scientific process (data) Standardized curricula/governing regulation English as the global language Prone to homogenization	International and intercultural case studies Interpretation of results via cultural, economic, political lens Marginalization of non-English speakers, non-Western ideas Mobility of ideas International issues around data collection, measurement, storage, publication, sharing, utility, and ownership Intercultural communication and collaboration strategies Interrelationship of local and global, homogenization and diversification

(*Continued*)

TABLE 3.2 (Continued)

Disciplinary Group	Attributes	Approaches to Global Learning
Hard-applied (technologies)	Competitive; purposive; functional Economic imperative Technology and product-driven International governing regulations International faculty/little technology transfer Relevance of language ability	International design, manufacturing, testing, packaging, marketing, and usage practices and regulations International content Intercultural communication and collaboration
Soft-pure (humanities)	Inherently international Inherently interdisciplinary Highly interpretative Value of human experience Relevance of local culture Multiple ways of knowing	Social construction of knowledge Critical self-reflection Empathic understanding of others' lived experiences Interdisciplinary approaches to problem solving Knowledge of diverse cultural beliefs, values, and practices Experiential learning Intercultural communication and collaboration skills Application of knowledge in service to others
Soft-applied (social sciences)	Value of reflective practice Relevance of local culture Challenge beliefs, values, assumptions Value human experience Application of learning Multiple ways of knowing	Critical self-reflection and reflective practices Empathic understanding of others' lived experiences Interdisciplinary approaches to problem solving Knowledge of diverse cultural beliefs, values, and practices Experiential learning Intercultural communication and collaboration skills Perspective taking

Source: Adapted from Agnew, 2012 and Landorf et al., 2018.

TABLE 3.3 Disciplines and Stein et al.'s (2016) Articulations of Internationalization

Disciplines	Stein's Articulations of Internationalization
Hard disciplines (e.g., technology, engineering, physics, chemistry)	**Global knowledge economy** • Improve CVs; develop differential human capital for success in global labor market
Soft disciplines (e.g., education, nursing, philosophy, psychology)	**Global public good** • Self-betterment; benevolent social entrepreneurship and public responsibility *(noblesse oblige)* **Anti-oppressive internationalization** • Act in solidarity with marginalized people and groups in pursuit of social justice; affirm critical hope **Relational Translocalism** • Political and disenchantment with existing imaginaries, relationships, existence (including currents and counter-currents).

and their basic approaches to internationalization. Table 3.2 then builds on these findings by connecting disciplinary attributes to specific global learning approaches, providing practical insights for engaging faculty. Finally, Table 3.3 elevates the analysis to a critical perspective by examining how different disciplines align with broader articulations of internationalization, revealing underlying power dynamics and systemic inequities.

As shown in Table 3.1, faculty in the *hard-pure disciplinary category* (e.g., physics, chemistry) indicated that hard-pure disciplines are inherently international, borderless, and universal and that science transcended context and therefore remains impersonal and value-free. Notably, researchers have consistently found it challenging to recruit faculty from hard pure disciplines for studies on internationalization in the context of the disciplines (Agnew, 2012; Bulnes & de Louw, 2022; Clifford, 2009; Eftekari, et al. 2025). Low participation may stem from these faculty members' belief that their work is already international and borderless by nature. Consequently, they might see little need to engage in additional internationalization efforts, leading them to decline invitations to participate in related studies or initiatives.

To address this challenge, Clifford (2009) suggests offering group professional development opportunities for faculty in the hard-pure disciplines. The sessions could focus on dialogue about internationalizing their curriculum, helping them to recognize the value of explicit internationalization efforts even in field perceived as inherently global. However, because it has been difficult to engage faculty in the hard-pure internationalization initiatives, new approaches are needed. It might be the case that engaging them by speaking directly to the ontology and epistemology of their disciplines will naturally interest them in this work. Specifically, framing internationalization in ontological and epistemological ways *and* as an opportunity to address global issues can be a way to invite faculty members and, especially those in the hard pure disciplines. Further, engaging them in larger conversations about global purposes to which their work could make highly significant impact to the health of our world could be an effective faculty recruitment strategy.

In *the hard-applied disciplinary category*, the divergence of local and global issues such as global warming and environmental effects of consumerism, for example, require university students to develop global competencies, such as language and communication abilities, and to engage with local culture. Language and communication competencies are critical in the hard-applied discipline because, as faculty reported (Agnew, 2012), a single product may be a result of individual pieces of that product being produced in different countries. This multinational product development emphasizes the need for language abilities of graduates to succeed in the global work environment. Also noted in Table 3.1 in the hard-applied category was the notion that while there were considerable international faculty there was little international content in the curriculum (Agnew, 2012; Bulnes & De Louw, 2022). The "absence of knowledge transfer" raises a significant concern regarding faculty member's capacity to question their own disciplinary epistemology with the intentional or unintentional result of privileging Western ways of knowing. Most disciplines endorse the need for global competence, reflection on values, and knowledge systems of the disciplines, and for including global perspectives in the curriculum (Agnew, 2012).

As shown in Table 3.1 *soft-pure disciplines* (such as sociology, philosophy) emphasize attributes that are innately international, inherently interdisciplinary, and highly relevant to local culture. These disciplines naturally lend themselves to internationalization due to their focus on understanding human experiences across different cultural contexts. Of particular importance in soft-pure disciplines is the notion that students should experience other cultures with depth and breadth. This immersion helps students more easily absorb, learn, and understand what it means to be human in another culture. Additionally, these disciplines often explicitly expect students to apply their knowledge to real-world problems, aiming to improve the lived experiences of others.

However, the interpretative nature of soft-pure disciplines presents unique challenges when it comes to standardization. Even within a single discipline, the degree of interpretation can vary significantly, adding complexity to decision-making processes in curriculum internationalization. This means that subsequent interpretation of concepts and theories cannot be easily standardized across different cultural contexts, requiring a nuanced approach to internationalization efforts in these fields.

The *soft-applied disciplinary* attributes as shown in Table 3.1 include the relevance of local culture and recognize that there are multiple ways of knowing (Agnew, 2012). The related approaches to global learning for those faculty members in the soft-applied disciplinary group are, for example, empathic understanding of others' lived experiences and knowledge of diverse cultural beliefs, values, and practices (Landorf et al., 2018). Therefore, suggestions for engaging faculty members in these disciplines might be to enlist them in developing exchange programs where faculty members can experience different cultures firsthand or organize workshops focused on specific cultural beliefs, values, and practices so that faculty can learn about different perspectives and integrate those perspectives into coursework. Additionally, identifying collaborative international research and/or interdisciplinary projects can provide faculty with global perspectives and opportunities to apply their knowledge in diverse contexts.

Epistemological orientations of the disciplines highlight the different ways in which the academic disciplines approach and value internationalization in higher education. The hard-pure disciplines view their fields as inherently international and borderless, while soft-pure and applied disciplines recognize more explicit needs for cultural integration and global competencies. Faculty perspectives and engagement with internationalization vary significantly across these disciplinary categories, with hard-pure faculty being particularly challenging to recruit for internationalization initiatives due to their belief that their work is already international by nature.

Challenges in Internationalizing the Curriculum

Internationalizing the curriculum presents several challenges. It requires coordination among disciplines, degree requirements, and other key elements. This coordination involves agreeing on internationally relevant content and aligning with the broader goals of internationalization. However, the process is complex due to several factors:

1 Coordination among disciplines, institutions, and national education systems.
2 Risk of undervaluing local knowledge and perspectives.

3 Potential for over-standardization and loss of diverse perspectives.
4 Faculty resistance to perceived threats to academic freedom.
5 The dominance of English as the universal language and the perception that internationalization always involves teaching in English.

These challenges highlight the delicate balance required when internationalizing educational curricula, emphasizing the need for thoughtful and inclusive approaches that respect both global and local perspectives. Given these challenges and the need for balance, an examination of disciplinary attributes can inform effective strategies for engaging faculty in the internationalization process.

Strategies for Engaging Faculty in Different Disciplines

Faculty Engagement and Global Learning

So why are the disciplinary attributes important to know? Table 3.2 presents a synthesis of disciplinary attributes by Agnew (2012) and corresponding approaches to global learning as outlined by Landorf et al. (2018). Knowing how faculty members in specific disciplines approach global learning can assist leaders of internationalization in their efforts to engage faculty in this important work.

While Table 3.1 identifies the core characteristics of each disciplinary category, understanding how these attributes translate into specific approaches to global learning is crucial for developing effective engagement strategies. Table 3.2 bridges this gap by explicitly connecting disciplinary attributes to practical approaches in global learning.

For example, as shown in Table 3.2, the soft-applied disciplinary attributes include the relevance of local culture and recognize that there are multiple ways of knowing (Agnew, 2012). The related approaches to global learning for those faculty members in the soft-applied disciplinary group are, for example, empathic understanding of others' lived experiences and knowledge of diverse cultural beliefs, values, and practices (Landorf et al., 2018). Therefore, suggestions for engaging faculty members in these disciplines might be to enlist them in developing exchange programs where faculty members can experience different cultures firsthand or organize workshops focused on specific cultural beliefs, values, and practices so that faculty can learn about different perspectives and integrate those perspectives into research and coursework. Additionally, identifying collaborative international research and/or interdisciplinary projects can provide faculty with global perspectives and opportunities to apply their knowledge in diverse contexts.

Referring to Table 3.2, the hard-pure attributes are characterized by attributes such as standardized curriculum, English as a global language, and that the discipline is borderless with a universal language (Agnew, 2012). Bulnes and de Louw (2022) found that the hard pure faculty has a clear preference for objectivity as the faculty were uncomfortable discussing anything related to subjective views and perspectives. Approaches to global learning identified by Landorf et al. (2018) for faculty in the hard pure category include, for example, the marginalization of non-English speakers and non-Western ideas, intercultural communication and collaboration strategies, and the interrelationship of the local and global. Therefore, suggestions for engaging faculty members in the hard pure disciplines might be to develop an inclusive curriculum by integrating diverse perspectives and non-Western ideas into their coursework. This could be supported by curriculum grants and workshops that focus on inclusivity and representation. Further, because the hard-pure disciplines approach global learning as though it is already international, it may be important to promote interdisciplinary courses and projects that bridge hard-pure disciplines with social sciences and humanities, for example.

Table 3.2 indicates that the hard-applied disciplines are characterized by attributes such as the divergence of local and global issues and the importance of language abilities (Agnew, 2012). The corresponding approaches to global learning include developing global competencies and engaging with local culture (Landorf et al., 2018). To engage faculty in these disciplines, leaders might focus on creating opportunities for international collaborations on applied projects, emphasizing the importance of cross-cultural communication skills in professional settings, and developing case studies that highlight the interplay between local and global issues in their field.

For the soft-pure disciplines, Table 3.2 shows attributes such as being innately international, inherently interdisciplinary, and highly relevant to local culture (Agnew, 2012). Their approaches to global learning emphasize experiencing other cultures with depth and breadth and applying knowledge to improve others' lived experiences (Landorf et al., 2018). Strategies for engaging these faculty might include supporting long-term international research projects, encouraging the development of courses that explore global themes through multiple disciplinary lenses, and facilitating partnerships with international organizations for applied learning experiences.

A deeper focus on the interconnectedness of knowledge across disciplines, cultures, and national contexts may scaffold the idea, importance, and added value of difference thereby using the idea of knowledge development to engage faculty across all disciplines. Aligning this work to the idea of preparing graduates to address complex global issues may pique the interests of faculty in any discipline.

This analysis of disciplinary approaches to internationalization provides valuable insights into how different academic fields can engage with global perspectives. To fully understand the impact of these approaches, however, they must be examined through a more critical lens.

A Critical View of the Disciplines

Critical Analysis of Disciplinary Approaches

Stein et al. (2016) provide a critical framework of four articulations of internationalization, outlining the various goals, institutional drivers, and educational aims for each articulation of internationalization—global knowledge economy, the global public good, anti-oppressive internationalization, and relational localism. The following analysis aligns the four articulations with the main disciplinary motivations of faculty to engage in internationalization.

Having examined both the characteristics of different disciplines and their approaches to global learning, we can now analyze these patterns through a more critical lens. Table 3.3 situates these disciplinary approaches within broader frameworks of internationalization, revealing how different academic fields either reinforce or challenge existing power structures in global higher education.

Hard academic disciplines like technology, engineering, physics, and chemistry, for example align with the global knowledge economy in several distinct ways as illustrated in Table 3.3. Their main goals focus on improving individual and national economic advantage within the global "knowledge society" while generating income to address deficits from public defunding. The institutional drivers behind these disciplines emphasize branding, developing novel resource streams, and enhancing performance and productivity. Their educational aims center on developing human capital and building competencies for innovation, leadership, and entrepreneurship in global markets.

In contrast, soft academic disciplines like education, nursing, philosophy, and psychology, for example, more readily align with Stein's et al. (2016) remaining three articulations: the global public good, anti-oppressive, and relational translocalism. Their goals, while somewhat nuanced differently are not aligned directly and solely with the global knowledge economy. They do instead align more closely to the betterment of the individual, community, and our interconnectedness. Examples of these goals include such aspects as expanding opportunities for social mobility, working toward systemic change, and centering interdependence. The institutional drivers for these disciplines focus on advancing liberal democratic ideals, positioning the university as the critical conscience of society, and revitalizing marginalized knowledge. Their educational aims prioritize the ideas of democracy, equality, inclusion, and social cohesion, while working to transform oppressive structures and the disillusionment and disenchantment with exiting imaginaries.

To critically analyze the internationalization of academic disciplines within the context of today's global marketplace, it is necessary to recognize the privileging of certain disciplines and the marginalization of others. The economic motivations and demands of the global market align well with the priorities of hard-applied disciplines, which focus on producing tangible, market-driven outcomes. This market alignment privileges these disciplines, as their research efforts are closely tied to economic benefits and the demands of a globalized economy, making their projects more likely to receive funding.

Internationalization has led to technological advancements and the standardization of English in research publications which operates to facilitate the global mobility of ideas and scholars. Those scholars researching in English have greater control of research agendas and related policies that determine what counts as knowledge. Similarly, families with strong economic means have a wider selection of elite institutions for their children, benefiting education, career prospects, and social mobility. However, the dominance of English simultaneously empowers many scholars worldwide while marginalizing non-English speakers and non-Western perspectives. The global standardization of English has created inequities in knowledge dissemination, which often leads to the undervaluation of marginalized scholars. Exclusive practices in higher education internationalization highlight the need for a more equitable approach to global knowledge production and dissemination in academia.

Disciplinary Challenges and Inequities: Marginalization of the humanities

When universities reduce funding for humanities programs, they undermine their own educational mission. This shift reflects how market forces have gained too much influence over educational goals in the balance between market demands, government oversight, and academic priorities, the triple helix. All disciplines are needed to solve complex global issues. The humanities play a vital role in fostering critical thinking, cultural understanding, and ethical reasoning—essential foundations of a well-rounded education and a global perspective. When humanities disciplines are underfunded, it undermines the capacity to engage with diverse cultural contexts as it limits the attributes that these disciplines offer. That is, attributes such as the value of human experience, the relevance of local culture, empathy, reflexive practice, and the understandings of multiple ways of knowing.

The marginalization of the humanities in favor of more economically driven disciplines limits the scope of internationalization by narrowing the focus to market-oriented outcomes. This approach overlooks the importance of developing global citizens who can navigate complex cultural landscapes, appreciate diverse perspectives, and contribute to solving global challenges. Internationalization in education may be, to some extent, about economic gains, but not at the expense of higher education foundational educational aims.

A critical analysis of the internationalization of academic disciplines reveals the privileging of certain fields and the marginalization of others. To achieve critical internationalization, it is imperative to foster an inclusive academic environment that values the humanities and ensures equitable dissemination of knowledge across all disciplines. This is not possible without consideration of the interplay between higher education culture (governance, autonomy, academic disciplines) and the external, enabling environment.

Conclusion

The contemporary landscape of higher education calls for a critical approach to internationalization that challenges traditional, economically driven, and Western-centric models. This chapter explores the pivotal role of governance structures, academic disciplines, and external influences in shaping how universities engage with internationalization. A critical approach emphasizes the need to address power imbalances, value diverse forms of knowledge, and rethink the economic imperatives that too frequently dominate internationalization strategies.

University governance, with its varied models—hierarchical, monarchical, oligarchic, and anarchical—profoundly influences institutional autonomy and decision-making, creating both opportunities and constraints for global engagement. Similarly, how faculty understand internationalization in the context of their disciplines is important to determining engagement strategies. Protecting and exercising academic freedom is necessary in tempering market forces and government demands in the process of upholding democratic ideals in service to society.

Implications for Ethical Policies and Practices

1 *Balancing market needs and government demands with educational aims.* There is an ethical imperative for universities to temper commercial and government threats such that fundamental educational aims can be preserved.

2 *Addressing colonial legacies.* There is an ethical responsibility for institutions to critically examine and address these legacies, working toward epistemic justice and valuing diverse knowledge systems.
3 *Protecting academic freedom.* It is important to protect academic freedom and institutional autonomy, which are under threat in most countries. Universities have an ethical duty to safeguard these principles, even in the face of external pressures.
4 *Ensuring inclusive governance.* There is an ethical imperative to create governance structures that are transparent, accountable, and representative of diverse voices within the university community.
5 *Privileging of disciplines.* Universities have an ethical responsibility to ensure more equitable approaches that value diverse perspectives and resist the pressure to marginalize non-Western knowledge or non-English speakers.
6 *Preserving humanities and critical thinking.* Defunding humanities undermines the development of critical thinking, cultural understanding, and ethical reasoning crucial for internationalization and the capacity to address global challenges.
7 *Addressing systemic inequities.* Power structures in academia can perpetuate systemic inequities. Universities have an ethical obligation to critically examine and address these issues in their internationalization efforts.

Notes

1 Academic Freedom Index is a comprehensive tool design to assess the state of academic freedom in countries around the world. https://academic-freedom-index.net.
2 This model of the Bi-Cameral Governance Structure represents a synthesis of the author's research, professional observations, and analysis on higher education leadership, culture, and change from 2005–2020.

References

AAC&U (n.d.). Definitions of global learning. American Association of Colleges and Universities. Retrieved on November 1, 2024 from https://www.aacu.org/office-of-global-citizenship-for-campus-community-and-careers/definitions-of-global-learning.

Academic Freedom Index (2024). Downloaded on July 21, 2024 from https://academic-freedom-index.net/research/Academic_Freedom_Index_Update_2024.pdf

Agnew, M. (2012). Strategic planning: An examination of the role of disciplines in sustaining internationalization of the university. *Journal of Studies in International Education*, 17, 183–202.

Buckner, E. & Stein, S. (2020). What Counts as Internationalization? Deconstructing the Internationalization Imperative. Journal of Studies in International Education 2020, Vol. 24(2) 151–166.

Bartell, M. (2003). Internationalization of universities: A university culture-based framework. *Higher Education*, 45, 43–70.

Becher T., & Trowler, P., (2001). *Academic Tribes and Territories: Intellectual Inquiry and the culture of disciplines*. The Society for Research into Higher Education & Open University Press.

Bulnes, C., & de Louw, E. (2022). Towards a typology of internationalisation at home activities in academic disciplines: A study conducted at a Dutch university of applied sciences. *Compare: A Journal of Comparative and International Education*, 52(8) 1–20.

Carillo, S. (2023). After a disastrous testimony, three college presidents face calls to resign. National Public Radio (NPR). Downloaded on October 15, 2023 from https://www.npr.org/2023/12/08/1218314691/after-a-disastrous-testimony-three-college-presidents-face-calls-to-resign

Clifford, V. (2009). Engaging the disciplines in internationalizing the curriculum. *International Journal for Academic Development*, 14(2), 133–143.

De Wit, H., & Altbach, P. (2021). *Internationalization in higher education: Global trends and recommendations for its future*. Routledge.

Eftekhari, P., Yousefzadeh, S., & Coelen, R. J. (2025). Internationalization of the curriculum at home (IoCaH): Why academic disciplines matter. *Journal of Studies in International Education*. https://doi.org/10.1177/10283153241307967

Fricker, M. (2007). *Epistemic injustice: Power and the ethics of knowing*. Oxford University Press.

Gonzales, L., Pasque, P., Farris, K., & Hansen, J. (2023). Epistemic injustice and legitimacy in U.S. doctoral education: A systemic review of literature. https://doi.org/10.3102/00346543231187628

Green, W., & Whitsed, C. (Eds.). (2015). *Critical perspectives on internationising the curriculum in disciplines: Reflective narrative accounts from business, education, and health*. Sense.

Greenfield, N. (2022). At Oberlin, a long tradition of shared governance is ended. *University World News*. Retrieved on November 11, 2024, from https://www.universityworldnews.com/post.php?story=20221203065247323

GlobalHigher Ed. (2011, October 24). Creating a future with Indigenous Knowledge: Universities as platforms of Indigenous thought. Retrieved from https://globalhighered.wordpress.com/2011/10/24/creating-a-future-with-indigenous-knowledge/

Jiang, X. (2010). Towards the internationalization of higher education from a critical perspective. *Journal of Further and Higher Education*, 32(4), 347–358.

Jones, E., & Killick, D. (2013). Graduate attributes and the internationalized curriculum: Embedding a global outlook in disciplinary learning outcomes. *Journal of Studies in International Education*, 17(2), 165–182. https://doi.org/10.1177/1028315312473655

Kanarek, Jaret (2014). Critiquing cultural relativism. *The Intellectual Standard*, 2(2), 1.

Landorf, H., Doscher, S., & Hardick, J. (2018). *Making global learning universal*. Routledge.

Leask, B. (2015). *Internationalization of the curriculum*. Routledge.

Reich, R. (2023). Academic freedom is the loser when big donors hound US university presidents. *The Guardian*. Retrieved on July 15, 2024 from https://www.theguardian.com/commentisfree/2023/dec/12/us-college-donors-influence-gaza-israel

Stein, S. (2017). The persistent challenges of addressing epistemic dominance in higher education: Considering the case of curriculum internationalization. *Comparative Education Review*, V61, S1.

Stein, S., Andreotti, V., Bruce, J., & Suša, R. (2016). Towards different conversations about the internationalization of higher education. *Comparative and International Education/Éducation Compar Ée et Internationale, 45* 45(1), 1–18.

Stier, J. (2004) Taking a critical stance toward internationalization ideologies in higher education: idealism, instrumentalism and educationalism. *Globalisation, Societies and Education.*, 2 (1), 83–97.

Sporn, B. (1996). Managing university culture: an analysis of the relationship between Institutional culture and management approaches. *Higher Education*, 32, 41-61.

Sporn, B. (1999). *Adaptive university structures: An analysis of adaptation to socioeconomic environments of US and European universities.* London, UK: Jessica Kingsley.

Stein, S., & Andreotti, V. (2016). Decolonization and higher education. In M. Peters (Ed.), Encyclopedia of educational philosophy and theory. Singapore: Springer.

Tuck, E., & Yang, K. W. (2012). Decolonialization is not a metaphor. *Decolonialization: Indigeneity, Education & Society*, 1(1), 1–40

Kezar, A., & Eckel, P., (2002). The Effect of Institutional Culture on Change Strategies in Higher Education, *The Journal of Higher Education*, 73(4), 435–460.

Kivinen, O., & Poikus, P. (2006) Privileges of Universitas Magistrorum et Scolarium and their justification in charters of foundation from the 13th to the 21st centuries.*Higher Education*, 52, 185–213.

PART 2
Strategic Dimensions of Internationalization
Critical and Cultural Readiness Approaches

4
A CRITICAL APPROACH TO INTERNATIONALIZATION OF TEACHING AND LEARNING

Jos Beelen

Introduction: terminology

The 5th Global Survey of the International Association of Universities acknowledges that internationalization at home and internationalization are two separate concepts but considers them as one and therefore investigates *internationalization of the curriculum at home*. (Marinoni & Cardona, 2024, p. 155). This conforms to practice in many policy documents, in which the terms are used interchangeably. Beelen and Jones (2015b) describe the common features as follows:

> They both aim to reach 100% of students, focus on the intercultural as well as the international; are embedded within the core formal and informal curriculum, not simply in the elective elements; are delivered through internationalised learning outcomes and assessment; do not depend on the presence of international students or staff and do not assume that their presence will automatically 'internationalise' the student experience; do not depend on teaching in English; and are specific to individual programmes of study and the academics who deliver them.
> *(p. 8)*

Definitions and their reception

Partly in response to the exclusive character of student mobility, attention over the past two decades shifted to opportunities for internationalization of teaching and learning at home institutions for all students. The move toward internationalization for all students can be considered a critical approach to the dominant modality of internationalization: study abroad. Originally, internationalization at home was defined as:

> Any internationally related activity with the exception of outbound student and staff mobility.
> *(Crowther et al., 2001, p. 8)*

One key issue with this definition is that it does not explicitly mention the focus on all students. Another is that it presents an activity-based approach to internationalization, that omits mentioning the purpose of these activities. There has been a shift toward an outcomes-oriented approach, requiring study programs to determine in advance what the learning outcomes of their internationalization practices should be.

The revised definition by Beelen and Jones mentions both these elements:

> the purposeful integration of international and intercultural dimensions into the formal and informal curriculum for all students within domestic learning environments.
> *(Beelen & Jones, 2015a, p. 78)*

This revised definition addresses the opportunities for international and intercultural learning from diversity, both from diverse cultures within the local student body and wider population as well as from working with students from other nations.

The revised definition sought to clarify the notion of internationalization at home, for those working in European international offices, who may have been charged with developing internationalization in their institutions and engaging academics in the endeavor, but who might not themselves relate as easily to the idea of internationalizing the curriculum, as defined by Leask (2015), and widely adopted elsewhere.

While the 2015 definition of IaH has been frequently cited as valuable in practice (see e.g. Jones & Reiffenrath, 2018), many practices labeled as 'internationalization at home' still simply focused on activities rather than on learning outcomes. (Beelen, 2023, p. 105).

Three remarks about the 2015 definition

To understand the second definition of internationalization at home the following aspects need to be considered:

1. It is important to note that internationalization at home cannot be considered an educational or pedagogical concept, but rather an approach to enable students to learn from perspectives from other countries, cultures and disciplines.
2. The 'purposeful' in the 2015 definition of internationalization at home does not only refer to (graduate) outcomes but also to learning outcomes to ensure that internationalized learning really takes place. Considerable research has been done into the internationalization of learning outcomes (see Jones & Killick, 2013; Clifford, 2014; Leask, 2015; Beelen, 2017).
3. Several authors have observed that internationalization of the home curriculum is enacted differently across academic disciplines and that a disciplinary approach is required instead of 'one size fits all'. Research into discipline specific internationalization is ongoing (see Agnew, 2012; Agnew & Kahn, 2015; Leask & Bridge, 2013; Bulnes & De Louw, 2022; Agnew et al., 2023).

Critical receptions of internationalization at home

Overall, internationalization of the home curriculum at home has been received positively, which led the International Association of Universities (2012, pp. 4–5) to call on all universities to "affirm internationalization's underlying values, principles and goals" through "pursuit of the internationalization of the curriculum as well as extra curricula [sic] activities so that non-mobile students, still the overwhelming majority, can also benefit from internationalization and gain the global competences they will need". Almeida (2018) discusses the values that underpin internationalization at home and stresses its inclusive focus on all students and calls it "an alternative discourse to the market-driven agendas".

Yet over the years, internationalization at home has also been critiqued. It has been called an "activist network" (Rizvi, 2007, p. 391). A "movement" rather than a concept, criticized for focusing on means rather than aims and shifting into "instrumental mode" (Brandenburg & De Wit, 2010, p. 16); for a tendency to focus on "activity and not results as indicators of quality" (Whitsed & Green, 2013); or pretending to be guided by high moral principles while not actively pursuing them (De Wit & Beelen, 2014).

It stands out as a western concept and has therefore been approached with criticism by African scholars (see Brewer & Leask, 2012, p. 247).

From a South African perspective Teferra (2019) sees internationalization as an imposed concept and includes internationalization at home in his critical approach. Heleta (2023, 820), also from a South African perspective, critiques the Policy Framework for Internationalisation of Higher Education in South Africa, which contains both the definitions of internationalisation at home and internationalization of the curriculum for "*copying of Eurocentric definitions*" and "*lack of reference to historical and contemporary global and South African higher education and internationalisation contexts*".

Internationalization at home has also been critiqued by the Global North. Stein (2017, p. 6) writes: "without addressing larger contexts and questions, curriculum internationalization may reproduce rather than interrupt Western dominance". Jones (2022, p. ii) raises the question if curriculum internationalization—and related concepts—can serve to address a range of issues, such as equality, diversity, inclusion, social justice and decolonization. She argues for 'interculturalization' over internationalization to do justice to the increasing pluriformity of local societies and the learning opportunities this entails. Leask (2023b, p. 228) echoes the importance of the intercultural dimension within internationalized curricula. She argues that the knowledge base of the curriculum needs to be diversified (p, 230).

The generally positive reception of internationalization of the home curriculum has led many universities to embrace it. In the 6th Global Survey of Association of Universities (IAU), 75% of respondents acknowledged a noticeable increase in the importance of internationalizing the curriculum at home within their institution over the past five years (Marinoni & Cardona, 2024, p. 155). However, in the same survey, 27% of respondents considered "enhanced internationalization of the curriculum" the most significant benefit of internationalization (Marinoni & Cardona, 2024, p. 64). This raises questions about whether the respondents perceive internationalization at home as an aim in itself or rather as an instrument for achieving other benefits, such as increased competences of students.

Both internationalization at home and Virtual Exchange/Collaborative Online International Learning (COIL) have been positively received for their potential to practice internationalization without reducing carbon footprint (see Nikula et al., 2024, p. 48).

Critiquing the 'home' and the 'domestic'

The notion of 'home' can be critically approached. While some students cross a national border (e.g. that between the Netherlands and Germany) daily, to study at a university across that border, they remain living in their own environment but nevertheless count as international students.

Students enrolled in programs offered through transnational or offshore modalities do not even leave their country but still study at a foreign institution. The same may apply to digitally delivered education, which creates a third space that is neither 'at home' or 'abroad'.

Another problematic use of 'home' is in the notion of a diffuse group of students that have some relation with the country where they go and study.

Their parents or grandparents may have migrated from the host country or may have lived and worked abroad for a period. They may speak the language of the host country fluently, to some extent, or not at all. They may speak the language of the host country fluently but never use it for academic purposes. They may or may not have the nationality of the host country.

They return to their roots in what can be termed 'heritage mobility'. These students take an intermediate position between domestic and international students, and it is difficult to determine what 'home' is for them.

Misconceptions around internationalization of the home curriculum

Below, we discuss a range of misconceptions about internationalization at home. Many practitioners in internationalization of higher education consider internationalization of the curriculum (Leask, 2015) and internationalization at home as different and somehow competing concepts, while they should be considered interwoven concepts that overlap and complement (Beelen & Jones, 2015b, p. 8).

Still, much time is lost in debating the difference between these definitions and much less in stressing that neither internationalization of the curriculum nor internationalization at home are aims in themselves, but instruments to enhance students' competences.

Alternative to mobility

During the COVID pandemic many practitioners turned to internationalization at home and virtual exchange, which they considered an alternative for mobility programs. Yet, well before the pandemic, it had been stressed that the home curriculum should be considered the fundamental basis of internationalization for all students. Mobility adds value for the limited group of students who are able and willing to study abroad. This was already pointed out by de Wit (2011, p. 13) and Jones phrased it as follows: "Mobility needs to be seen as adding value to an internationalised curriculum, not as the focal point of internationalisation efforts" (Jones, 2020, p. 181).

Internationalization at home is studying with international students

When internationalization at home is understood as home students studying in electives with international students, the language of instruction generally switches to English. Friess and Mucha (2020) studied one aspect of internationalization at home: that of international students and domestic students studying together. They note false dichotomies between international and domestic students (p. 62). Jones (2015) also emphasizes that the distinction between home and international students should be minimized or eliminated in favor of a more integrated and inclusive approach to education. This implies that it is an oversimplification that domestic and international students are two distinct groups, both monocultural.

Most students outside the Anglophone world will not study with international students and will participate in education in the local language.

In diverse cities and universities with a diverse student population, domestic programs delivered in the local language are more culturally and socially diverse than international programs delivered in English. The latter will tend to attract a more homogenous socio-cultural, socio-economic and elitist student body, composed of international and domestic students.

Pars pro toto

A common misconception is that specific components of internationalization at home are confused with the concept as a whole. For example, the idea that integrating incoming international students at their host university is equivalent to internationalization at home. However, at many continental European universities, only a minority of home students may study together with incoming international students. Therefore, a commitment to integrating international students does not reach the full potential for internationalization at home, which should be for all students. This approach can be considered a 'pars pro toto' effect, by which a specific part of internationalization at home is seen as equivalent to delivering the whole (Beelen, 2019, p. 41).

Internationalization at home is inclusive by default

Internationalization at home, while aiming to involve all students, is not inclusive by default. Van Mol and Perez-Encinas (2022) found that the socio-economic background of students may impact the choice of students not to engage with modules with an international component.

What is less obvious is issues of teaching and learning, pedagogies, assessment and the hidden curriculum (Leask, 2015, p. 8) favor some students and exclude others.

Critical perspectives on the implementation of internationalization of the home curriculum

The misconceptions of internationalization at home described above play a role in the implementation processes. Below is a critical discussion of known and current processes in internationalization of home curricula.

Disengagement of academics

Lack of engagement of academics has long been identified as a key obstacle to the implementation of internationalization of the home curriculum (see e.g. Leask & Beelen, 2010).

Mestenhauser (2006) already advocated a systemic approach to internationalization at home to move beyond the small group of academic staff and students with an intrinsic interest in internationalization. In this systemic approach, academics, as the facilitators of learning, are considered the 'owners' of the internationalization process.

To explain lack of engagement, Mestenhauser (2011) examined university staff' mindsets, which had developed over lengthy periods of time, deeming these "dispositions". These dispositions may lead to ethnocentrism, reinforced by the national origin of education systems. The sources of these dispositions are not only formal education but also general experiences, such as travel, employment, relationships with other people (including foreigners), media, reading materials, family socialization, political orientation, economic class, acculturation, and religious beliefs. Mindsets are therefore relevant to the question of if, and to what extent, a lecturer engages with internationalization.

The study by Van den Hende (2024) indicates that lack of engagement of academics is not sufficiently addressed by institutional policies and support.

More recently, Weissova and Johansson (2022) surveyed academics at a Swedish university and found that personal international experiences and commitment to internationalization still are identified as the primary enablers for staff to work with internationalization of the curriculum (p. 31). They advocate support and time as enablers for staff engagement. As an initial step, Weissova (2022) suggests using Appreciative Inquiry in the engagement process.

Professional development

'Traditional' approaches to professional development for internationalization of the home curriculum tend to be ineffective since they attract mainly those academics who are already engaged.

Action research with academics of a specific study program, which may include the formulation of learning outcomes, is an alternative to traditional professional development (Beelen, 2017).

Another alternative to traditional professional development for academics is through professional learning communities. The Erasmus project 'Supporting Academics to Become International Educators through Professional Learning Communities' (SABIO)[1] explored local and international professional learning communities across seven universities in Europe and the US and found that this form of networked learning can lead to inspirational, international and interdisciplinary learning experiences.

Disengagement of educational developers

Considerable research has gone into development of internationalized curricula.

Killick (2018) focused on developing intercultural practice in an Anglophone context while Gregersen-Hermans and Lauridsen (2021) aimed to understand the role that educational developers can play in the internationalization of higher education, particularly in international classrooms taught in English. Cozart and Gregersen-Hermans (2021) also developed a competence profile for educational developers.

However, Wimpenny et al. (2019) identified gaps in academic research in relation to the role of educational developers in internationalization: how they perform their role and tasks, how they prepare for their tasks, and what motivates them.

Most of the scholarly work on the role of educational developers focuses on international classrooms taught in English or for other education in English. Yet, the overwhelming majority of students do not study abroad but study at home in the local language.

Educational developers can be instrumental in 'mainstreaming' internationalization in domestic curricula.

Leadership for an internationalized curriculum

Van den Hende (2024), in her case study of the University of Groningen, concludes that internationalization of the curriculum entails an organizational change process that is complex and currently "largely inadequate for academic staff and their specific disciplinary contexts" (p. 127). Beelen (2018) argues that top-down institutional leadership for internationalization at home should be focused on bottom-up development in departments and study programs.

Likewise, based on their case study Weissova and Johansson (2022, p. 32), argue that a fully internationalized curriculum is a "long-term transformative process" that requires a top-down strategy and engagement of academic staff, management and administrative support.

Internationalization and decolonization

There is ongoing discussion on what decolonizing the curriculum means and also what it requires from academics. Wimpenny et al. (2021a) raise the question of how '*decolonizing* the academic self' relates to '*internationalizing* the academic self' (Sanderson, 2008) and explore these concepts through auto-ethnographic research by five western European curriculum developers.

Virtual Exchange/COIL with partners in the Global South brings issues of decolonization within reach of every academic (Wimpenny et al., 2021b), both for the colonizers and the colonized.

Colonial assumptions are often part of the hidden curriculum, defined by Leask (2015, p. 8) as "the various unintended, implicit and hidden messages sent to students". The hidden curriculum is also a focus area within internationalization at home, just as with internationalization of the curriculum, alongside formal and informal curricula. Internationalization can be an instrument for bringing in a range of perspectives from different national, cultural and disciplinary angles. Decentering dominant paradigms and highlighting emerging paradigms are key elements of Leask's theoretical framework for internationalization of the curriculum (Leask, 2015, p. 27) and also figures in the articulation of 'relational translocalism' Stein et al., 2016, p. 13).

Meanwhile, the urgency to decolonize curricula seems low. The 6th Global Survey Report of the International Association of Universities (Marinoni & Cardona, 2024) asked about the most pressing concerns for internationalization. Decolonization of the curriculum scored low at 4% as a world average (p. 210). Regionally, the highest score was in Sub-Saharan Africa with 14%, followed by North Africa & the Middle East (6%) and Asia & Pacific (6%).

A shift toward COIL and Virtual Exchange

Soulé et al. (2024) did a scoping study of internationalization at home-related search terms in English medium peer-reviewed journals. They identified 58 papers that matched their search criteria of which 10% discussed in-campus activities for internationalization at home while 90% involved various modes of online collaboration, such as COIL, Virtual Exchange and telecollaboration. The authors found that "these collaborations predominantly feature a more substantial role for the "Global North", raising concerns about the insufficient efforts to articulate a decolonized, internationalized, and inclusive curriculum that incorporates interactions with diverse perspectives" (p. 38). Their study also identified the need for "well supported implementation strategies" to overcome technological and organizational barriers.

Decolonization and equitable North–South perspectives were an explicit focus of the iKudu project, an Erasmus+ capacity-building project in which five European and five South African universities collaborated to build capacity for COIL. Apart from generating 55 North–South COIL practices, the project generated a wealth of insights and experiences around designing, executing and evaluating COIL practices.[2]

While COIL/Virtual Exchange can be considered a prominent component of internationalization at home, it usually reaches only small groups of students. COIL/Virtual Exchange also needs alignment with the other components of an internationalized curriculum.

Coventry University and The Hague University of Applied Sciences, who consider COIL the most intensive form of Virtual Exchange (see O'Dowd, 2023) conducted a comparative case study on the two institutions' practices for COIL (Beelen et al., 2021). With a top-down approach to COIL at Coventry University versus a bottom-up approach at The Hague University of Applied Sciences, at both institutions, the alignment of COIL with other instruments for an internationalized curriculum was not obvious. The study found a tendency to develop 'stand-alone' COIL practices that were not connected with other components of an internationalized curriculum, such as comparison of cases and literature, comparative.

Research and engagement with local international and cultural groups and organizations.

Therefore, the prevalence of Virtual Exchange/COIL practices -particularly when they are electives, is not a reliable indicator of the degree of internationalization of a curriculum.

Critical perspectives on COIL/Virtual Exchange

During the COVID pandemic, both internationalization at home and Virtual Exchange suddenly stood in the spotlight. In reaction, institutions developed responses that they labeled 'internationalization at home' but which were online electives. An example of this was a report by Universities UK International (2021). It was titled *Internationalisation at home; Developing global citizens without travel; international activities delivered at home: showcasing impactful programmes, benefits and good practice*. It contains examples from three Anglophone countries: the UK, the US and Australia. The report focuses on activities, and it is not clear how the idea of 'global citizens' in the title is understood or intentionally addressed.

This confusion is not limited to the relation between Virtual Exchange and internationalization at home but also extends to Virtual Exchange itself. A variety of alternative terms is used, such as telecollaboration and COIL (see O'Dowd & Beelen, 2021). This makes the discussion diffuse, with different people advocating or critiquing different versions (see e.g. Van Hove, 2021). One form of Virtual Exchange used under the label of internationalization at home is that of preparation for mobility of students, but this is obviously limited to the mobile minority of students.

Virtual Exchange provides 'third space' learning opportunities (Doscher, 2024, pp. 78–79) that have the potential to reach all students, in many cases they remain electives for a limited group of students. Indeed, 'upscaling' such practices to include all students and 'scale up' requires considerable effort and coordination with partner universities. This means that a COIL practice does not only require collaborative work by students but also by academics, both in design and in execution.

Accessibility and inclusion

There have been several critical approaches to digital learning in general, among others that of Farag et al. (2021). Based on Freire's concept of 'literacy', they develop Critical Media Literacy (CML) to help educators to work with Learning Management Systems and mitigate the danger of Freire's 'banking model' of education. In this model, teachers, who are the epistemological authority, deposit knowledge into passive students, whose pre-existing knowledge is ignored in the process.

While Freire did not apply the banking model to internationalization of education, it fits the situation since student's previously acquired competences in in internationalization from primary and secondary education are often ignored and diversity is not leveraged. The 'banking model' therefore fits in the articulation of the global knowledge economy (Stein et al., 2016).

More specifically about COIL, Borger (2022) has investigated accessibility issues that may tend to exclude students from the learning environment. Similarly, Aldrich and Whatley (2024) applied an equity-based lens to digital internationalization and noticed inequalities in access and connectivity. Exclusion in COIL seems to have been understood mostly in relation to access and media literacy. Beelen and van Stapele (2021) point at other factors that may exclude such relation to language, pedagogical approaches and assessment methods.

As far as COIL design is concerned, Kolm et al. (2022, 183) conducted a systematic review of literature on teaching and assessing students' International Online Collaboration Competencies (IOCCs) and found that "Methods to teach and evaluate IOCCs acquisition are underdeveloped but urgently needed to equip professionals for global virtual teamwork".

Also, about COIL design, De Louw and Beelen (2024), in a case study on the engagement of educational developers in COIL, found that Collaborative Learning, while being the core of COIL, is not a topic that developers and academics discuss. In addition, Van Mol and Perez-Encinas (2022) stress socio-economic background of students as significant factor in non-participation of students in internationalization activities in the home curriculum.

DeWinter and Klamer (2021) have looked at ways in which to make COIL more inclusive in the framework of an Erasmus+ capacity-building project that aimed to develop skills for COIL at South African universities (see above).

Taking stock of Virtual Exchange and COIL

Virtual Exchange, in particular COIL, has taken prominence within internationalization at home, to the extent that it is often considered equal to it. Specific issues include:

- Accessibility and connectivity favor students and institutions in the Global North.
- COIL design does not include International Online Collaboration Competencies and there are questions about Collaborative Learning being included.
- Virtual Exchange/COIL practices tend to be electives for a minority of students.
- In many cases, COIL is not aligned with other international components of the curriculum or with values and goals at faculty or institutional levels.
- As a research field, Virtual Exchange/COIL is evolving from case studies into investigating broader topics, such as global citizenship through COIL.

Conclusions on the state of internationalization of the home curriculum

The 6th Global Survey of the International Association of Universities (Marinoni & Cardona, 2024) identifies institutional leadership and the international office as the main drivers of institutional internationalization (p. 43). This is not surprising because these stakeholders tend to be the respondents of the Global Surveys. However, they are not directly involved in internationalized teaching and learning: the international office because developing curriculum is not their primary task, and institutional leadership is too far away to be aware of what is practiced within individual study programs. The study by Van den Hende (2024) demonstrates how complex leadership for internationalization of the home curriculum is to engage and support academics through professional development.

The difficulties in engaging stakeholders such as academics and educational developers, make it difficult to make internationalization of the home curriculum systemic. Also, internationalization at home is not inclusive by default and nor is COIL/Virtual Exchange, which tends to reach only a minority of students.

We have not made much progress since the introduction of the first definition of internationalization at home in 2001 in moving internationalization of the home curriculum from activities-based to outcomes-oriented. We lack publications about programs that have successfully internationalized their entire curriculum. Soria and Troisi (2014) claim that students can acquire intercultural competences at home that match those acquired abroad. Mace (2021) explores the pitfalls and possibilities of an ecosystem for global learning and internationalization at home.

Therefore, Leask (2023a, p. 28) asks these two questions about the future of internationalization of the curriculum: "How strong is our commitment to providing all students with access to a high quality, state-of-the art internationalised education experience for the global common good?" and "How prepared are we as a global collective to embrace what has until now been on the margins, as the 'new normal' for internationalisation?" equally relevant and perhaps more pointed questions are: what has prevented us from making more progress in this area after a quarter century of knowing? What are our collective personal motivations to maintain the status quo?

Implications for Ethical Policies and Practices

1 *Research into internationalization at home in non-Anglophone contexts*: Research into internationalization of teaching and learning comes mostly from Anglophone contexts in the Global North, whereas most students across the world study in programs in local languages. How to internationalize these programs through pluriform perspectives and leveraging local diversity through 'interculturalization' is an important topic of research.
2 *Inclusion of students in an internationalized curriculum*: Internationalized curricula focus on all students in the compulsory curriculum, also those students who would, because of their background,

not choose electives with an international character. How these students can be fully included is a topic that also merits further research. Future research can clarify the of 'heritage' students in both international and domestic classrooms.
3 *Stakeholders and leadership*: Leadership should bring stakeholders together. These include educational developers. Educational developers can play a systemic role in the internationalization of teaching and learning and professional development of academics.
4 *Professional development*: Alternative forms of professional development such as action research and Professional Learning Communities should be developed.

Notes

1 Supporting Academics to become International Educators through Professional Learning Communities 2021-1-CZ01-KA220-HED-000032178.
2 www.ufs.ac.za/ikudu/research/dissemination-of-ikudu-knowledge-and-news.

References

Agnew, M. (2012). Strategic planning: An examination of the role of disciplines in sustaining internationalization of the university. *Journal of Studies in International Education, 17*(2), 183–202. https://doi.org/10.1177/1028315312464655

Agnew, M., De Louw, E., & Eftekhari, P. (2023). Demystifying the role of the academic discipline in internationalisation. *EAIE: European Association for International Education Annual Conference*, Rotterdam, The Netherlands, September 26–29, 2023.

Agnew, M., & Kahn, H. (2015). Internationalization at home: Grounded practices to promote intercultural, international, and global learning. *Metropolitan Universities, 25*(3), 3146.

Aldrich, C., & Whatley, M. (2024). Access and Equity in Virtual Environments. In: T. Woodman, M. Whatley & C. Glass (Eds.), *Digital Internationalization in Higher Education*, pp. 57–70. Routledge.

Almeida, J. (2018). *Internationalisation at home: An epistemology of equity*. https://www.eaie.org/resource/internationalisation-at-home-an-epistemology-of-equity.html

Beelen, J. (2017). *Obstacles and enablers to internationalising learning outcomes in Dutch universities of applied sciences* (Doctoral dissertation Università Cattolica del Sacro Cuore).

Beelen, J. (2018). Watering a hundred flowers: Institutional leadership for internationalization at home. In J. Beelen, & J. Walenkamp (Eds.), *Leading internationalization in higher education: People and policies* (pp. 65–80). The Hague University of Applied Sciences.

Beelen, J. (2019). Internationalisation at home: Obstacles and enablers from the perspective of academics. In E. Hillebrand-Augustin, G. Salmhofer, & L. Scheer (Eds.), *Responsible university. Verantwortung in Studium und Lehre; Sammelband Tag der Lehre 2017 der Karl-Franzens-Unversität Graz* (Grazer Beiträge zur Hochschullehre, Band 9) (pp. 29–54). Grazer Universitätsverlag.

Beelen, J. (2023). Internationalisation at home and virtual exchange: Addressing old and erroneous approaches. In F. Hunter, R. Ammigan, H. de Wit, J. Gregersen-Hermans, E. Jones, & A. Murphy (Eds.), *Internationalisation in higher education: Responding to new opportunities and challenges* (pp. 101–112). Ten years of research at the Centre for Higher Education Internationalisation (CHEI).

Beelen, J., & Jones, E. (2015a). Redefining internationalization at home. In A. Curai, L. Matei, R. Pricopie, J. Salmi, & P. Scott (Eds.), *The European higher education area: Between critical reflections and future policies* (pp. 67–80). Springer.

Beelen, J., & Jones, E. (2015b). Looking back at 15 years of internationalisation at home. *Forum, 0*, 6–8.

Beelen, J., & Van Stapele, N. (2021). Towards the new exclusive in internationalisation. *Symbiosis Express IntlEd, 4* 19–21.

Beelen, J., Wimpenny, K., & Rubin, J. (2021). Internationalisation in the classroom and questions of alignment: Embedding COIL in an internationalised curriculum. In P. Nixon, V. Dennen, & R. Rawal (Eds.), *Digital learning and new technologies in the internationalisation of higher education; Universities in the information age* (pp. 29–45). Routledge.

Borger, J. (2022, 28 October). Getting to the CoRe of Collaborative Online International Learning (COIL). *Frontiers, 7.* https://doi.org/10.3389/feduc.2022.987289

Brandenburg, U., & de Wit, H. (2010, winter edition). The end of internationalization. *Boston College Newsletter, 62*, 15–17.

Brewer, E., & Leask, B. (2012). Internationalization of the curriculum. In D. Deardorff, H. de Wit, D. Heyl & T. Adam (Eds.), *The Sage handbook of international higher education* (pp. 245–266). Sage.

Bulnes, C., & De Louw, E. (2022). Towards a typology of internationalisation at home activities in academic disciplines: A study conducted at a Dutch university of applied sciences. *Compare: A Journal of Comparative and International Education.* https://doi.org/10.1080/03057925.2022.2108376

Clifford, V. (2014) Engaging the disciplines in internationalising the curriculum. *International Journal for Academic Development, 14*(2), 133–143.

Cozart, S. M., & Gregersen-Hermans, J. (2021). An international competence profile for educational developers. In Gregersen-Hermans, J., & Lauridsen, K. M. (Eds.), *Internationalising programmes in higher education: An educational development perspective.* Routledge.

Crowther, P., Joris, M., Otten, M., Nilsson, B., Teekens, H., & Wächter, B. (2001). *Internationalisation at home; A position paper.* European Association for International Education.

De Louw, E., & Beelen, J. (2024). Exploring unchartered territory: The role of an educational developer in COIL. Manuscript submitted for publication. https://www.tandfonline.com/journals/rija20

De Wit, H. (2011). Internationalization misconceptions. *International Higher Education,* (64). https://doi.org/10.6017/ihe.2011.64.8556

De Wit, H., & Beelen, J. (2014, May 2). Reading between the lines; Global internationalisation survey. *University World News.* Retrieved from www.universityworldnews.com

DeWinter, A., & Klamer, R. (2021). Can COIL be effective in using diversity to contribute to equality? Experiences of iKudu, a European-South African consortium operating via a decolonised approach to project delivery. In M. Satar (Ed.), *Virtual exchange: Towards digital equity in internationalisation* (pp. 29–40). Research-publishing.net

Doscher, S. (2024). Curriculum internationalization in the digital era. In C. Woodman, M. Whatley, & C. Glass (Eds.), *Digital internationalization in higher education* (pp. 73–85). Routledge.

Farag, A., Greeley, L., & Swindell, A. (2021). Freire 2.0: Pedagogy of the digitally oppressed. *Educational Philosophy and Theory*, 54(13), 2214–2227. https://doi.org/10.1080/00131857.2021.2010541

Friess, W., & Mucha, A. (2020). International students as learning space inventory? On the functional production of difference in the context of the university strategy Internationalization at Home – A post-structuralist analysis. In W. Friess, A. Mucha, & D. Rastetter (Eds.), *Diversity management und seine Kontexte celebrate diversity?!* (pp. 55–67). Verlag Barbara Budrich.

Gregersen-Hermans, J., & Lauridsen K. (2021). *Internationalizing programmes in higher education; An educational development perspective*. Routledge.

Heleta, S. (2023). Critical review of the policy framework for internationalisation of higher education in South Africa. *Journal of Studies in International Education*, 27(5), 817–833.

International Association of Universities. (2012). *Affirming academic values in internationalization of higher education: A call for action*. International Association of Universities.

Jones, E. (2015). Internationalisation and the student experience: The role of the international student in the global university. In *Internationalisation of higher education* (pp. 231–247). Routledge.

Jones, E. (2020). From mobility to internationalization of the curriculum at home: Where are the students in the intelligent internationalization conversation? In K. A. Godwin, & H. de Wit (Eds.), *Intelligent internationalization: The shape of things to come* (pp. 179–183). Brill/Sense Publishing.

Jones, E. (2022). Problematizing the Idea of Curriculum 'Internationalization'. *Journal of International Students*, 12(1), i–v ISSN: 2162-3104 (Print), 2166-3750 (Online). https://doi.org/10.32674/jis.v12i1.4592

Jones, E., & Killick, D. (2013). Graduate attributes and the internationalised curriculum: Embedding a global outlook in disciplinary learning outcomes. *Journal of Studies in International Education*, 17(2), 165–182.

Jones, E., & Reiffenrath, T. (2018, August 21). Internationalisation at home in practice. *EAIE*. https://www.eaie.org/blog/internationalisation-at-home-practice.html

Killick, D. (2018). *Developing intercultural practice. Academic development in a multicultural and globalizing world*. Routledge.

Kolm, A., de Nooijer, J., Vanherle, K., Werkman, A., Wewerka-Kreimel, D., Rachman-Elbaum, S., & van Merriënboer, J. J. G. (2022). International online collaboration competencies in higher education students: A systematic review. *Journal of Studies in International Education*, 26(2), 183–201. https://doi.org/10.1177/10283153211016272

Leask, B. (2015). *Internationalization of the curriculum*. Routledge.

Leask, B. (2023a). Does internationalization of the curriculum have a post pandemic future? *IaU Horizons*, 28(1), 27–28.

Leask, B. (2023b). Reimagining internationalization of the curriculum. In R. J. Tierney, F. Rizvi, & K. Erkican (Eds.), *International encyclopedia of education* (Vol. 8, pp. 220–232). https://doi.org/10.1016/B978-0-12-818630-5.02038-8

Leask, B., & Beelen, J. (2010). Enhancing the engagement of academic staff in international education. In *Proceedings of a Joint IEAA-EAIE Symposium* (pp. 28–40). International Education Association of Australia.

Leask, B., & Bridge, C. (2013). Comparing internationalisation of the curriculum in action across disciplines: Theoretical and practical perspectives. *Compare*, 43(1), 79–101.

Mace, M. (2021). Creating a campus global learning ecosystem by employing internationalization at home strategies. In S. Kommers, & K. Bista (Eds.), *Inequalities in study abroad and student mobility; Navigating challenges and future directions* (pp. 129–239). Routledge.

Marinoni, G. & Cardona, S. (Eds.) (2024). Internationalization of Higher Education: Current Trends and Future Scenarios (6th IAU Global Survey Report). International Association of Universities.

Mestenhauser, J. (2006). Internationalization at home; Systems challenge to a fragmented field. In H. Teekens (Ed.), *Internationalization at home: A global perspective* (pp. 61–77). Nuffic.

Mestenhauser, J. (2011). *Reflections on the past, present and future of internationalizing higher education; discovering opportunities to meet the challenges.* University of Minnesota.

Nikula, P.-T., Lamont, A., & Renders, E. (2024). Digital approaches to sustainability. In C. Woodman, M. Whatley, & C. Glass (Eds.), *Digital internationalization in higher education* (pp. 45–56). Routledge.

O'Dowd, R. (2023). *Internationalising higher education and the role of virtual exchange.* Routledge.

O'Dowd, R., & Beelen, J. (2021, September 7). Virtual exchange and internationalisation at home navigating the terminology. EAIE. www.eaie.org/blog/virtual-exchange-iah-terminology.html

Rizvi, F. (2007). Internationalization of curriculum: A critical perspective. In M. Hayden, J. Levy, & J. Thompson (Eds.), *The Sage handbook of research in international education* (pp. 390–403). Sage.

Sanderson, G. (2008). A foundation for the internationalization of the academic self in higher education. *Journal of Studies in International Education, 12*(3), 276–307.

Soria, K. M., & Troisi, J. (2014). Internationalization at home alternatives to study abroad: Implications for students' development of global, intercultural and international competencies. *Journal of Studies in International Education, 18*(3), 261–280. https://doi.org/10.1177/1028315313496572

Soulé, M. V., Parmaxi, A. and Nicolaou, A. (2024). Internationalization at home in higher education: A systematic review of teaching and learning practices. *Journal of Applied Research in Higher Education, 17*(7), 29–60. https://doi.org/10.1108/JARHE-10-2023-0484

Stein, S. (2017). The persistent challenges of addressing epistemic dominance in higher education: Considering the case of curriculum internationalization. *Comparative Education Review, 61*, S25–S50.

Stein, S., Andreotti, V., Bruce, J., & Susa, R. (2016). Towards different conversations about the internationalisation of higher education. *Comparative and International Education, 45*(1), article 2.

Teferra, D. (2019, 23 August), Defining internationalisation - Intention versus coercion. *University World News.* www.universityworldnews.com/post.php?story=20190821145329703

Universities International (2021). Internationalisation at home – Developing global citizens without travel; international activities delivered at home: Showcasing impactful programmes, benefits and good practice https://www.universitiesuk.ac.uk/universities-uk-international/insights-and-publications/uuki-publications/internationalisation-home-developing

Van den Hende, F. (2024). *Curriculum internationalisation: A dynamic organisational change process.* Doctoral dissertation University of Groningen.

Van Hove, P. (2021, September 23). Words matter: Why we should stop talking about 'virtual mobility'. EAIE. www.eaie.org/blog/words-matter-virtual-mobility.html

Van Mol, C., & Perez-Encinas, A. (2022). Inclusive internationalisation: Do different (social) groups of students need different internationalisation activities? *Studies in Higher Education.* https://doi.org/10.1080/03075079.2022.2083102

Weissova, L. (2022). Staff engaged: Using appreciative inquiry to implement internationalisation at home. *CIHE Perspectives, 19,* 57–58. https://www.bc.edu/content/dam/bc1/schools/lsoe/sites/cihe/publication/Perspectives/Perspectives%2019.pdf

Weissova, L., & Johansson, A. (2022). Making the invisible visible: Current practices and perceptions of internationalisation of the curriculum. *Journal of Student Affairs, 18,* 23–32.

Whitsed, C., & Green, W. (2013, January 26). Internationalisation begins with the curriculum. *University World News.* Retrieved from www.universityworldnews.com

Wimpenny, K., Beelen, J., Hindrix, K., King, V., & Sjoer, E. (2021a). Curriculum internationalization and the 'decolonizing academic'. *Higher Education Research & Development, 41*(7), 2490–2505. https://doi.org/10.1080/07294360.2021.2014406

Wimpenny, K., Beelen, J., & King, V. (2019). Academic development to support the Internationalization of the curriculum (IoC): A qualitative research synthesis. *International Journal for Academic Development, 25*(3), 218–231.

Wimpenny, K., Hagenmeier, C., Jacobs, L., & Beelen, J. (2021b, January 21). Decolonisation through inclusive virtual collaboration. *University World News.* https://www.universityworldnews.com/post.php?story=20210121054345601

5
EXPLORING INCOMING MOBILITY THROUGH A CRITICAL AND INCLUSIVE INTERNATIONALIZATION LENS

Eva Janebová, Christopher Johnstone, and Thi Nguyen

Dimensions of Inclusive Internationalization

Over the past three decades the concept of "inclusiveness" has become increasingly socially desirable. Global instruments like the Sustainable Development Goals, for example, have called for inclusive education as part of a broader commitment to quality education at all levels (United Nations Department of Economic and Social Affairs (2015). The inclusiveness movement can be found in higher education discourses worldwide (Kelly et al., 2023), but vagueness around what exactly inclusion means, and what it means for both higher education and internationalization is required for conceptual transparency. Indeed, researchers have noted that without a critical lens toward inclusiveness, narratives of inclusivity become performative acts that may lack the substance or capacity to transform systems (Gibbs et al., 2023).

Such was the rationale for our original mapping of inclusive internationalization. Drawing inspiration from Stein et al. (2016), Bedenlier et al. (2018) and others, we sought to identify ways in which inclusive internationalization might be present in institutions and the ways that aspects of might be confused, conflated, or coopted for particular interests. In this chapter, we use our "dimensions" of inclusive internationalization (theoretical, representational, and participatory) to highlight ways in which institutions might critically engage with internationalization and, specifically, mobility.

Theoretical Dimensions

Theory is an important tool for understanding and evaluating internationalization and inclusive internationalization. Theories create frameworks, inform approaches to internationalization, and guide policies. Historically, there have been debates among scholars and practitioners about neoliberal vs. liberal aims and missions of internationalization. Historically, internationalization has been framed as both a strategy to help universities meet their strategic goals and a tool to help universities promote global public goods (Knight, 2004). As the privatization, competitiveness, and corporatization of universities arose in the early 2000s, however, scholars pointed out, and critiqued the linkages between internationalization and neoliberal economic theory and practice (Bamberger et al., 2019).

An early antidote to neoliberal internationalization was the calls by scholars to reorient internationalization toward its liberal, public good aspects of internationalization. DeLaquil (2019) and de Wit and Jones (2018), for example, connected concepts of inclusive internationalization and the public good mission of universities. In this way, internationalization itself could be inclusive of broader efforts to improve societies through taking a social responsibility approach. Streitwieser et al. (2019) further called for internationalization to be more "humanistic" in its approaches and to work on global challenges such as access to higher education for refugee populations.

Increasingly in the mid-2010s, critical scholars began to influence the field. Critical researchers in internationalization have focused their work on highlighting the ways in which historic power and social relations impact the dynamics of internationalization. Critical research begins with an assertion that there are dominant narratives and relationships that guide how work is done in higher education. These relationships came about through long histories of colonization, economic injustices, racism, sexism, and ableism. Critical researchers often seek to highlight these inequities or challenge normative frameworks that continue to oppress and suppress persons with diverse identities, geographies, and resources.

We now turn to three key focal points of critical internationalization scholars as a foreground for interrogating international mobility. In the paragraphs below we highlight efforts in decolonization, anti-neoliberalism, and climate-focused research as genres of critical internationalization studies, relevant to inclusive internationalization, and frames of reference for evaluations of mobility.

Decolonization

Decolonization and inclusivity do not always sit well together. When narratives of social cohesion dominate understandings of inclusion, there may be underpinnings about social normativity and assimilation of non-dominant groups into dominant social norms in order to increase cohesion. Scholars who seek to decolonize internationalization, however, often focus on understanding inclusivity internationalization to be reflected of plurality. From a decolonial perspective, inclusivity does not mean that all ideas and perspectives align or cohere, but instead may be in a healthy tension in pluralistic higher education settings. Such tension is useful in questioning narratives, assumptions, and power related to whose knowledge "counts" in higher education and internationalization.

A critical and decolonizing orientation toward internationalization focuses on the role of both settler and exploitation colonialism and the requisite forms of knowledge that go along with legacies or contemporary versions of such colonization. Inclusion, from the standpoint of critical and decolonizing education, is an act of disrupting academic spaces to envision new or recapture ancient ways of knowing. For example, Wimpenny et al. (2021) provided an overview on how they, scholars in a European-South African capacity building project, reflected on colonial legacies in their own institutions and partially addressed them through internationalization of the curriculum and internationalization at home. Many critical accounts of internationalization, however, acknowledge and document that the promise of the benefits of internationalization (including, but not limited to mobility) are often distributed unequally on racial, gender, economic, and other hierarchies (Andreotti et al., 2018; Stein and Silva, 2020).

Anti-Neoliberalism

Often related to decolonization, anti-neoliberalism scholarship, as it relates to internationalization, examines and critiques how internationalization is tied into globalization, and how globalization is driven by neoliberal economic theory and practice. Neoliberalism is a guiding principle for most of the world's economy today that is based on free markets and the shaping of individuals as market actors (Toft, 2021). Ampuja (2021) suggests that neoliberalism became both a global economic driver and largely unquestioned global philosophy after the transition of Eastern Bloc countries to capitalist economies in the late 1980s and 1990s. Bamberger et al. (2019) explain how, at present, both higher education and internationalization are "entangled" in neoliberal ideas. To the extent that internationalization is often portrayed as a positive element in universities, reinforcing ideas of understanding and cosmopolitanism, Bamberger et al. (2019) argue that humanistic ideas are often co-opted by larger neoliberal agendas, and folded into the broader aims of profiteering and competition for influence among higher education institutions. In this case, internationalization has either become a willing partner or has been co-opted to reinforce values of competition, market values, and stratification within educational pursuits.

The role of neoliberalism in internationalization is manifested in a variety of ways. For example, Le Ha and Barnawi (2015) and Wei and Johnstone (2020) both presented examples of "excellence" campaigns in nations that were designed to promote internationalization, increase global rankings and reputation, and attract talent and partnerships. Discourses guiding excellence programs frequently cite global competition and market-related outcomes for participants. In the case of the work by Le Ha and Barnawi, a further embrace of English, the lingua franca of the global economy, was present. Chen and Huang (2024) recently studied internationalization in Japan, concluding that internationalization is simply a cultural outgrowth of an existing higher education system that is "competitive, exclusionary, and pragmatic" (p. 1909). Scholars critical of the neoliberal nature of higher education internationalization point out that, despite promising values of greater intercultural understanding, internationalization often aligns with other aspects of neoliberal higher education. In the case of mobility, incoming students may be appreciated for little more than the economic or reporting capital they can provide. Outgoing students, in turn, may face competition for opportunities or find those opportunities to be narrowly focused on market-preferred outcomes.

Climate-Centric Critique

Rumbley (2020) stated that while student mobility had long been viewed as the manifestation of internationalization's role in the betterment of societal and human conditions globally, it was ironically damaging to the broader ecosystem. The first part of the climate-centric critique pertains to the high dependence of international mobility activities on carbon-intensive air travel. Shields (2019) estimated that worldwide, approximately 40 megatons of greenhouse gas per year were associated with student mobility, which was as much as the amount produced by Jamaica, Tunisia, and Croatia combined. In the case of the United States, a leading country in global carbon emissions[1] flights taken by over 350,000 US students studying abroad in the 2018–2019 academic year (before the pandemic) were predominantly to Europe and Asia, which inflated the students' carbon footprints (IIE, 2022a). Not to mention, most of these experiences lasted eight weeks or less (IIE, 2022b).

The second part of the climate-centric critique underlines the ongoing disconnect between ecological needs and the economic agenda that drives internationalization. International mobility initiatives at higher education institutions have historically been grounded by market-based, consumerist rationales, which center individualistic desires and prioritize short-sighted productivity goals, such as enrollment numbers, program variety, and corporate profit, over issues of social ethics—environmental responsibility included (Baer, 2023; Campbell & Nguyen, 2023). Most notably, Baer (2023) highlighted that the parameters of capitalism—within which many internationalization efforts had been taking place—functioned as an enabler of extractive models of engagement and an overarching driver of climate change.

The third and last part of the climate-centric critique concerns how the power imbalances embedded in the internationalization landscape intertwine with the perpetuation of environmental injustices. It is well-recognized that while a majority of students from the Global South migrate to the Global North for long-term socioeconomic advancement (Chen, 2017; Mazzarol & Soutar, 2002), students from the Global North likely view mobility to the Global South through the lens of short-term charitable service and/or hedonistic tourism (Namakkal, 2013; Sharpe, 2015; Zuchowski et al., 2017). Additionally, narratives of saviorism and Orientalism are often coded into discursive contents of education abroad programs and global academic partnerships in manners that position the Western, White-bodied individual as the default expert or "main character" of internationalization efforts (Vavrus & Pekol, 2015; Onyenekwu et al., 2017), while sidelining the presence of those who do not fit into that image (Acevedo, 2022; Blake et al., 2020).

Summary: Theoretical Dimensions

This section provided an overview of three critical dimensions of inclusive internationalization. Although inclusion is not always a central feature in critical internationalization studies, there are themes that overlap, such as the importance of plural ways of knowing, multilingualism, earth care, and detachment from capitalistic overtones of internationalization. Some critical scholars seek to expose the ways in which internationalization reified colonial practices and adopted market ideologies. Others, like Beck (2021) suggest it is time to rid the world of internationalization. Building on Beck's work, for example, we question if we have not already arrived in a new era for reconsideration of the global work of universities.

In reality, there are numerous theoretical perspectives that drive how internationalization is enacted in higher education. This section focused specifically on critical theories and orientations, in line with the general themes of this book. Later in this chapter, a closer look at Czech mobility will be undertaken and informed by these critical theories. In any instance when institutions or individuals seek to be more inclusive, this inclusion is guided by philosophy and social theory. *We argue that critical social theories are helpful for informing any attempt to make internationalization more inclusive.* Without recognition (and critique) of the colonizing aspects of internationalization, the alignment of internationalization goals with neoliberal economics, and the dangers internationalization poses to the environment, there is no chance that internationalization can achieve its goals of promoting a better world through global engagement. In the interconnected world in which we all currently live, there is little doubt that global engagement will continue in higher education institutions. How that engagement occurs and what philosophical and theoretical stances will guide that work are critically important questions. We argue that without a grounding in the atrocities and continued influence of colonization, without an acknowledgment of the ways in which internationalization can be co-opted by neoliberal aspirations, and without an acknowledgment of climate risk due to internationalization, inequities in global engagement run the risk of doing more harm than good.

Representational Dimensions

Representation, in the case of this chapter, refers to the presence of people in positions who can influence internationalization strategy and direction. Case studies in internationalization of higher education reveal that governance around internationalization *can* be shared if there is institutional will. For example, in the 1990s, Bradford College (United States) began making efforts to become more inclusive and involving stakeholders from across the university (Freysinger, 1993). Hudzik (2015) affirmed educational hierarchies in his writing, but also specifically called for "bottom-up" leadership of internationalization to come from academics and student support units. Sometimes representational equity or equality is achieved through strategic leadership at universities (i.e., any initiative benefits from diverse thinking from those who guide it). Equitable and inclusive representation, however, must sometimes also at times it must be fought for through unions and other collaboratives.

For example, organizations like the Erasmus Student Network (ESN) have pushed for student representation in internationalization decision-making (Green, 2019). Brooks (2019) further advocated for strong representation across campus units to drive the internationalization agenda. Similarly, Diversity Abroad (2018) suggested the importance of diversity and equity staff in conversations about internationalization, and the Academic Cooperation Association (2019) also called for both academics and community engagement personnel to be drivers of internationalization. More recently, Pattison (2024) noted that staff dedicated to internationalization and academics need to forge effective working relationships because both perspectives are needed to ensure internationalization represents diverse campus perspectives.

Participatory Dimensions

Janebová and Johnstone's (2020) final dimension described participation. In the 2020 work, we focused mainly on three supports to participation that would enhance inclusive internationalization. The first support was internationalization at home. This enables students to participate in international learning within their institution's everyday activities, including academic and extracurricular activities (Beelen & Jones, 2015). Mobility programs pose a greater threat to participation. In response to these threats, universities have employed both accommodations and accessibility efforts to enhance inclusion for mobility (Johnstone & Edwards, 2020).

Accommodations are small or large changes to programs that support individuals' participation. Accommodations might include allowances for differential timing or submission. From a critical perspective, accommodations may be helpful but do little to change exclusionary structures. From a systems perspective, inclusive internationalization can only occur if it is accessible to all interested. Regarding mobility, accessibility may include programming or options that are shorter in duration, lower in cost, or utilize digital technologies. These programs may be designed for students with family care needs or other travel constraints (O'Dowd & Beaven, 2019). As noted above, programming that focuses on curriculum, such as internationalization at home or Collaborative Online International Learning (COIL) (Radjai & Hammond, 2024; University of Minnesota, n.d.), provided participants have access to requisite technology and language barriers are addressed. Despite moves toward accessible internationalization, Bernardo et al. (2018) noted that the field and the strategy are still marked by "(1) power, paternalism, and neoliberalism, (2) paucity of critical dialogue and research, and (3) linguistic and financial barriers to internationalization" (p. 982). So, while accessibility provides a helpful framework for understanding participatory inclusion, there is also a constant need for reflection on the power structures that dominate internationalization practice.

Exploring, Reflecting Upon, and Critically Analyzing Czech Mobilities

The above sections provide an overview of dimensions that allow for conceptual analysis of Czech mobility. In this section we examine various aspects of Czech mobility through our framework of inclusive internationalization, informed by the concept of critical internationalization. It is clear that internationalization does not happen in a bubble; It is guided by national and university policies and Czech mobility presents an interesting case study in the "how" and "why" of internationalization. As stated previously Czechia joined the European Union in 2004 and has since had access to European mobility schemes afforded by membership especially for short-term and semester-long mobilities. The analysis in this section is based on the latest research of incoming full-time international students in the Czech Republic at all levels of studying, as prepared by the Czech National Agency (2024). This research includes data from 52 higher education institutions in the Czech Republic and explores motivations of international students to come to the Czech Republic, their perception of quality of their study experience including social needs. Unfortunately, there are no similar national data collections on outgoing students, so this section, by necessity, is focused on the incoming students (Table 5.1).

Since joining the EU, international student mobility has increased substantially in the Czech Republic and with that mobility has come an increase in international students, defined in the National Agency report as those with non-Czech citizenship, to 18% (54, 770) of the total number of Czech students (304,518 in 2022). The report shows that the majority of international students in higher education institutes in the Czech Republic come from Eastern or Central European countries (over 70%) with 52,6% enrolled in bachelor's degree programs, 37,5% in master programs, and 10% in doctoral programs (p. 11). A total of 92,4% are studying in

TABLE 5.1 Number of international students from the most represented countries, their percentage, and their increase/decrease in the last 5 years

Country	Number of international students	Percentage (%)	Percentage change over 5 years (%)
Slovakia	20,920	38	−2,6
Russia	7,645	14,0	32,9
Ukraine	6,224	11,4	104,0
Kazakhstan	2,747	5,0	68,0
India	1,815	7,1	165,4
Belarus	1,074	4,7	43,0

full-time study and 7.7% in part-time study. Thus, the following analysis focuses on majority of students, who study full-time.

Colonial Dimensions of Czech Mobility

The Czech Republic was never a colonizing country. For centuries it was part of the Austro-Hungarian empire and more recently it was occupied by both Germany and the Soviet Union. Some argue that it did not enjoy true sovereign freedom until after the Velvet Revolution in 1989. An analysis of student demographics of international students reveals several patterns, however, that reflect what Vavrus and Pekol (2015) described as a northern discrepancy in international mobility (i.e., long-term mobilities have historically been more accessible to students from the Global North). However, data from the report indicate an increase in students from formerly colonized countries, especially from three specific countries: Nigeria, Ghana, and Bangladesh. Although there is a smattering of agreements between universities, there has not been a concerted effort for partnership in the Global South for Czech institutions. Czech academics from the Global South are virtually nonexistent in Czech higher education institutions. This means that although Czech students and academics might have exposure to international students from the Global South, exposure at the collegial level is nonexistent. This may have implications for their deeper understanding of issues connected with Global North-South inequities and their willingness to include non-traditional knowledge.

Decolonization theory (Lin, 2023; Da Silva et al., 2024) is a helpful lens for understanding how internationalization and student mobility are influenced by colonial histories. It is possible that countries that have engaged in exploitative colonization (e.g., France, the Netherlands, Germany, and England) or are now governed by settler colonists (e.g., New Zealand, Australia, the United States, and Canada) are taking more reflective approaches to decolonization. However, in the Czech Republic where a focus could be given to reconciliation activities with German or Russian students, who both study regularly in the Czech Republic, there is no evidence, anecdotal or otherwise, that this is happening.

Another concerning pattern aligns with the "maintenance of historical sustained hierarchy" (da Da Silva et al. (2024), p. 1). The National Agency report shows that the Czech Republic is an attractive destination for students from Eastern parts of Europe with Slovakia (38%) and Ukraine, Kazakhstan, Belarus, and Russia (32%) together amounting for 70% of all international students in the Czech Republic (p. 27). These countries belonged to the former Soviet Union. Such a regional discrepancy in incoming students seems to reproduce the structures of Eastern and Western Europe in the 20th century.

Furthermore, this pattern of mobility, coupled with unintentional economic implications of a brain drain (as described below), creates even more inequalities among the regions of Europe. More investigation is needed into the positionality of the Czech Republic in these mobility patterns. Is the Czech Republic a transition country in terms of a door to the West for students from Eastern Europe? What role do Czech higher education institutions play in keeping the hierarchy of East and West? How could a national and institutional policy counter that and attract a much more diverse student body?

Neoliberal Dimensions of Czech Mobility

While the connections between Czech mobility and decolonization are at best indirect, the linkages in relation to neoliberalism are not. Like most accepting countries in the world, Czech institutions have focused much of their activity on attracting international students as a revenue stream and the current discourse tends to stress the recruitment of high numbers of incoming students for their economic benefit for the Czech Republic (Uhl, 2024). Current targets are placed at 30% of overall enrollment. As some policy makers point out "selfish benefits need to be balanced by unselfish benefits of internationalization" (Miller, 2024). In general, with a few notable exceptions, there is less focus on understanding the impact on the quality of education and how that is enhanced by international students; even less so on the potential of international mobility to improve societies (de Wit & Jones, 2018). Janebová's personal experience with working with policies and strategies of three major Czech universities, Charles University[2], Palacky University[3]; Masaryk University[4] -which all published strategic plans for their internationalization in 2021- shows that much more emphasis needs to be placed on connecting international students with the humanistic ideas of addressing societal challenges, Although Palacky University explicitly connects the level of internationalization at the university with its societal impact on the local community and region.

International mobility is often defined in economic terms not only by institutions but also by students themselves. Students from Eastern and Central Europe often study abroad seeking economic opportunity, especially in countries that may provide opportunities for permanent migration. This brain drain concerns only specific groups of international students in Czechia: Only 6% of German students plan to stay in Czechia after their studies, compared to 54% of Slovaks, 52% of southern and Eastern European students, and 42% of African students. Students from Slovakia tend to easily find work, https://www.statista.com/statistics/270499/co2-emissions-in-selected-countries/especially in the Metropolitan area of Prague, and over a third who study in the Czech Republic do not return to Slovakia. The Czech Republic is already the dominant economic power in the Slovakian–Czech relationship, and this will only exacerbate the power imbalance.

Despite this emphasis on the economic motivation, a trend is emerging across Czech higher education to refocus more on the benefits of the public good through internationalization. However, there are several recent examples of inclusive gatherings, of senior leadership, academics, and non-academic staff, which target a broader range of participants than the traditional workshops focused on international offices and study departments. For example, at a recent conference (November 2024) on Driving Quality Institution-Wide Internationalization in Prague, co-organized by the Mestenhauser[5] Institute for International Collaboration and the Czech Ministry of Education, Youth and Sports in partnership with the University of Minnesota (Ministry of Education, Youth and Sports of the Czech Republic, 2024) several speakers, such as Christopher Johnstone, Barbara Kappler and Harvey Charles, from the University of Minnesota, pointed to the importance of integrating Justice, Equity, Diversion and Inclusion (JEDI) into strategic management thinking. Furthermore, a recent international conference organized by Charles University brought attention to the quality of teaching and learning in the discourse.[6] It remains to be seen if these initiatives signal long-term move to bridging agendas and of distancing internationalization from the neoliberal rationale.

Seeing mobilities through the critical lens, we are reminded that incoming students should not be viewed only in terms of neoliberal lens of a potential economic capital to a region but also in terms of what impact they bring to the quality of education and overall study and work experience of students and staff at the university. However, there is little focus on the overall study and work experience of international students and staff at Czech universities. More studies that seek to more holistically understand the experiences of international students may help to offset neoliberal narratives needed.

The Climate Case for Czech Mobilities

Above we described a Northern and Central European bias for mobility. While this bias has consequences for not addressing historic economic inequalities or colonial legacies, the long-term mobility by students in nearby nations and the possibility of their long-term stay has positive consequences in regard to climate impact. According to recent statistics, 38%

of the international student population (out of 54,770) comes from neighboring Slovakia. Many of these students travel home regularly, primarily using trains or buses, which results in a relatively low carbon footprint. Similarly, a significant number of students are recruited from the former USSR, including Russia (14%), Ukraine (11.4%), Kazakhstan (5%), and Belarus (2%). Notably, the number of students from Ukraine has been steadily increasing. These students frequently face financial constraints and therefore are also more likely to rely on trains or buses for travel. We see a growing trend of recruitment from distant countries such as Bangladesh, Nigeria, and Turkey, which has increased by 476% for Bangladesh, 156% for Turkey, and 210% for Nigeria. These may raise concerns about the future of higher carbon footprints due to air travel of incoming students from these countries.

Beyond the potentially and comparatively smaller climate impact of Czech mobilities in comparison to other nations, blended mobilities—combining physical and virtual mobility—are on the rise thanks to the Erasmus+ scheme. These programs often support short-term mobilities, making international experiences more accessible to those who have barriers to longer-term participation. However, although virtual engagement has positive climate dividends, blended mobilities frequently have much the same carbon footprint as longer-term mobilities.

Representational Dimensions

As previously stated, the representational dimension is about who can influence internationalization strategy and direction because the participation dimension often reflects governance structures.

Universities in the Czech Republic follow a dual asymmetrical governance model, with a Senate that tends to rate low on the Inclusivity scale. The Senate elects the Rectors who appoint the Rector's "Board" of academic Vice-Rectors. This Board determines overall strategies, policies, and procedures for the university. Within this hierarchical structure, internationalization portfolios are usually handed down to Deans (also elected) and Vice Deans of Internationalization (appointed by the Dean). This hierarchical model is the norm in the Czech higher education system.

University autonomy has important implications on individual institutional approaches to internationalization and mobility, meaning the right of the university to determine its organization and administrative procedures, to decide on priorities and budget, hire personnel and admit students, etc. (Matei, 2017). While Czech universities are autonomous in this regard they must operate within national priorities. For example, the national Strategy on Internationalization (Ministry of Education, Youth and Sports of the

Czech Republic, 2021, p. 8) focuses on the quality of Internationalization at Home and in terms of student mobility on complex quality services for international students, development of internationally welcoming campuses and measures to ensure the equal quality of study programs taught in Czech and in other languages. These priorities are adopted and managed within institutional priorities to different degrees and are implemented with little knowledge of other institutional strategies. The newly established Mestenhauser Institute for International Collaboration[7] will play a crucial role in supporting a shared understanding of quality internationalization and in translating national strategies to institutional settings and in facilitating interinstitutional exchange (Ministry of Education, Youth and Sports of the Czech Republic, 2024).

While autonomy can be seen as a positive it compounds the discontinuity of priorities and strategies caused by the three-year cycle of elected Rectors in public higher education institutions in the Czech Republic. The short terms of Rectors and the senior leadership team make it nearly impossible to maintain what Zumeta (2011, p. 134) the "social contract" between higher education and the "society of which it is a part", in which internationalization for society should play a pivotal role. Holding rectors and senior leadership accountable for such society-focused internationalization is almost impossible.

Senior-level leadership in Czech universities is relatively homogeneous. Leaders are Czech nationals who have not been exposed to a culture of inclusive participatory leadership unless they have had an international study or work experience. As Mestenhauser pointed out, the Czech academic culture tends much more toward higher power distance (i.e., clear boundaries and roles, inequality in workplace is accepted) according to Hofstede's dimensions (2010) than for example in the United States (Janebová, 2023, p. 113). Furthermore, university leadership is still predominantly male, although there is greater gender diversity at faculty level. That situation is slowly changing with the introduction of gender equality efforts through the European Commission's HR Award for Excellence to which higher education institutions in the Czech Republic aspire, a recent notable change being the inauguration of the first female President of Charles University, the country's oldest and most prestigious university. There is also a lack of international academics in management positions who would complement the presence of international students and provide a real-life demonstration of the benefits of internationalization.

Because of the Czech-born, male-dominated, hierarchical, top-down approach of senior leadership, it is not surprising that there is a continued focus on the "bottom line" of mobility. However, as internationalization becomes more institutionalized and a broader understanding of the benefits grows, less hierarchical forms of leadership may emerge. For example, at a recent internationalization conference held at the Ministry of Education in Prague (Ministry of Education, Youth and Sports of the Czech Republic, 2024) representatives from a variety of constituencies including academics, administrators, student support personnel, and mobility coordinators were all present. An emphasis on bottom-up change to internationalization strategy and inclusive methodologies such as Professional Learning communities (Andersson et al., 2023) may influence the neoliberal narratives that currently drive mobility. However hierarchical structures are seldom pillars of inclusive governance and are very resistant to change.

Participatory Dimensions

The final dimension of inclusive internationalization is the participatory dimension. We have mentioned the misalignment in the representation of international students and staff with the mostly Czech-born top decision-makers. From a critical perspective, understanding power structures and drivers can provide insights into who actually is and is not engaging in mobility to the Czech Republic.

It is important to revisit the "diversity make up" of international students in the Czech Republic. From the latest National Agency report (p. 12), it is evident that the international student body does not represent the global spectrum of students—the majority of international students come from regions with similar history, perhaps Slavic language affiliation, similar traditional educational backgrounds and even some shared history during communism. This prompts a question about the diversity impact of international students on the benefits of internationalization on the quality of the formal and hidden curriculum.

The most recent data on inbound mobility suggests that the explanation for this lack of diversity is that the dominant driver of incoming mobility is familiarity (linguistic, cultural, or personal). For example, 27% of students who chose to study in the Czech Republic did so because of cultural or linguistic affinity (in the case of Slovak students it was 43%, presumably because of similarities between Czech and Slovak languages and cultural traditions). For students who speak Slavic languages there is also the incentive of free education as students who participate in Czech language programs pay nothing or nominal fees, compared to those who participate in English-medium programs. Another 12% chose to study in the Czech Republic because they had a friend or family member in the country (again for Slovak students it was higher at 56%). For other students the quality of life was a major drawcard (24%), for others it was a specific higher education institution (20%). Students from nations wealthier than the Czech Republic (such as Germany, Israel, and the United States) presumably have different motivational pressures. In the case of the United States, it might have been ancestral roots or the lower cost of HE; in the case of Germany, it may simply be the fact that it is a neighboring country.

In many ways, becoming an international student in a context that is linguistically or culturally like one's home can have benefits—time for adaptation is reduced, barriers for engaging in everyday activities are reduced, and cultural learning may be accelerated. However, if over 70% of international students in Czech higher education institutions are coming from Eastern or Central European countries, the benefits of learning from diverse global perspectives may be reduced. While the aim of having 30% international students on campuses is laudable, unless there is a focus on realizing the quality benefits of international students in Czech institutions this target is only helping the universities' bottom line. The difficulty of realizing the benefits is exacerbated by students self-selecting Czech mobilities based on linguistic affinity or personal connections. This cultural isomorphism challenges the delivery of internationalization at home programs designed to build intercultural capacity in all students and claims about the "diversity bonus" may remain theoretical wishful thinking rather than practical benefits.

Another participatory issue is whether all international students have genuine opportunities to engage with home students both inside and outside the classroom. The Czech language is a difficult language to learn for citizens of non-slavic countries and Czech and non-speaking Czechs are usually taught in separate instructional settings. Whether or not this is a deliberate institutional strategy or a matter of convenience, it impacts on the ability of students to interact inside the classroom. The National Agency report demonstrates that the language of instruction is cutting across the domestic and international students groups, creating new grouping in terms of: A) Czech-born and students from Slavik countries (in particular Slovakia) studying in Czech-language taught courses together, and B) the rest of international students who study in English-taught courses without the presence of Czechs or Slovaks and without the supportive structures provided to Czech-speaking students. The dual offering also has implications for integration of students outside the classroom and reinforces the language divide and subsequent inequalities among the Check-speaking and international students.

The report also demonstrates of international students studying in Czech (Slovaks, some Russians, Ukrainians, and Kazakhstanis who can understand Czech) feel much more integrated at the university than the rest of international students who study in English. In total, 95% of these students reported satisfaction with their studies and integrated into campus life. In contrast, only about a third of students in English programs (primarily North Americans, South Asians, and Western Europeans) were satisfied with their level of integration on campus. Less satisfied students reported a lack of instructor interest and poor attitudes toward international students as their biggest complaints. Obviously linguistic integration plays a key role in satisfaction with students, but the results also call for strengthening of support services to international students (e.g. Josek et al., 2016; ISANA guide, 2011; Ministry of Education, Youth and Sports of the Czech Republic, 2021, pp. 13–14); Glass, 2023), As Perez-Encinas (2018, p. 112) points out in her collaborative approach to internationalization strengthening of these services must not be done separately but provided by the same services that offer support to home students.

The National Agency Report (2024) has other findings that are relevant to identifying barriers for international students studying in the Czech Republic—91% of all international students identified "Lecture" as the main method of instruction. This is the least appropriate pedagogical method in terms of enabling interactions among students. What is needed is a curriculum that incorporates inclusive content and pedagogical strategies that encourage students to voice, analyze, and transfer their unique cultural perspectives into learning discussions. Unfortunately, the report cites one of the respondents: "Most teachers don't know how to make their teaching engaging, they just read the text from their slides" (p. 104). This may result in unequal learning experiences of students studying in programs taught in English as against Czech. The National Agency report also raises the question of whether there is a disparity in the content and quality of education provided for each group—free Czech-taught programs and fee-based English programs, maybe because of different standards for syllabi, instructional methods, or resources (Czech written scholarship versus Global English written sources). This question and the issue of quality in academic teaching require further research if dual-track internationalization is not going to undermine trust in internationalization as a means to achieve quality education for all. The Centers of Teaching and Learning currently being established in Czech higher education will improve the quality of teaching and learning and the student experience but now they are targeting only home students. With the increasing numbers of international students this quality initiative would benefit from a collaborative approach (Perez-Encinas, 2018), improving quality of education for both home and international students without recreating the separation of study agendas for international and home students.

The clear division between those who feel integrated and satisfied compared to those who do not, based on linguistic assimilation, leads to creating artificial identities. Similar to what Frieß and Mucha (2020) note about the negative effect of creating artificial identities between domestic and international students, these "artificial identities" in the Czech Republic are not by home v international student groups but based on language within the group of international students. The unintended consequence of this is the reconstruction (instead of deconstruction) of the historical patterns of Western versus Eastern European block, in this case through mobility. Furthermore this international divide between Czech (Slavonic) speaking students and international students who learn in English needs focused attention and strategies for inclusion inside and outside of the classrooms, from all representational stakeholders including national policy makers, university leadership, international offices, and study departments.

Conclusion

This chapter introduced Janebová and Johnstone's (2020) dimensions of inclusive internationalization as an analytical framework for understanding Czech mobilities. We started by examining the theoretical dimensions of inclusive internationalization—focusing on decolonization, anti-neoliberalism, and climate-centric dimensions. The Czech Republic's lack of direct engagement with colonization (either as colonists or as a colonized nation) likely led to a lack of reflection or action related to decolonizing curriculum or mobilities. The Czech government's policy and approach to international student mobility, however, can be easily understood through a neoliberal framework. International student recruitment is primarily for the purpose of attracting fee-paying students. As a result, students from low- or lower-middle income countries are under-represented in Czech universities, and there are little specific policies or programs aimed at addressing these inequalities.

In practice, most international students in the Czech Republic are from countries in its immediate vicinity. This has an unintended, but positive influence on the nation's climate impact. At present, students primarily engage in long-term mobility (with many staying in the country even after graduation), which may be possible by rail or other more climate-friendly transportation forms than airplanes. Virtual mobilities, which are common in Czech universities also help to minimize climate impact, but are increasingly attached to short-term mobility, which could eventually have long-term climate impacts.

The final two dimensions of Janebová and Johnstone's model inform the inclusivity of such mobility. Czech mobility, and all internationalization efforts, are governed autonomously by strong and vertical hierarchies of leadership operating within national priorities. In general, there is little international representation in these hierarchies and, although recent changes are emerging, hierarchies are still heavily gendered, and male-dominated. This chapter did not rely on primary research, but a future research project might interrogate how a lack of shared governance may narrow visions of the purposes and potential benefits of mobilities. For now, Czech mobility is defined by regionalism and cultural/linguistic/geographical bonds with nearby countries. This regionalism has positive climate implications and also allows for a more naturalistic internationalization than over-reliance on strong global partners. At the same time, it may reduce the potential classroom benefits of diverse perspectives in classrooms.

Czech mobility presents an interesting case study in the "how" and "why" of internationalization. Internationalization does not happen in a bubble. It is guided by national and university policies and may or may not reflect broader global social theories (i.e., there appears to be an easy connection to neoliberalism in Czech mobilities but less specific connection with colonization). It is important, nonetheless, to understand the nuances and context of mobility to avoid sweeping generalizations on the contemporary status of mobility. The Czech example provides a localized and contextualized example to better understand the phenomenon of mobility beyond the numbers.

Implications for Ethical Practices and Policies

1 Inequities in Mobilities: Policies governing student mobilities should address whether mobility programs are inclusive and accessible to diverse participants or if they disproportionately benefit certain groups due to financial, geographic, or social inequalities. Furthermore, it's essential to evaluate whether these programs exacerbate regional disparities, such as brain drain, particularly in areas shaped by historical power dynamics.
2 Humanistic Approach: Adopting a critical and inclusive humanistic perspective allows for a nuanced understanding of how student mobilities influence university communities and broader societal structures. This lens emphasizes the multifaceted cultural, social, and ethical impacts of mobility.
3 Representational Approach: Institutional leadership that includes international student and staff may bring more diverse perspectives that can drive innovation, transform local communities, and influence institutional and national higher education policies through their unique ideas and needs.

4 Participatory Approach: Efforts must be made to identify, understand, and address inequities within international student and staff groups. Such inequities may lead to some individuals feeling alienated while others are well-integrated, with potentially significant implications for satisfaction with their studies.
5 Delocalization and Climate-Conscious Approach: Recruitment strategies should promote diversity without reinforcing traditional Global North-South or East-West mobility patterns. They should also prioritize environmental sustainability, minimizing the carbon footprint associated with international mobilities.
6 Collaborative Approach: Collaboration is key to creating equitable inclusive institutions. Efforts should ensure that the quality of the study experience is consistent for both international and domestic students, with equal access to resources and opportunities.

Notes

1 https://www.statista.com/statistics/270499/co2-emissions-in-selected-countries/.
2 https://cuni.cz/UKEN-1473.html.
3 https://strategie.upol.cz/fileadmin/userdata/cm/strategie/doc/sz/SZ_2021__UP.pdf.
4 https://www.muni.cz/media/3359367/strategic_goals_mu_2021_2028.pdf.
5 http://www.miic.world.
6 https://paedagogium.cuni.cz/wp-content/uploads/2024/12/programme-en-esf.pdf.
7 https://miic.world.

References

Academic Cooperation Association. (2019). *Internationalisation for all? Wider inclusion in the internationalisation of higher education: ACA reflection paper.* Brussels: Author. http://www.aca-secretariat.be/fileadmin/aca_docs/event_presentations/ACA-2019-April_Reflection_Paper_Inclusion.pdf

Acevedo, R. M. (2022). Ideational obstructions to mobility justice in U.S. study abroad. *Mobilities, 18*(6), 872–887. https://doi.org/10.1080/17450101.2022.2156807

Ampuja, M. (2021). Globalisation and neoliberalism: A new theory for new times? In J. Zajda (Ed.), *Third international handbook of globalisation, education and policy research.* Springer. https://doi.org/10.1007/978-3-030-66003-1_3

Andersson, I., Tomaskova, R., & Janebová, E. (2023). Creating international professional learning communities: Toward inclusive internationalization. Paper presented at the *Czeducon Conference,* Brno, Czech Republic.

Andreotti, V., et al. (2018). Mobilising different conversations about global justice in education: Toward alternative futures in uncertain times. *Policy & Practice: A Development Education Review, 26,* 9–41.

Baer, H. A. (2023). Grappling with climate change and the internationalization of higher education: An eco-socialist perspective. *Journal of Studies in International Education, 27*(4), 638–653. https://doi.org/10.1177/10283153231172024

Bamberger, A., Morris, P., & Yemini, M. (2019). Neoliberalism, internationalization and higher education: Connections, contradictions and alternatives. *Discourse, 40*(2), 203–216. https://doi.org/10.1080/01596306.2019.1569879

Beck, K. (2021). Beyond internationalization: Lessons from post-development. *Journal of International Students, 11*(S1), 133–151. https://doi.org/10.32674/jis.v11iS1.3847

Bedenlier, S., Kondakci, Y., & Zawacki-Richter, O. (2018). Two decades of research into the internationalization of higher education: Major themes in the *Journal of Studies in International Education* (1997–2016). *Journal of Studies in International Education, 22*(2), 108–135. https://doi.org/10.1177/1028315317710093

Beelen, J., & Jones, E. (2015). Redefining internationalization at home. In A. Curai, L. Matei, R. Pricopie, J. Salmi, & P. Scott (Eds.), *The European higher education area: Between critical reflections and future policies* (pp. 67–80). Springer. Retrieved from http://doi.org/10.1007/978-3-319-20877-0

Bernardo, A. B. I., Begeny, J. C., Earle, O. B., Ginns, D. S., Pilar Grazioso, M., Soriano-Ferrer, M., Suzuki, H., & Zapata, R. (2018). Internationalization within school and educational psychology: Perspectives about positive indicators, critical considerations, and needs. *Psychology in the Schools, 55*(8), 982–992. https://doi.org/10.1002/pits.22160

Blake, D., Gasman, M., Esmieu, P. L., Castro Samayoa, A., & Cener, J. (2020). Culturally relevant study abroad for students of color: Lessons from the Frederick Douglass Global Fellowship in London. *Journal of Diversity in Higher Education, 13*(2), 158–168. https://doi.org/10.1037/dhe0000112

Brooks, R. (2019). Diversity and European higher education students: National perspectives in a global age. In L. E. Rumbley (Ed.), *Encompassing all voices* (pp. 11–14). European Association for International Education.

Campbell, A. C. & Nguyen, T. (2023). Climate action and aspirations for international education professionals. In K. McBride, & P. T. Nikula (Eds.), *Sustainable education abroad: Striving for change* (pp. 121–136). Forum on Education Abroad.

Chen, J. M. (2017). Three levels of push-pull dynamics among Chinese international students' decision to study abroad in the Canadian context. *Journal of International Students, 7*(1), 113–135. https://eric.ed.gov/?id=EJ11257

Chen, L., & Huang, F. (2024). Neoliberalism, internationalization, Japanese exclusionism: The integration experiences of international academics at Japanese universities. *Studies in Higher Education, 49*(11), 1900–1913

Czech National Agency for International Education and Research. (2024). *Report on research at Czech higher education institutions 2024*. Dům zahraniční spolupráce.

Czech National Agency for International Education and Research (DZS). (2024). *Report on research at Czech higher education institutions 2024*. Prague, Czech Republic: Dům zahraniční spolupráce.

Da Silva, K. A., Pereira, L. S. M., & Aparecido da Silva, K. (2024). Introduction: The emergence of a decolonial approach in the internationalization of higher education. In *Decolonizing the internationalization of higher education in the Global South* (Vol. 1, pp. 1–3). Routledge. https://doi.org/10.4324/9781003409205-1

De Wit, H., & Jones, E. (2018). Inclusive internationalization: Improving access and equity. *International Higher Education, 94*, 16–18.

DeLaquil, T. (2019). Inclusive internationalization as innovative internationalization: Purpose-driven higher education against inequity in society. In R. Schendel,

H. de Wit, & T. DeLaquil (Eds.), *Inclusive and innovative internationalization of higher education: Proceedings of WES-CIHE Summer Institute* (pp. 5–8). Boston College.

Diversity Abroad. (2018). *Collaborative leadership: Advancing diversity, equity, and comprehensive internationalization in higher education*. Diversity Abroad. Retrieved from https://www.diversityabroad.org/DIVaPublic/Resources-Services/Research-Reports/Internationalization_HE/DEIReport_Form.aspx

Freysinger, R. C. (1993). Towards total internationalization: Comprehensive institutional reform and global studies—The case of Bradford College. *The Journal of General Education, 42*(3), 177–190.

Frieß, W., & Mucha, A. (2020). International students as learning space inventory? On the functional production of difference in the context of the university strategy Internationalization at Home: A post-structural analysis. In W. Frieß, A. Mucha, & D. Rastetter (Eds.), *Diversity management und seine kontexte: Celebrate diversity?!* (pp. 55–68). Verlag Barbara Burdich.

Gibbs, C., Achebe, N., Johnson, B., Nwaiche, C., & Ortiz, D. V. (2023). Constructing college-level diversity, equity, and inclusion (DEI) minors—Moving from performative to transformative DEI. *Radical Teacher, 127*(127), 41–50. https://doi.org/10.5195/rt.2023.977

Glass, C. (2023). Global perspectives on student affairs and services: A handook by B. Schreiber, R. B. Ludeman, C. R. Glass & G. Blanco (2023). Boston, US: Center for International Higher Education. *Journal of Student Affairs in Africa, 11*(2), 159–160. https://doi.org/10.24085/jsaa.v11i2.4899

Green, W. (2019). Engaging students in international education: Rethinking students' engagement in a globalized world. *Journal of Studies in International Education, 23*(1), 3–9.

Hofstede, G., Hofstede, G. J., & Minkov, M. (2010). *Cultures and organizations: Software of the mind* (3rd ed.). McGraw-Hill.

Hudzik, J. K. (2015). Integrating institutional policies and leadership for 21st-century internationalization. *International Higher Education, 83*, 5–7.

IIE. (2022a). *Host regions and destinations of US study abroad students, 2005/06-2020-21* [Data set]. https://opendoorsdata.org/data/us-study-abroad/host-regions/

IIE. (2022b). *Duration of U.S. study abroad, 2005/06-2020-21* [Data set]. https://opendoorsdata.org/data/us-study-abroad/duration-of-study-abroad/

ISANA International Education Association. (2011). Guidelines for international student support and services.

Janebová, E. (2023). The challenge of culture: The Czech path to international education. In A. M. D'Angelo, M. K. O'Brien, & G. Marty (Eds.), *Mestenhauser and the possibilities for future international education* (p. 112). Routledge.

Janebová, E., & Johnstone, C. (2020). Mapping the dimensions of inclusive internationalization. In: S. Kommers & K. Bista (Eds.), *Inequalities in study abroad and student mobility: Navigating challenges and future directions* (pp. 115–128). Routledge.

Johnstone, C., & Edwards, C. (2020). Accommodations, accessibility, and culture: Increasing access to study abroad for students with disabilities. *Journal of Studies in International Education, 24*(4), 424–439.

Josek, M., Alonso, J., Perez-Encinas, A., Zimonjic, B., De Vocht, L., & Falisse, M. (2016). *The international-friendliness of universities: Research report of the ESNsurvey 2016*. Erasmus Student Network. Retrieved from https://esn.org/ESNsurvey

Kelly, A. M., Padden, L., & Fleming, B. (Eds.). (2023). *Making inclusive higher education a reality: Creating a university for all*. Routledge. https://doi.org/10.4324/9781003253631

Knight, J. (2004). Internationalization remodeled: Definition, approaches, and rationales. *Journal of Studies in International Education*, 8(1), 5–31. https://doi.org/10.1177/1028315303260832

Le Ha, P., & Barnawi, O. Z. (2015). Where English, neoliberalism, desire, and internationalization are alive and kicking: Higher education in Saudi Arabia today. *Language and Education*, 29(6), 545–565. https://doi.org/10.1080/09500782.2015.1059436

Lin, G. Y. (2023). Alluvial zones of decolonizing internationalization of higher education. *Journal of Contemporary Issues In Education*, 18(2), 37–52.

Matei, L. (2017). Three ideas of academic freedom. In M. Ignatieff, & S. Roch (Eds.), *Academic freedom. The global challenge*. CEU Press.

Mazzarol, T., & Soutar, G.N. (2002). "Push-pull" factors influencing international student destination choice. *International Journal of Educational Management*, 16(2), 82–90. https://doi.org/10.1108/09513540210418403

Miller, J. (2024). Value-driven internationalization. *Presentation by the Deputy Minister at Driving the Quality of Institution-wide Internationalization*, Prague, Czech Republic.

Ministry of Education, Youth and Sports of the Czech Republic (2021). Strategie internacionalizace 2021+ [Internationalization strategy 2021+]. https://msmt.gov.cz/uploads/odbor_30/DH/SZ/Strategie_internacionalizace_2021_.pdf

Ministry of Education, Youth and Sports of the Czech Republic (2024). *Conference on driving quality institution-wide internationalization*. https://msmt.gov.cz/vrchni-reditelka-wildova-na-konferenci-k-internacionalizaci

Namakkal, J. (2013, August 29). Study abroad as neocolonial tourism. *CounterPunch*. https://www.counterpunch.org/2013/08/29/study-aboard-as-neo-colonial-tourism/

O'Dowd, R., & Beaven, A. (2019). Examining the impact of virtual exchange. *Forum*, 14–16. https://www.academia.edu/41333601/Examining_the_impact_of_Virtual_Exchange

Onyenekwu, I., Angeli, J., Pinto, R., & Douglas, T. (2017). (Mis)representation among U.S. study abroad programs traveling to the African continent: A critical content analysis of a Teach Abroad program. *Frontiers: The Interdisciplinary Journal of Study Abroad*, 29(1), 68–84. https://doi.org/10.36366/frontiers.v29i1.386

Pattison, S. (2024). *The elephant in the room: Humanizing the international higher education practitioner-faculty relationship*. Dissertation from the University of Minnesota.

Perez-Encinas, A. (2018). A collaborative approach in the internationalization cycle of higher education institutions. In A. Curaj, L. Deca, & R. Pricopie (Eds.), *European higher education area: The impact of past and future policies* (pp. 107–123). Springer. https://doi.org/10.1007/978-3-319-77407-7

Radjai, L., & Hammond, S. (2024). Internationalizing the curricula through COIL in Japanese higher education: Towards inclusive, accessible, and pluralistic internationalization. *Journal of Virtual Exchange*, 7, 84–106 https://doi.org/10.21827/jve.7.41033

Rumbley, L. E. (2020). Internationalization of higher education and the future of the planet. *International Higher Education*, 100, 32–34.

Sharpe, E. K. (2015). Colonialist tendencies in education abroad. *Journal of Teaching & Learning in Higher Education*, 27(2), 227–234. https://www.isetl.org/ijtlhe/pdf/IJTLHE1970.pdf

Shields, R. (2019). The sustainability of international higher education: Student mobility and global climate change. *Journal of Cleaner Production*, 217, 594–602. https://doi.org/10.1016/j.jclepro.2019.01.291

Stein, S., Andreotti, V., Bruce, J., & Suša, R. (2016). Towards different conversations about the internationalization of higher education. *Comparative and International Education/Éducation Comparée et Internationale*, 45(1), 2.

Stein, S., & Silva, J. E. D. (2020). Challenges and complexities of decolonizing internationalization in a time of global crises. *ETD Educação Temática Digital*, 22(3), 546–566.

Streitwieser, B., Loo, B., Ohorodnik, M., & Jeong, J. (2019). Access for refugees into higher education: A review of interventions in North America and Europe. *Journal of Studies in International Education*, 23(4), 473–496.

Toft, J. (2021). Neoliberalism. In *Encyclopedia of social work*. NASW Press and Oxford University Press. https://doi.org/10.1093/acrefore/9780199975839.013.1409

Uhl, M. (2024). Policy vision for the future: EU and beyond. *Presentation by the Director of the Czech National Agency for International Education and Research at Driving the Quality of Institution-wide Internationalization*, Prague, Czech Republic. https://www.dzs.cz/en/article/future-education-internationalization-tool-excellence-and-innovation

United Nations Department of Economic and Social Affairs (2015). *Transforming our world: The 2030 agenda for sustainable development*. Retrieved from https://sdgs.un.org/sites/default/files/publications/21252030%20Agenda%20for%20Sustainable%20Development%20web.pdf

University of Minnesota (n.d.). *Collaborative online international learning*. Retrieved from https://global.umn.edu/oci/coil

Vavrus, F. & Pekol, A. (2015). Critical internationalization: Moving from theory to practice. *FIRE: Forum for International Research in Education*, 2(2), 5–21. http://preserve.lehigh.edu/fire/vol2/iss2/2

Wei, Y., & Johnstone, C. (2020). Examining the race for world-class universities in China: a culture script analysis. *Higher Education*, 79(3), 553–567

Wimpenny, K., Hagenmeier, C., Jacobs, L., & Beelen, J. (2021, January 21). Decolonisation through inclusive virtual collaboration. *University World News, Africa* https://www.universityworldnews.com/post.php?story=20210121054345601

Zuchowski, I. S., Gopalkrishnan, N., King, J., & Francis, A. (2017). Reciprocity in international student exchange: Challenges posed by neo-colonialism and the dominance of the Western voice. *Aotearoa New Zealand Social Work*, 29(1), 77–87. https://doi.org/10.11157/anzswj-vol29iss1id235

Zumeta, W. (2011). What does it mean to be accountable? Dimensions and implications of higher education's public accountability. *Review of Higher Education* 35(1), 131–148.

6
A CRITICAL APPROACH TO RESEARCH INTO INTERNATIONALIZATION FROM A GLOBAL SOUTH PERSPECTIVE

*Lynette Jacobs, Nelia Oosthuysen,
Cornelius Hagenmeier, and Tafadzwa Ruzive*

Introduction

While many see internationalization as a field of practice in Higher Education, research into internationalization is forthcoming from different world regions. It originated in what is often referred to as the *Global North* (also referred to as *the West* or *the Minority World*, as opposed to the *Global South/Rest/Majority World*). The last two decades of the 20th century saw scholars such as Hans de Wit (Boston College, USA), Joseph Mestenhauser (University of Minnesota, USA), John Hudzik (Michigan State University, USA) and Jane Knight (University of Toronto, Canada), laying the foundation for the conceptualization of internationalization by defining the concept; formulating models and engaging in scholarly thinking. Key works published during this time set the process in motion by activating the initial conceptualization of internationalization of higher education (Knight (1997) (later revised); unpacking strategies for internationalization (Knight & De Wit, 1995), and exploring the rationales for internationalization (De Wit, 1998) amongst others.

The turn of the century saw the discourse broadening with Mestenhauser (2000) introducing the role of management and leadership in internationalization, and specifically the importance of integrating international and global dimension into the being of the university. Agnew and VanBalkom (2009, p. 452) introduced the Cultural Readiness for Internationalization (CRI) model as "an assessment tool to determine cultural readiness for internationalization for the purpose of facilitating organizational adaptation" (also see Chapter 1). Scholars started to question the inclusivity of

DOI: 10.4324/9781315623337-8

internationalization, with Brandenburg and De Wit calling for internationalization to better serve societal needs (Brandenburg & De Wit, 2011). The notion of comprehensive internationalization was introduced by John Hudzik (2011) while Laura Rumbley looked amongst other matters at challenges in embedding global engagement within institutional strategies (Helms & Rumbley, 2017).

Betty Leask developed a framework for internationalization of the curriculum (2015), based on earlier work dating back to the late nineties, that is still applied by many researchers and practitioners. Similarly, while internationalization at home as a concept was introduced earlier in a different form, Jos Beelen and Elspeth Jones redefined it (Beelen & Jones, 2015) focusing on the intercultural development of all students moving away from mobility and the underlying neoliberal thinking. Internationalization of the home curriculum is discussed in more depth in Chapter 4.

The work co-authored by Eva Egron-Polak (and its subsequent iterations) on global trends and regional perspectives examines the various approaches to internationalization from different regions (Egron-Polak & Hudson, 2010) while another key topic was discussed by Fiona Hunter (2018) namely the development of administrative staff to become key players in the internationalization.

However, at the same time, scholars from the Global North started critiquing the western-centric view on internationalization. Phillip Altbach and others criticized the dominance of Western institutions in higher education internationalization (Altbach & Knight, 2007; Altbach, 2007) while Simon Marginson (2006) commented on the power dynamics and inequalities in global higher education and rankings (Marginson & Van der Wende, 2007). Rajika Bhandari, herself a first-generation immigrant in the USA, probed international student mobility, including motivations and challenges, and advocated for equitable access to internationalization opportunities (Bhandari, 2011, 2017).

The connection between higher education and the societies they serve is longstanding. This relates to notions such as the public good, producing graduates in line with societal needs and service to society (see also Chapter 11). However, Jones et al. (2021, p. 330) argued that there is an "urgent need to align internationalisation and university social responsibility agendas through the construct of Internationalisation in Higher Education for Society" (IHES). At the same time Kostrykina (2021) warned against the so-called white knight complex, and to take an approach to working with society using the same principles as service learning, working together with communities on projects they condone.

Most recently, the important work of Sharon Stein and her colleagues within the Critical Internationalization Studies Network raised awareness for different drivers for internationalization. (e.g. Buckner & Stein, 2020; Stein, 2019). Her work, along with other critical frameworks and theories is discussed throughout this book.

Main discourses in the South

Higher education in the Global South (also referred to as *the Rest*[1] or *the majority world*) has presented unique challenges and perspectives in the realm of internationalization. While Western academic discourse often focuses on the mechanics and benefits of internationalization, scholars from the Global South emphasize decolonization, the recognition of indigenous knowledge systems and the reclamation of intellectual spaces and languages following centuries of oppression, colonization and marginalization. After years of exploitation, slave trade, colonialism and imperialism, followed by difficult local histories in some cases, including the oppression by governments (e.g. the Apartheid regime in South Africa in the 20th century, political dictatorships in different countries over time (e.g. in Venezuela, Zimbabwe, Uganda), and genocide (e.g. Rwanda), marginalization, social justice and human rights are pivotal topics.

Although there are differences across the various regions in the Rest, common themes do exist. In the section that follows we discuss the topics that cut across, after which we funnel it down to the 2022 South African definition of internationalization of higher education as a case study. The collective concept that runs across spaces is "decoloniality". While this term is generally used across regions, in Africa the term "Africanization" is frequently found, indicating a call to respect and recognize African knowledge systems, philosophies, and languages with ways of being foregrounded in the discourse (Canagarajah, 2013).

The call for epistemic recognition and respect

The first point to note in this broader discourse is the demand for recognition and respect in terms of how knowledge comes about. Achille Mbembe and many other scholars including Sabelo Ndlovu-Gatsheni critiqued the Eurocentric epistemologies that dominate African universities. They called for an epistemological shift that centers African histories, experiences and knowledge systems and advance epistemic freedom while dismantling colonial knowledge hierarchies (Mbembe, 2001; Ndlovu-Gatsheni, 2013, 2015; Rodney et al., 2024). Their work resonates with what Stein (e.g. in Stein et al., 2016, p. 13) referred to as "Relational Translocalism", an alternative concept to internationalization, that allows for contextualization and the decentering of global capitalist discourse and thinking to promote pluriversality.

A call to decolonize the curriculum and university structure

Building on the call for epistemic recognition, Ali Mazrui, a Kenyan diaspora scholar and others (e.g. Okpewho et al., 2001; Mazrui, 2002; Le Grange, 2016), some who have moved to the West, emphasized the need to decolonize curricula, to center African philosophies and knowledge systems in the curriculum but also critiqued structures in the university that perpetuate colonial epistemologies leading to students not recognizing themselves in the curricula (Niemczyk, 2019).

Inclusion and recognition for indigenous languages

Epistemic freedom also relates to the language that is used in higher education. Whereas in many parts of the Rest, the colonial languages are pragmatically used as common language (e.g. Spanish, Portuguese and Dutch in Latin America and Africa, and mainly English and French in Africa) there are strong voices in favor of indigenous languages. For instance, Canagarajah (2013) highlighted the importance of integrating African languages as part of reclaiming African epistemologies and Ngũgĩ wa Thiong'o[2] advocated, through artistic expressions, discourse and research, for the use of African languages in African education, as opposed to the dominance of colonial languages. He argued that language is central to cultural liberation (wa Thiong'o, 1986).

Decoloniality and gender

Decolonial scholars have argued that gender is socially constructed within Western thinking. Oyěwùmí (1997) made sense of the Western perception of gender from an African perspective. María Lugones (2010), an Argentinian scholar, developed the concept of coloniality of gender, examining how colonialism introduced hierarchical gender systems that intersect with race and class oppression. Her work brought feminist and intersectional perspectives into the decoloniality discourse.

Decolonization and border thinking from Latin America

Walter D. Mignolo became a leading voice in the decoloniality movement and advocating for pluriversality. He developed the idea of the geopolitics of knowledge to dissect Western epistemic hegemony and the way modernity is inextricably linked to coloniality (Mignolo, 2011, 2012). He warned to be

> aware that there are people on both sides of the border and be aware of what side you dwell in. You have not chosen it; you came to the world when the world was already delineated by international relations, global linear thinking, racism, sexism, and so on.
>
> *(E-International Relations, 2017, p. 8)*

Other well-known scholars were Paulo Freire, with the notion of pedagogy for the oppressed (Freire, 1970), and Rigoberta Menchú (1984), who wrote about the struggles and oppression that women experience in Latin America.

Southern philosophies

The philosophies from the South are often built on the collective nature of the communities. For instance, *Ubuntu* is an African philosophy that can be simplified to mean "I am because we are" (Le Grange, 2016, p. 9). Consideration should be given on how *Ubuntu* informs collaboration in higher education. While Ramose (1999) advocated *Ubuntu*, as a foundation for decolonizing knowledge and fostering a sense of shared humanity in education, le Grange (2016) proposes its link to decolonize the curriculum. Many indigenous philosophies and value systems, such as those of Native American, Maori and Aboriginal cultures, resonate with *Ubuntu* and emphasize relationality, interconnectedness with nature and communal responsibilities. Such thinking resonates not only with learning and teaching but informs participatory forms of research.

Internationalization themes from the Global South

The discourse on internationalization to some extent focused on the practice of internationalization. While these themes are not dissimilar from the discussion in the West, and in many cases was written with scholars in the West, or diaspora living in the West, the contextualization was imbedded. One of the main arguments in the higher education discourse was that African universities mirrored Western models, while marginalizing indigenous knowledge systems and Africanization in the face of globalization. Presenting critical perspectives on how global dynamics shape educational policies and practices, is Argentinian sociologist, Carlos Alberto Torres. He highlights the intersection of globalization, education and citizenship (e.g. Burbules & Torres, 2013).

Injustice and social justice

Following years of marginalization and violence, the call for social justice remains. For instance, in his book *Black Reparations in the Era of Globalization*, Mazrui (2002) analyzed the economic and political consequences of reparations and their importance in the Africanization discourse. The concept of social justice and reparations is closely linked with the philosophy of *Ubuntu* (Mukwambo et al., 2024) in that it represents fairness, solidarity and tolerance. In later works Mazrui as well as Teferra commented on the migration of African professionals resulting in brain drain and how that impacts Africanization (Mazrui & Kaba, 2016; Teferra & Altbach, 2004; Teferra, 2005; Teferra, 2008). Leal et al. (2022, p. 246) problematized how internationalization remains "immersed in a Eurocentric agenda that projects itself universally" while Francis Nyamnjoh (originally from Cameroon) focused on neocolonial dynamics of internationalization and the marginalization of African perspectives in the internationalization space (Nyamnjoh, 2021). Damtew Teferra's (Ethiopia) research focused on internationalization and, specifically, issues related to partnerships, academic mobility and the challenges of internationalization in African higher education systems (Teferra & Altbach, 2004; Teferra, 2005, 2008). He also addresses matters related to capacity building, and global academic networks (Teferra & Altbach, 2004; Teferra, 2005, 2008). We conclude that in the internationalization discourses in the South, the engagement with internationalization lies within the understanding of decolonization.

Scholarship from South Africa

Nico Jooste, a prominent South African scholar whose extensive research and leadership have significantly influenced the thinking and practice on internationalization of higher education in South and Southern Africa, initiated a debate in South Africa with the annual and later biannual Colloquia Series at Nelson Mandela Metropolitan University (NMMU). During the first Colloquium a definition of internationalization of higher education was developed by Jooste and Naude:

> an acute awareness of different nations in the world and the active, willing movement across national boundaries in processes of exchange. Internationalisation is intensified by globalisation but respects and supports the idea of nationalities and the sovereignty of nation-states.
> *(Jooste & Naude, 2005, p. 47)*

Jooste emphasizes internationalization strategies, the role of higher education in societal transformation, and the challenges of implementing internationalization in developing contexts. He co-edited *The Globalisation of Internationalisation: Emerging Voices and Perspectives*, which explores diverse global perspectives on internationalization (De Wit et al., 2017) and commented on the published *Policy Framework for the Internationalisation of Higher Education in South Africa* as a compass for comprehensive internationalization (Jooste & Hagenmeier, 2022).

Charl Wolhuter is another established South African scholar who amongst others, explores the unintended consequences of internationalization. Some examples are regionalization of the student body due to an influx of students from neighboring countries, brain drain resulting from the outflow of top South African talent to the Global North, and challenges to indigenization and decolonization efforts within South African higher education. He argued the importance of developing contextually appropriate internationalization strategies (Wolhuter, 2023).

Chika Sehoole's work on mobility is influential. He systematically analyzed patterns of student mobility in Africa (Sehoole, 2011; Sehoole & Lee, 2021). Mobility and migration indeed remain a point of discussion. Although Laakso (2021) considers international mobility as a form of freedom but argues that it does not come without challenges. One such is the inability of mobility to translate to epistemic diversity as pointed out by Jacobs et al. (2022). An important conceptual contribution linked with movement came from Hagenmeier et al. (2017, p. 81) who argued that the "concept of intellectual *métissage*, as a form of intellectual cross-fertilization across international borders, is a necessary and appropriate tool to drive internationalization with the aim of fulfilling the developmental mandate of African universities".

Discussion

The academic discourse in the Global South presents a distinct narrative focused on reclaiming space in global academia following centuries of exploitation and marginalization. Scholars from Africa and Latin America emphasize decolonization and the recognition of indigenous knowledge systems. African scholars have been particularly vocal in this discourse, advocating for decolonizing curricula, integrating African knowledge systems, promoting *Ubuntu* philosophy and including African languages in education exemplifying efforts to center African epistemologies.

Latin American perspectives, contribute critical concepts like the geopolitics of knowledge and coloniality of gender. Their work challenges Western epistemic dominance while promoting pluriversality and intersectional perspectives.

In South Africa, scholars have made significant contributions to internationalization discourse and have developed frameworks for internationalization in African contexts, being critical of the negative side of internationalization and providing longitudinal studies on certain focus areas such as mobility patterns and regional dynamics.

The narrative culminates in recent developments, such as Hagenmeier's concept of intellectual *métissage*, which proposes cross-border intellectual exchange as a tool for advancing African universities' developmental goals. This ongoing discourse reflects the Global South's efforts to reshape international higher education while maintaining cultural integrity and advancing decolonial objectives.

Coming together

Although many Western scholars are interacting and co-publishing with Southern scholars (e.g. Teferra & Altbach, 2004; Wimpenny et al., 2024) and contributing to the "otherwize" thinking as Stein puts it (e.g. Wimpenny et al., 2022) the brief review suggests a misalignment between the discourses in *the West* and *the Rest* as well as it being stratified. Indeed, Jacobs and Mitchell (2021) found an imbalance, with the decolonial debate in professional publications mainly happening amongst the *Rest*. Yet over the past 10+ years, the evolution of higher education internationalization in the Global South has been marked by two significant publications that have the potential to reshape discourses and bring them together.

The 2014 Global Dialogue on the Future of Higher Education Internationalization in Port Elizabeth (now Gqeberha) established key commitments to ethical and inclusive practices, while the 2022 definition of internationalization by Heleta and Chasi introduced a critical, justice-oriented framework specifically for South African higher education. These developments are recognized here for their potential impact on bridging Western and non-Western perspectives on internationalization.

Global Dialogue and declaration

As an outcome of the Global Dialogue, "nine national, six regional, and nine additional organisations from around the world, with national, regional and global responsibilities" declared their "commitment to emphasise the importance of decision-making and practices in the development of internationalization activities that are imbued with ethical considerations and inclusivity" (IEASA, 2014, p. 2).

The declaration identifies three integrated areas of development for the future agenda of international higher education:

1 Enhancing the quality and diversity of mobility programs for students, academic, and administrative staff.
2 Increasing focus on the internationalization of the curriculum and related learning outcomes.
3 Gaining commitment on a global basis to equal and ethical higher education partnerships.

To actualize these goals, the declaration outlines specific high-priority action steps that relate to joint professional development, increase access through certain initiatives, encourage and enable joint research and publications and build a network of experts. It is important to note one statement in which participants committed "to apply ethical standards to their own activities and urge their members or constituencies to do likewise" (IEASA, 2014, p. 3). This commitment to ethical standards is crucial because it represents a shift from simply promoting internationalization to ensuring it is implemented responsibly and equitably. A commitment to ethical standards is indicative of efforts to address "internationalization drift" (passim), a movement away from market-induced practices. In a field historically shaped by power imbalances between Global North and South institutions, this explicit commitment to ethical practice signals an intention to prevent the reproduction of colonial or exploitative relationships in international partnerships. The significance of participants not only committing themselves but also pledging to urge their constituencies to follow suit must be noted. It suggests a systemic approach to embedding ethical considerations throughout international higher education networks.

The declaration thus obliges higher education institutions to promote international higher education and research that recognize the richness and diversity offered by all regions. It advocates for a global higher education agenda that is equitable, ethical, socially responsible, accessible and accountable. While the declaration has certainly influenced the practice and thinking in internationalization circles and remains part of the framing specifically amongst internationalization practitioners, we could find no study that tracked the implementation of the declaration to date. This is particularly problematic given that the declaration itself emphasizes the importance of responsible implementation and ethical practices, suggesting a possible gap between stated commitments (espoused values) and action (enacted values) for ensuring their fulfillment. The incongruence between espoused and enacted values undermines the credibility of such declarations and highlights the need for systematic monitoring and evaluation of internationalization initiatives.

A definition for internationalization in South Africa

Secondly, in 2022, Heleta and Chasi published a definition of Higher Education Internationalization for South Africa that reads as follows:

> Internationalisation of higher education is a critical and comparative process of the study of the world and its complexities, past and present inequalities and injustices, and possibilities for a more equitable and just future for all. Through teaching, learning, research and engagement, internationalisation fosters epistemic plurality and integrates critical, anti- racist and anti-hegemonic learning about the world from diverse global perspectives to enhance the quality and relevance of education.
>
> *(Heleta & Chasi, 2022, p. 8)*

The definition focuses specifically on South Africa and has the potential to act as a bridge between the understanding of *the West* and *the Rest* and influence the conceptual thinking on internationalization.

Heleta and Chasi's definition offers a unique bridge between the Global North and the Global South approaches to internationalization by weaving together practical academic activities with transformative social justice goals. While acknowledging historical inequities, the definition does not dwell in the past but rather charts a path forward through epistemic plurality and critical engagement. By emphasizing both "quality and relevance" alongside "anti-hegemonic learning", it creates a common ground where Western institutions can recognize familiar elements of academic excellence while engaging with diverse knowledge systems and perspectives. The definition's strength lies in its ability to validate multiple ways of knowing while maintaining focus on concrete educational outcomes, making it accessible and applicable across different cultural and institutional contexts.

In the section that follows we thus discuss how the new conceptualization was used since publication.

Influence of the 2022 definition on scholarship

We identified all citations of the 2022 conceptual paper between the time of publication and five December 2024. We used Google Scholar's citation function to identify all articles and chapters in which Heleta and Chasi (2022) were cited (a total of 37 identified). Of those, two were self-citations, and the full text of two of the publications was not available through either open access or our university library extensive subscriptions. That left us

TABLE 6.1 Countries where Heleta and Chasi (2022) was cited

Africa	Europe	Latin America	North America	Australasia	Middle East
Mozambique	Italy	Brazil	USA	Australia	Qatar
RSA	Netherlands	Chile		China	
Zimbabwe	Sweden	Colombia		Hong Kong	
	UK			Indonesia	

with 35 abstracts and 33 full texts to analyze (not counting the citation in Chapter 2 of this book).

We first examined authors from which countries cited the article containing this definition. Analysis of the authors' affiliations showed they were based in 16 countries (Table 6.1).

From this brief analysis it can be concluded that scholars from all world regions refer to this new definition of internationalization.

Our second analysis evaluated how deeply authors engaged with the new conceptualization, moving beyond simple citation to the quality of theoretical engagement. We developed a systematic five-point scale to assess engagement levels:

1 Minimal (1 point): Citation appears with others in a paragraph without discussion.
2 Limited (2 points): Brief mention of the definition.
3 Moderate (3 points): Some discussion of the definition's concepts.
4 Substantial (4 points): Detailed engagement with the definition's ideas.
5 Deep (5 points): Multiple citations with thorough conceptual discussion and/or critique.

To ensure reliability, the first and second authors independently rated each citation's level of engagement, while the third and fourth authors reviewed these assessments.

The results are displayed in the table below (Figure 6.1):

The analysis reveals that most citations of the 2022 definition demonstrate superficial engagement rather than substantive theoretical discussion.

Yet, a deeper level of engagement exists, for example, Mukwambo, et al. (2024) used the framing by the 2022 definition in their explorative study on the experiences of international students from Africa at South African Universities during the COVID-19 pandemic and noted the "unequal and hierarchical Eurocentric knowledge bases" (p. 47). They argue that the

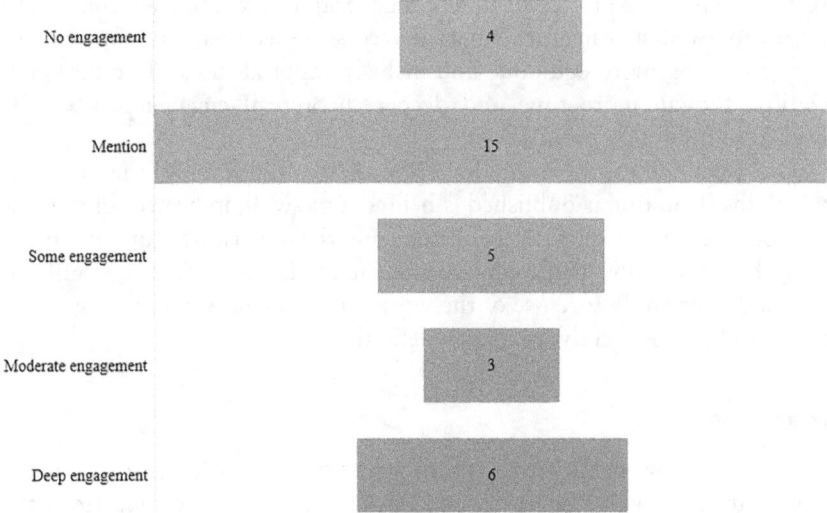

FIGURE 6.1   Levels of engagement from other authors with Heleta and Chasi (2022) (n-33).

2022 definition is aligned with the fundamental African value of Ubuntu, as it is linked with the collectiveness that the South builds on tolerance, fairness and equality.

Pap, situated in New York, also used the definition as a lens and argued that it provides for a "more inclusive and more nationally customized internationalization of higher education where all academics, research methods, teaching, and learning strategies have equal representation" (2024, p. 95). Ndaipa (2023, p. 2) situated in Sweden, argued that unlike Heleta and Chasi (2022), "many African researchers just replicate the interpretation of the internationalization of HE as presented by their counterparts from the Global North". He applauded their effort and continued to use their definition in building decolonial theory in his thesis. Wimpenny et al. (2024, p. 33) appreciate how the conceptualization by the 2022 definition "bring together positionality, criticality and plurality, and what we should be doing across our education contexts from a border thinking perspective" but then acknowledge that "we are not there yet in such appreciation of one another's visions as a conscious coming together". As such, it remains work in progress.

While early engagement with Heleta and Chasi's definition shows promising signs of its potential to bridge different approaches to internationalization, its full impact on reshaping international higher education discourse and practice is yet to be realized. The definition's ability to resonate with scholars across different geographical contexts—from South Africa to Sweden—suggests it may indeed serve as a valuable framework for developing more equitable and inclusive approaches to internationalization, though more time and deeper theoretical engagement will be needed to fulfill this promise.

Our own comment on the definition is two-fold. Firstly, the article in which the definition is published is behind a paywall, indicative of the tension between the business of publishing and the idealistic nature of what it publishes. Secondly, while appreciated, it reads more than a manifesto than a definition. Future use of the work will show how people align with this manifesto or merely use it as a definition.

Discussion

In this chapter we deliberated on the current trends in scholarship on internationalization of higher education, by juxtaposing discourses from the Global North and the Global South over the past decades. Our analysis examined several aspects of Heleta and Chasi's (2022) definition of internationalization in South African Higher Education. First, we investigated its impact on current academic discourse. Second, we evaluated whether this definition could help bridge the divide between different regional perspectives on internationalization. Finally, we assessed how effectively the definition advances both local and global agendas while fostering a shared understanding of internationalization.

In many ways the 2022 definition is less of a definition and more of an ambition. This might, however, also be said of most definitions used in the higher education discourse, as pointed out by De Wit (2024). While Heleta and Chasi may not represent mainstream thinking, the definition certainly keeps the debate alive and provides new input that enables the discourses on internationalization and on decolonization to come together. This critique of internationalization is emerging as a new direction in the field, steadily gaining acceptance in academic discourse.

Critical approaches to internationalization appear in both Northern and Southern scholarship. Northern critical approaches, such as Stein, and other Northern colleagues raise awareness of inequalities and marginalization in internationalization of higher education, but this Northern critique still remains selective. The Southern scholarship consistently foregrounds these concerns of inequality and marginalization as central themes across many publications. (e. g. Jacobs et al., 2022; Leal et al., 2022; Mignolo, 2012; Wimpenny et al., 2024).

The development of higher education theory reflects distinct regional contributions and historical contexts. Western scholars have primarily shaped the conceptual foundations of internationalization, while scholars from the Global South have focused their theoretical contributions on decolonization. This division in academic focus is not arbitrary but deeply rooted in local contexts and histories. While all regions participate in global scholarly discussions, their distinct perspectives emerge from their particular historical and social circumstances. This is especially evident in how Global South institutions continue to grapple with colonial legacies in higher education. The widespread adoption of the Humboldtian university model serves as a prime example—a Northern/Western concept that became the blueprint for universities worldwide through colonial and post-colonial influence.

What this means for future scholarship

One observation is that the discourse on internationalization in the Global South is often highly theoretical and only has limited impact on internationalization practice. This disconnect between discourse and practice is gradually being resolved. For example, the successful endeavors of stakeholders including the International Education Association of South Africa to entrench a research culture amongst internationalization practitioners have yielded success. IEASA has in the past 15 years invested considerably in encouraging practitioners, especially the younger generation, to undertake research on internationalization.

A new generation of practitioner researchers[3] has started to reshape the discourse on South African Higher Education Internationalization. Recently, several South African internationalization practitioners completed their PhD's and started disseminating their findings. Included in this group of practitioners now actively contributing to the discourse are Divinia Jithoo, Segun Obadire, Judy Peter, Tasmeera Singh and Cornelius Hagenmeier. Their scholarship is buttressed by research support at higher education institutions. In some cases, such as with established scholars Lynette Jacobs (Interim Director UFS Office for International Affairs) and Felix Maringe (Deputy Vice-Chancellor for Institutional Development, Research, and Innovation, University of Kigali), internationalization management and leadership are combined with solid research practice and theory.

Additionally, scholars from other fields have started to investigate internationalization. Examples include the authors of the recently published book *Perspectives on Comprehensive Internationalization of Higher Education* (Dorasamy & Mugano, 2022), and the various scholars who hail from other disciplines, but contributed to the scholarship emerging from the EU-funded iKudu capacity building project.[4] Interactions through visiting scholarships, virtual engagement, joint projects and more such initiatives are building understanding of the different contexts and have led to more collaborative thinking and publishing.

Reflecting on the insights gained, we can ask the following question: To what extent does the scholarship of internationalization influence policy and practice, particularly the scholarship emerging from the South? The authors argue that to theorize in the relatively closed internationalization grouping without the discourse transcending to university leadership and faculty approaches prevents impact.

Implications for ethical policies and practices

Reflecting on the insights gained, we can ask the following questions: To what extent does the scholarship of internationalization influence policy and practice, particularly the scholarship emerging from the South? Which directions should higher education internationalization and its scholarship go on the African continent, where Higher Education mostly reflects the former colonial contexts?

The authors argue that to theorize in the relatively closed internationalization grouping without the discourse transcending to university leadership and faculty approaches prevents impact.

1 *Bridging the gap between discourse and practice*: One observation is that the discourse on internationalization in the Global South is often highly theoretical and only has limited impact on internationalization practice. However, this disconnect between discourse and practice is gradually being resolved.
2 *Meeting the needs of local societies*: We posit that scholarship from the Rest should focus on developing a local knowledge-imbued inclusive internationalization process which also responds to the developmental needs of its contexts. Universities from the Rest should be committed to contributing to the societies in which they are embedded, and care should be taken to co-create and further develop validating and participatory ways of knowing that are aligned with being and doing in the South.
3 *Encouraging young practitioners to undertake research*: The International Education Association of South Africa (IEASA) has in the past 15 years invested considerably in encouraging practitioners, especially the younger generation, to undertake research and entrench a research culture amongst internationalization practitioners.
4 *Combining management and leadership with research into internationalization*: A new generation of practitioner researchers[1] has started to reshape the discourse on South African Higher Education

Internationalization, amongst whom are Divinia Jithoo, Segun Obadire, Judy Peter, Tasmeera Singh and Cornelius Hagenmeier. In some cases, such as with established scholars Lynette Jacobs (University of the Free State) and Felix Maringe (University of Kigali), internationalization management and leadership are already combined with solid research practice and theory.

5 *Researchers into internationalization entering from other disciplines*: Scholars from other fields have started to investigate internationalization. Examples include the authors of the book *Perspectives on Comprehensive Internationalization of Higher Education* (Dorasamy & Mugano, 2022), and the various scholars who hail from other disciplines, but contributed to the scholarship emerging from the EU-funded iKudu capacity building project[2].

The authors want to acknowledge their own limitations because they are not able to engage with academic discourses in languages other than English. It has certainly impacted the focus of the chapter, but also opens possibilities for further studies.

Notes

1 We use in the discussion that follows *the West* and *the Rest* intentionally to label what is mostly referred to as Global North/Global South, to disrupt the traditional Western/Northern focus while removing it from the geo-political classification to rather an identity of otherness that does not align with modernity. Similarly, the *minority world* represents the Global North while the *majority world* is those in the Global South, highlighting the inequality of power.
2 https://www.youtube.com/watch?v=FOXqc-8zCPE.
3 The authors do not claim that this is a complete list. However, these are examples of scholars who are linked to the international offices in South Africa, and who conduct research on internationalization.
4 https://www.ufs.ac.za/ikudu/research/dissemination-of-ikudu-knowledge-and-news, see also Chapter 4.

References

Agnew, M, & VanBalkom, W. D. (2009). Internationalization of the university: Factors impacting cultural readiness for organizational change. *Intercultural Education, 20*(5), 451–462, https://doi.org/10.1080/14675980903371324

Altbach, P. (2007). Globalization and the University: Realities in an Unequal World. In J. J. Forest, & P. Altbach (Eds.), *International Handbook of Higher Education*. Springer. https://doi.org/10.1007/978-1-4020-4012-2_8

Altbach, P. J., & Knight, J. (2007). The internationalization of higher education: Motivations and realities. *Journal of Studies in International Education, 11*(3–4), 290–305. https://doi.org/10.1177/1028315307303542

Beelen, J., & Jones, E. (2015). Redefining internationalization at home. In A. Curai, L. Matei, R. Pricopie, J. Salmi, & P. Scott (Eds.), *The European higher education area: Between critical reflections and future policies* (pp. 57–72). Springer. https://doi.org/10.1007/978-3-319-20877-0_5

Bhandari, R. (2011). International Student Mobility: Patterns and Trends. In R. Bhandari, & P. Blumenthal (Eds.), *International Students and Global Mobility in Higher Education: National Trends and New Directions*. Palgrave Macmillan.

Bhandari, R. (2017). *The gender dimensions of academic mobility*. Institute of International Education. Retrieved from https://www.iie.org/wp-content/uploads/2022/12/Women-and-Academic-Mobility.pdf

Brandenburg, U., & De Wit, H. (2011). The end of internationalization. *The Internationalization Debate, 62*. https://doi.org/10.6017/ihe.2011.62.8533

Buckner, E., & Stein, S. (2020). What counts as internationalization? Deconstructing the internationalization imperative. *Journal of Studies in International Education, 24*(2), 151–166. https://doi.org/10.1177/1028315319829878

Burbules, N. C., & Torres, C. A. (2013). *Globalization and education: Critical perspectives*. Routledge.

Canagarajah, S. (2013). *Translingual practice: Global English and cosmopolitan relations*. Routledge.

De Wit, H. (1998). Rationales for Internationalisation of Higher Education. *Millenium, 11*. 1–8

De Wit, H. (2024). 'Everything that quacks is Internationalisation'—Critical reflections on the evolution of higher education internationalization. *Journal of Studies in International Education, 28*(1), 3–14. https://doi.org/10.1177/10283153231221655

De Wit, H., Gacel-Ávila, J., Jones, E., & Jooste, N. (Eds.). (2017). *The globalization of internationalization emerging voices and perspectives*. Routledge.

Dorasamy, N., & Mugano, G. (Eds.). (2022). *Perspectives on comprehensive internationalisation of higher education*. AOSIS.

Egron-Polak, E., & Hudson, R. (2010). *Internationalization of higher education: Global trends, regional perspectives; IAU 3rd global survey report*. International Association of Universities.

E-International Relations. (2017). Interview—Walter D. Mignolo. https://www.e-ir.info/2017/06/01/interview-walter-d-mignolo/

Freire, Paulo. (1970). *Pedagogy of the oppressed*. Translated by Myra Bergman Ramos. Herder and Herder.

Hagenmeier, C., Lansink, A., & Vukor-Quarshie, G. (2017). Internationalisation and African intellectual métissage: Capacity-enhancement through higher education in Africa. *South African Journal of Higher Education, 31*(1). https://doi.org/10.20853/31-1-821

Heleta, S., & Chasi, S. (2022). Rethinking and redefining internationalisation of higher education in South Africa using a decolonial lens. *Journal of Higher Education Policy and Management, 45*(3), 261–275. https://doi.org/10.1080/1360080X.2022.2146566

Helms, R. M., & Rumbley, L. E. (2017). Global: National policies for internationalization—do they work? In *Understanding higher education internationalization*. https://doi.org/10.1007/978-94-6351-161-228

Hudzik, J. K. (2011). *Comprehensive internationalization: from concept to action*. NAFSA.

Hunter, F. (2018). Training administrative staff to become key players in the internationalization of higher education. *International Higher Education, 92*, 16–17. https://doi.org/10.6017/ihe.2018.92.10217

IEASA. (2014). *Nelson Mandela bay global dialogue declaration on the future of internationalisation of higher education*. Port Elizabeth. https://www.iau-aiu.net/IMG/pdf/nelson_mandela_bay_declaration.pdf

Jacobs, L., Kruger, E., & Madiope, M. (2022). The potential of African diaspora academics and diaspora academics in Africa in reshaping international higher education. In D. Lock, A. Caputo, P. Igwe, & D. Hack-Polay (Eds.), *Borderlands: The internationalisation of higher education teaching practices* (pp. 31–43). Springer Nature.

Jacobs, L., & Mitchell, L.-M. (2021). What was in the news? Conversations on internationalisation of higher education in university world news in 2020. In N. Popov, C. Wolhuter, L. de Beer, G. Hilton, J. Ogunleye, E. Achinewhu-Nworgu, & E. Niemczyk (Eds.), *New challenges to education: Lessons from around the world. BCES conference books* (pp. 23–29). BCES.

Jones, E., Leask, B., Brandenburg, U., & De Wit, H. (2021). Global social responsibility and the internationalization of higher education for society. *Journal of Studies in International Education*, 25(4), 330–347. https://doi.org/10.1177/10283153211031679

Jooste, N., & Hagenmeier, C. (2022). Policy framework for the internationalisation of higher education in South Africa: A compass for comprehensive internationalisation? *Journal of Studies in International Education*, 26(4), 415–435. https://doi.org/10.1177/10283153221105318

Jooste, N., & Naude, P. (2005). Towards an Internationalisation Policy for South Africa; Global, National and Institutional imperatives. In N. J. Jooste, & E. Naude (Eds.), *Internationalisation of higher education – A policy framework* (pp. 34–51). Nelson Mandela University Publication.

Knight, J. (1997). Internationalization of higher education: A conceptual framework. In J. Knight, & H. De Wit (Eds.), *Internationalisation of higher education in Asia Pacific countries* (pp. 5–19). European Association for International Education.

Knight, J., & De Wit, H. (1995). Strategies for internationalisation of higher education: Historical and conceptual perspectives. In H. de Wit (Ed.), *Strategies for internationalisation of higher education: A comparative study of Australia, Canada, Europe and the United States of America,* (pp. 5-32). European Association for International Education.

Kostrykina, S. (2021). Overcoming the White knight complex: Social license and internationalization for society. *Journal of Studies in International Education*, 25(4), 369–387. https://doi.org/10.1177/10283153211016267

Laakso, L. (2021). Academic Mobility as Freedom in Africa. *POLITIKON*, 47(4), 442–459. https://doi.org/10.1080/02589346.2020.1840023

Le Grange, L. (2016). Declonising the university curriculum. *South African Journal of Higher Education*, 30(2), 1–12. https://doi.org/10.20853/30-2-709

Leal, F., Finardi, K., & Abba, J. (2022). Challenges for an internationalization of higher education from and for the global south. *Perspectives in Education*, 40(3), 241–250. https://doi.org/10.38140/pie.v40i3.6776

Leask, B. (2015). *Internationalizing the curriculum*. Routledge.

Lugones, M. (2010). Toward a decolonial feminism. *Hypatia*, 25(4), 742–759.

Marginson, S. (2006). Dynamics of national and global competition in higher education. *Higher Education*, 52, 1–39.

Marginson, S., & Van der Wende, M. (2007). To rank or to be ranked: The impact of global rankings in higher education. *Journal of Studies in International Education*, 11(3–4), 306–329. https://doi.org/10.1177/1028315307303544

Mazrui, A. A. (2002). *Black reparations in the era of globalization*. Institute of Global Cultural Studies.

Mazrui, A. A., & Kaba, A. J. (2016). *The African Intelligentsia: Domestic Decline and Global Ascent*. Africa World Press.

Mbembe, A. (2001). *On the postcolony*. University of California Press. Retrieved from https://www.jstor.org/stable/10.1525/j.ctt1ppkxs

Menchú, Rigoberta. (1984). *I, Rigoberta Menchú: An Indian Woman in Guatemala*. Edited by Elisabeth Burgos-Debray, translated by Ann Wright. Verso Books

Mestenhauser, J. A. (2000). Missing in action: Leadership for international and global education. In H. De Wit (Ed.), *Internationalization of higher education: An institutional perspective* (pp. 23–62). UNESCO.

Mignolo, W. D. (2011). *The darker side of western modernity: Global futures, decolonial options*. Duke University Press.

Mignolo, W. D. (2012). *Local histories-global designs: Coloniality, subaltern knowledges, and border thinking*. Princeton University Press.

Mukwambo, P., Mkwananzi, F., & Seshoka, W. (2024). The policy and practice of internationalization in the Global-South: African international students' experiences in South Africa during COVID-19. *Journal of Comparative & International Higher Education, 16*(5), 45–59. https://doi.org/10.32674/afwhbb79

Ndaipa, C. J. (2023). *The interpretation and translation of global ideas into local practices. A study of the internationalisation of higher education in Mozambique*. KTH Royal Institute of Technology: Doctoral Thesis in Technology and Learning.

Ndlovu-Gatsheni, S. (2013). *Coloniality of power in postcolonial Africa*. African Books Collective.

Ndlovu-Gatsheni, S. J. (2015). Decoloniality as the future of Africa. *History Compass, 13*(10), 485–496.

Niemczyk, E. (2019). Glocal education in practice: Teaching, researching, and citizenship. In N. Popov, C. Wolhuter, L. de Beer, G. Hilton, J. Ogunleye, E. Achinewhu-Nworgu, & E. Niemczyk (Eds.), *BCES Conference Books* (pp. 11–18). Sofia.

Nyamnjoh, F. B. (2021). Keynote address: Mobility, globalisation, and the policing of citizenship and belonging in the twenty-first century: Delivered at the 27th Biennial Conference of the Southern African Historical Society, Rhodes University, 24 June 2019. *South African Historical Journal, 73*(2), 241–256. https://doi.org/10.1080/02582473.2021.1909121

Okpewho, I., Davies, C. B., & Mazrui, A. A. (Eds.). (2001). *The African diaspora: African origins and new world identities*. Indiana University Press.

Oyěwùmí, O. (1997). *The invention of women: Making an African sense of western gender discourses*. University of Minnesota Press.

Pap, A. (2024). University administrators, leadership, and faculty views on the internationalization of curriculum (a perspective through decolonial lenses from the Global South). *Journal of Higher Education Theory and Practice, 24*(6), 83–105. https://doi.org/10.33423/jhetp.v24i6.7059

Ramose, M. B. (1999). *African philosophy through Ubuntu*. Mond Books Publishers.

Rodney, W., Gikandi, S., & Santos, B. (2024). International institutions are no longer suitable. *Revue Project, 398*, 87–90.

Sehoole, C. (2011). Student mobility and doctoral education in South Africa. *Perspectives in Education, 29*(3), 53–63.

Sehoole, C., & Lee, J. J. (Eds.). (2021). *Intra-Africa student mobility in higher education. Strengths, prospects and challenges*. Palgrave MacMillan.

Stein, S. (2019). Critical internationalization studies at an impasse: Making space for complexity, uncertainty, and complicity in a time of global challenges. *Studies in Higher Education*, 46(9), 1771–1784. https://doi.org/10.1080/03075079.2019.1704722

Stein, S., Andreotti, V., Bruce, J., & Suša, R., 2016. Towards different conversations about the internationalization of higher education. *Comparative and International Education/Éducation Comparée et Internationale*, 45(1). 1–18.

Teferra, D. (2005). Brain circulation: Unparalleled opportunities, underlying challenges, and outmoded presumptions. *Journal of Studies in International Education*, 9(3), 229–250.

Teferra, D. (2008). The international dimension of higher education in Africa: Status, challenges, and prospects. *Higher education in Africa: The international dimension*, 5, 44–79.

Teferra, D., & Altbach, P. (2004). African higher education: Challenges for the 21st century. *Higher Education*, 47, 21–50.

wa Thiong'o (1986). *Decolonising the Mind: The Politics of Language in African Literature*. Heinemann.

Wimpenny, K., Finardi, K., Orsini-Jones, M., & Jacobs, L. (2022). Knowing, being, relating and expressing through third space global South-North COIL: Digital inclusion and equity in international higher education. *Journal of Studies in International Education*, 26(1), 279–296. https://doi.org/10.1177/10283 15322109408

Wimpenny, K., Jacobs, L., Dawson, M., & Hagenmeier, C. (2024). The potential of collaborative online international learning as a border thinking third space for global citizenship education. *International Journal of Development Education and Global Learning*, 16(1), 29–42. https://doi.org/10.14324/IJDEGL.16.1.03

Wolhuter, C. (2023). Internationalization of higher education in South Africa. In S. Kamyab, & R. L. Raby (Eds.), *Unintended consequences brought from contextual contours*. Routledge. https://doi.org/10.4324/9781003189916

7
INTERNATIONAL DEVELOPMENT, HIGHER EDUCATION'S THIRD MISSION AND THE INTERNATIONALIZATION OF SERVICE

Toward an International Community-Centered University Service Model

Julian Prieto and Annie Everett

Introduction

Higher education institutions (HEIs) often operate within the context of an isomorphic tripartite mission, including education, research, and service (DiMaggio & Powell, 1983). Leaders and policymakers in post-secondary education have acknowledged the importance of incorporating an international perspective in each of these missions by adopting strategies toward

> an intentional process of integrating an international and intercultural dimension into the teaching, research, and service functions of the institution to enhance the quality of education and research for all students and staff, and to make a meaningful contribution to society.
>
> *(De Wit et al., 2015)*

Research on the practice of internationalization in higher education has shown how HEIs typically align their teaching and research missions with the type of intentional process encouraged by De Wit (2015) and colleagues (Deardorff & Van Gaalen, 2022; Woldegiyorgis et al., 2022). Notably, scholars in the field have documented power imbalances between the Global North and the Global South when developing global engagement initiatives (Blanco Ramírez, 2014; De Wit & Altbach, 2021; George Mwangi et al., 2021; Lee, 2021). In particular, practices that fall under the internationalization of service, often described as a university's "third mission," have been criticized for perpetuating neocolonial structures, and scholars have proposed the need to develop social responsibility and

DOI: 10.4324/9781315623337-9

inclusivity strategies within an institution's internationalization process (Jones et al., 2021; Pashby & De Oliveira Andreotti, 2016; Silva, 2015; Stein et al., 2016, 2021).

This chapter critically analyzes HEI international "service" practices and introduces an international community-centered university service model. We draw extensive inspiration from the U.S.' Cooperative Extension System and by the Cultural Readiness for Internationalization change model (Agnew & VanBalkom, 2009) presented in Chapter 1. Our analysis addresses three key questions regarding international development service activities:

1 Who is in control?
2 Who are the beneficiaries?
3 What accountability mechanisms exist?

Understanding who controls decision-making helps avoid top-down approaches and promotes inclusivity, fostering collaboration with local stakeholders. Identifying beneficiaries is equally vital for assessing equity and effectiveness, promoting the idea that the benefits of initiatives are distributed equitably among diverse populations, addressing disparities, and prioritizing the specific needs of marginalized groups. Moreover, the presence of robust accountability oversight, evaluation, and continuous improvement strategies ensures that programs are accountable to internal and external stakeholders, including funding organizations and the communities being served.

This chapter begins with an overview of international development as a field. We then engage with the evolution of higher education's third mission, with a focus on the U.S. Land-Grant Universities' Cooperative Extension System (CES) model as an example of community-centered service engagement. We review scholarly discussions on the internationalization of service and introduce an alternative service model that combines best practices from CES and the Cultural Readiness for Internationalization (Agnew & VanBalkom, 2009) model, and we provide an overview of ethical implications for research and practice. We ultimately argue that integrating inclusive decision-making, equitable benefit sharing, local empowerment, transparent accountability, cultural sensitivity, adaptability, and a community-centered approach enhances the relevance, impact, and sustainability of international development efforts led by HEIs.

Defining International Development

Current understandings of international development emerged post-1945 in the context of the Cold War. Two competing visions of "development" emerged in the form of President Truman's Marshall Plan and the Soviet

Union's Molotov Plan (later known as the Council for Mutual Economic Assistance). Truman's Marshall Plan doctrine significantly shaped modern notions of international development (Haslam et al., 2017). In his Inaugural Address, Truman explained his reasoning behind the need to support and invest in international aid:

> We must embark on a bold new program for making the benefits of our scientific advances and industrial progress available for the improvement and growth of underdeveloped areas. More than half of the people of the world are living in conditions approaching misery. Their food is inadequate, they are victims of disease. Their economic life is primitive and stagnant. Their poverty is a handicap and a threat both to them and more prosperous areas. For the first time in history, humanity possesses the knowledge and the skill to relieve the suffering of these people.
> *(Truman, 1949)*

Outcomes related to the Marshall Plan in Europe have been used as evidence that successful "development" is based on the establishment of democratic political systems and neoliberal capitalist economies (Schaffer et al., 2017). Eventually, Marshall Plan principles were applied beyond Europe, as U.S. policymakers used international aid programs as tools to counter the spread of communism (Boschini & Olofsgård, 2007; Taffet, 2007).

Over time, the language of "development" has been standardized into two categories. Economic development standards, using gross domestic product as an indicator of growth, inequality, and poverty, classified countries as "developed" or "underdeveloped" (Haslam et al., 2017). Countries deemed "underdeveloped" became subject to external intervention and support from those labeled "developed." These patterns of international aid and intervention were institutionalized in 1969 through the Organization for Economic Cooperation and Development (OECD), which established that 0.7 percent of the donor country's gross national product would be committed to Official Development Assistance (ODA) programs (OECD, n.d.). ODA financial commitments triggered the creation of a development industry with practitioners in government agencies working alongside NGOs who organize the management and implementation of projects in "developing" countries. The international development agenda was conceived under unequal geopolitical power dynamics, with "developed" countries imposing their path to economic development on emerging economies using a uniform capitalist and neoliberal paradigm (Springett & Redclift, 2015). The directionality of aid generally flows from Global North countries to "underdeveloped" countries in the Global South, implying the perpetuation of unequal power dynamics and possibly neocolonial relations (Schaffer et al., 2017). Economists have particularly emphasized poverty reduction and economic growth, both at the individual and societal levels, as key development measures (Escobar, 1995).

Efforts to address these power imbalances were introduced through the United Nations Sustainability Development Goals (SDGs) in 2015, which require countries in the Global North to report and comply with their progress on all targeted indicators (Caballero & Londoño, 2022). Under the SDGs, all countries report on their progress in poverty reduction, universal education, and healthcare, and must act to conserve natural resources as a means of adapting to environmental planetary boundaries. However, despite these efforts, the flow of investment still largely moves from the Global North to the Global South, perpetuating global hierarchies and inequities.

Conceptualizing the *Third Mission* of Higher Education

Two multilateral organizations, UNESCO and the OECD, offer valuable insights into defining the service mission and its promotion. As a United Nations agency, UNESCO recognizes the commitment of HEIs to actively contribute to advancing the SDGs. UNESCO's Global Convention on the Recognition of Qualifications concerning Higher Education (2019) defines the service mission as a multifaceted approach that fosters social inclusion and addresses global challenges. UNESCO (2017) aligns this mission with its Education for Sustainable Development goals, emphasizing the integral role of HEIs in building a more sustainable and just world. The organization promotes a holistic approach to the third mission, advocating for the integration of community engagement, knowledge transfer, and social responsibility into the core functions of higher education. Additionally, UNESCO provides practical guidelines for the integration of community service, including initiatives like the Global Network of UNESCO Chairs on Community-Based Research and Social Responsibility in Higher Education (UNESCO, n.d.).

Similarly, the OECD acknowledges the significance of the service mission in higher education, primarily as a driver of economic development and social progress. Through its definition of "engagement with the wider world," the OECD recognizes universities as contributors to innovation, regional development, and overall societal well-being (OECD, 2019). The OECD's focus lies in providing frameworks for assessing the impact of HEIs on regional development, emphasizing indicators related to knowledge transfer, entrepreneurship, and community engagement. The organization actively encourages effective university-industry collaboration, technology transfer, and entrepreneurship to maximize the societal impact of higher education.

Together, these organizations contribute to the global discourse on integrating community service into higher education, fostering positive impacts on communities and societies worldwide. However, while UNESCO and the OECD provide valuable frameworks for understanding the service mission in global higher education, it is essential to critically assess their roles and inclusiveness. Criticism of the parochialism and relativism embedded in UNESCO's approach to culture and education goes back decades (Eriksen, 2001; Finkielkraut, 1987). One significant critique is that, due to their historical and institutional contexts, these organizations may inadvertently act as a foreign policy tool for Europe and other "developed" regions (Zahavi & Friedman, 2019). UNESCO, although a global entity, often sees higher participation and influence from European countries and other developed nations, potentially reinforcing a Eurocentric perspective on what constitutes effective community engagement.

Similarly, the OECD, with its origins rooted in economically advanced nations, tends to prioritize issues and metrics that resonate more with "developed" economies. This focus can marginalize the unique challenges and priorities of HEIs in the Global South, potentially overlooking vital aspects of social inclusion and local relevance in those contexts. Despite these critiques, however, UNESCO and the OECD play a pivotal role in shaping global discourse on the third mission of higher education, fostering a more equitable and inclusive global education landscape.

Adoption of the Third Mission Around the World

The "third mission" has various interpretations and implementation practices around the world. The U.S.' system of land-grant institutions (LGIs) represents the oldest model of a tripartite university mission. Established in the late 19th century, LGIs allowed the nation to consolidate its public higher education system, broadening access to higher education across diverse segments of the American population and establishing colleges focused on fields like agriculture, engineering, and practical education (Geiger, 2015). Generally, the LGI tripartite mission reflects principles of community service through training and educational programs that address the needs of agricultural workers and industrial labor, and by conducting applied research that responds to community needs (Kellogg Commission, 1999). Over the years these institutions have transformed into a combination of on-campus instruction, world-class research, and off-campus outreach and service.

Other nations interpret the third mission in a variety of ways (e.g., Izadi et al., 2020; Krčmářová, 2011; Nabaho et al., 2022; Preece, 2011; Sataøen, 2018; Schnurbus & Edvardsson, 2022; Tonelli & Gibson, 2023; Thorn &

Soo, 2006). In Europe, the third mission is often referred to as the "knowledge exchange" (Zawdie, 2010). Many European institutions emphasize collaboration with industry, regional development agencies, and local communities. Examples include the Knowledge Transfer Partnerships in the UK (SQW, 2023), the Quadruple Helix model in France (Alfonsi et al., 2021), and the Fraunhofer-Gesellschaft model in Germany (Fraunhofer-Gesellschaft, 2022). In Latin America, universities often align their third mission with a commitment to social justice and community development (Mora et al., 2018), while Asian countries, particularly in East Asia, often connect service missions to innovation and entrepreneurship (Symaco & Tee, 2019). African universities have also been found to frequently link their service missions to sustainable development goals, engaging in projects related to healthcare, agriculture, and environmental sustainability (Raditloaneng, 2013).

In short, the "service mission" of international higher education plays a crucial role in contributing to social, economic, and cultural development across the globe. At its core, this mission involves universities actively engaging with communities, addressing pressing issues, and translating academic knowledge into practical solutions. HEIs can make a significant impact on social development, contributing to alleviating poverty, reducing inequality, and promoting social justice through community-based projects and outreach initiatives (Haj Taieb, 2024; Zuti & Lukovics, 2014). Economically, universities act as catalysts for growth, fostering innovation, technology transfer, and collaboration with industries, resulting in job creation and a skilled workforce (Jaeger & Kopper, 2014). Additionally, HEIs contribute to cultural development and preservation through initiatives such as cultural exchange programs and collaborative research that fosters an understanding and appreciation of diverse cultural heritages (Smith, 2013).

U.S. Land-Grant Universities and the Third Mission: Lessons from the Cooperative Extension System

As noted above, in the U.S., institutional service missions first emerged with LGIs, which were designed to serve the public by applying academic knowledge to address societal needs (Christy & Williamson, 1992). Established by the Morrill Acts of 1862 and 1890, and further expanded to include tribal colleges in 1994, LGIs represent a cornerstone of the nation's higher education system. Historically, LGI's are considered a democratizing force for U.S. higher education, making higher learning accessible to broader segments of the U.S. population (Eddy, 1957; Nevins, 1962; Ross, 1942). However, it is important to acknowledge that the federal land allocated to states via the Morrill Acts stems from the sale of stolen native lands (R. Lee et al., n.d.). Additionally, historically Black colleges and universities created by the 1890 Morrill Act have faced chronic underfunding (National Education Association, 2022; Williams & Davis, 2019), making the land-grant commitment to equitable access historically uneven. Despite such pitfalls, the land-grant mission has evolved to encompass a wide range of disciplines, and in many ways, the institutional commitment to serving the needs of their local communities, states, and the nation itself remains steadfast. Today, LGIs play a pivotal role in advancing education, research, and outreach, with a focus on promoting accessibility, diversity, and social engagement.

One key way that LGIs connect with local communities occurs through the Cooperative Extension System (CES), a multi-institutional and multi-actor framework that guides how land-grants translate research into action. CES partners at the federal, state, and local levels to "translate science for the public, engage the public to act, prepare people for a better life, provide rapid response in disasters, develop partnerships, and connect people online" (Association for Public Land-Grant Universities, n.d.). Established by the 1914 Smith-Lever Act, the CES formalized relationships between LGIs and the U.S. Department of Agriculture (U.S. Department of Agriculture, n.d.). At the time, more than 50 percent of the U.S. population still lived in rural areas, with 30 percent of the workforce engaged in farming (National Institute of Food and Agriculture, n.d.). The CES helped drive an agricultural revolution by connecting universities with local communities to share knowledge, increase productivity, and solve local challenges. It is a clear example of the higher education service mission in action, actively engaging with communities to disseminate information and provide education.

The CES establishes a dynamic and interactive relationship between LGIs and the local community, serving as a knowledge dissemination platform and a space for mutual learning, collaboration, and the co-creation of solutions to address the unique needs of each community. The CES functions through knowledge transfer, needs assessment, educational programs, demonstration projects, and feedback mechanisms (Rasmussen, 1989).

The effectiveness of various CES initiatives has been measured using a combination of quantitative and qualitative methods, providing a comprehensive picture of their impact (Warner & Christenson, 1984; Workman & Scheer, 2012). CES programs are regularly evaluated to assess their goals, objectives, and outcomes (Duttweiler, 2008). This includes measuring the effectiveness of educational workshops, training sessions, and outreach initiatives (Borron et al., 2019). Evaluation methods may include surveys, interviews, focus groups, and pre-post assessments to quantify changes in knowledge, behavior, or practices among participants. Researchers also conduct economic impact studies to quantify the financial benefits or savings associated with the adoption of extension-recommended practices (Wang, 2014). This could include assessing changes in agricultural productivity, cost savings, or improvements in overall community well-being.

Some evaluations focus on longer-term outcomes, tracking changes in community resilience and sustainability (Robertson et al., 2008). The establishment and maintenance of partnerships between LGIs, extension services, and local communities are also indicative of the success of CES programs (Pardello & Michaels, 2020), with ongoing collaborations reflecting that the CES meets community needs and fosters a mutually beneficial relationship. Published research resulting from collaborations between extension agents and university researchers further demonstrates the CES' contribution to academia and its role in addressing real-world challenges.

The CES serves as an exemplary model for institutional service, aligning university resources with community needs to address societal challenges and contribute to the public good (Rasmussen, 1989). Its success is built on a collaborative, service-oriented approach that includes inter-institutional accountability mechanisms. Figure 7.1 illustrates the CES model's engagement cycle, which typically includes needs assessment, knowledge transfer, education, feedback, and impact assessment.

It should be noted that CES initiatives are not purely altruistic. A complex relationship exists between economic development and nationalism (Duara, 2019). U.S. higher education has historically bolstered nationalism by contributing to global competitiveness and security through education and research that enhance U.S. leadership (Tannock, 2007). This underscores the dual nature of extension work: while it can uplift communities, it can also reinforce nationalistic and economic policies. An analysis of investment in CES from 2017 to 2024 helps us understand how the projects of nationalism and extension services intertwine. The level of CES investment has fluctuated over time since 2017 ($509.8 million), peaking in the fiscal year 2020 ($609.5 million), and decreasing to $561.7 million by the fiscal year 2024 (Bickell, 2024). The impact of such investment is felt both locally and nationally. For example, between 1983 and 2010, nearly 500,000 more farmers transitioned out of U.S. agriculture than entered, though Goetz and Davlasheridze (2017) find that the impact of federal extension expenditures helped prevent the exit of nearly 137,000 more farmers during that period. In a more general economic sense, extension programming has also been found to yield high returns in terms of its

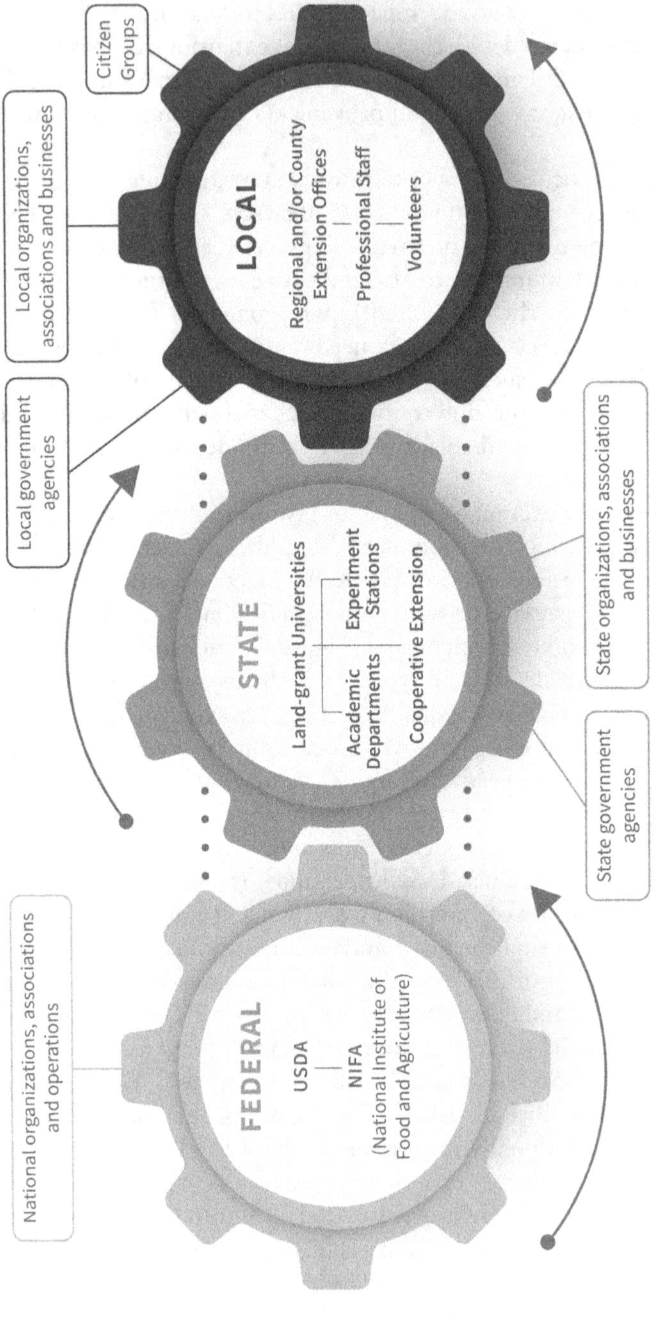

FIGURE 7.1 Illustration of How Cooperative Extension Works. Graphic courtesy of USDA's National Institute of Food and Agriculture.

internal rate of return or benefit-cost ratio and has been shown to contribute to productivity growth (Wang, 2014).

Three key questions emerge from our analysis of CES programming: **who benefits, who is in control, and what accountability mechanisms exist?** The CES addresses these questions effectively, providing a blueprint for other institutions to enhance their service missions.

Who benefits? CES programs benefit a wide range of individuals and communities, particularly in agriculture. Farmers gain access to the latest research and practices, while rural communities benefit from programs addressing local challenges. CES also supports families and consumers with education on topics like nutrition, health, and financial management. Its youth programs, like 4-H, offer hands-on learning and leadership development, preparing youth for future roles in agriculture and community leadership (Ohio Cooperative Extension Service, 1986).

Who is in control? Control of CES initiatives is collaborative, involving stakeholders such as LGIs, university administrators, faculty, and extension agents. Extension agents, acting as liaisons between universities and communities, play a critical role in program design and outreach. Community input is vital, guiding CES programs through needs assessment and engagement, while state and federal agencies, industry partners, and funding organizations share in decision-making.

What accountability mechanisms exist? CES ensures transparency and effectiveness through accountability mechanisms. Needs assessments involving communities guide program development. Advisory boards provide feedback and ensure relevance, while regular evaluations and impact assessments measure program success (Borron et al., 2019). Reporting mechanisms document activities, outcomes, and financial expenditures, ensuring programs are accountable and serving community needs.

Variations on the CES model have been implemented globally, primarily within agricultural extension (e.g., Chapman et al., 2003; Davis et al., 2010; Ferroni & Zhou, 2012; Fleischer et al., 2002; Hellin, 2012; Lioutas et al., 2019; Yitayew et al., 2021). Though the CES model is closely associated with agriculture, it stands as a model for institutional service that extends beyond its original focus, especially when considering the wide range of third mission activities available to HEIs.

The CES exemplifies holistic community engagement, addressing needs across agriculture, health, education, and economic development. It emphasizes knowledge transfer and collaboration, providing valuable lessons for HEIs worldwide in adopting comprehensive strategies that integrate the third mission's goals of community engagement and societal impact. The CES demonstrates that a focus on diverse beneficiaries, sharing control, and the presence of robust accountability mechanisms contribute to the overall success and impact of institutional service initiatives. Institutions seeking to improve their service mission can draw valuable lessons from the CES model, ensuring that their efforts are equitable, community-driven, and accountable to the diverse needs and aspirations of the communities they serve.

Higher Education's Third Mission and International Development

In a globalized context, the third mission extends beyond local impact to address the needs of diverse communities worldwide (E3M, 2010). Universities are encouraged to promote global citizenship by engaging in international partnerships, research collaborations, and initiatives that positively impact the global good (Pashby et al., 2020; Pinheiro et al., 2015; Stein, 2015; Stein et al., 2016). In addition, through international collaborations, it is expected that HEIs extend their role in addressing societal changes and social justice, contribute to the well-being of communities (Larrán Jorge & Andrades Peña, 2017; Gómez et al., 2018), promote civic participation and democratic values (Sengupta et al., 2020), developing opportunities for lifelong and adult learning (Adamuti-Trache & Schuetze, 2008; Knowles et al., 2015), and integrating SDG principles into their service mission agendas (United Nations, 2023).

International service practices were initially categorized under "service-learning," combining academic, research, and volunteer work with communities. Berry and Chisholm (1999) developed a typology of international service-learning activities by studying 97 colleges and universities worldwide, identifying three main categories of service: teaching, health care services, and community development. The concept of service-learning has also been applied to study-abroad programs that have a special focus on community engagement and intercultural competencies (Bringle et al., 2012).

Brandenburg et al. (2020) advance one of the most well-known frameworks for understanding "service" as a component of internationalization. Their report on the internationalization of higher education for society (IHES) offers a vision of service that aligns an institution's third mission and internationalization agendas to tackle local and global social issues. Activities include the development of education, research, and service initiatives that benefit the wider community, at home and abroad. This approach promotes a clear, intentional internationalization strategy with a focus on the potential impact on beneficiaries.

Following the IHES theoretical framework, HEIs worldwide have implemented internationalization strategies linked with social responsibility, focusing on social justice, economic development, and public good (Hazelkorn, 2016). A report on IHES initiatives that assessed 69 service programs across 48 different HEIs found that 63 percent of the activities mapped in the study considered developing "global citizens" as the main goal of IHES programs, while another 61 percent mentioned supporting the UN SDGs, and 52 percent focused their actions on activities that promote the education of the general public and capacity building and knowledge transfer (Bogdan et al., 2021). The report also finds that local and regional stakeholders are willing to collaborate when projects include applied research, innovation, and design thinking to engage young people in solving real-world problems.

Critical Voices in the Internationalization of Service

Critical voices in the internationalization of service have highlighted controversial aspects of expanding higher education's service mission globally. Many critics, using neo-colonial and decolonization theories, argue that an institution's definition of "service" in the international arena often assumes that capitalism, neoliberalism, and democracy are universal values—and approach which may perpetuate global power imbalances and radicalized inequities (Sant et al., 2018; Stein et al., 2016). Scholars have especially problematized the assumptions guiding the internationalization of higher education and sustainable development strategies.

Bamberger et al. (2019) acknowledge that the internationalization of higher education has encouraged the global spread of cosmopolitan, multicultural, social justice, and diversity values. However, critics have pointed out how international service activities also support a global imaginary that perpetuates capitalist social relations with intrinsic inequalities and racialized hierarchies (Silva, 2015). Classifying countries as "underdeveloped" imposes a singular model of development centered on economic progress, which disregards and minimizes alternative paths toward social well-being and contributions from indigenous knowledge (Stein et al., 2021). In cases where in indigenous knowledge is recognized, it is sometimes used for profit-making, such as in pharmaceutical development, to benefit institutions rather than the communities themselves (Nandy, 2000).

Scholars have also documented programs such as the "21 Day International Challenge," a New Zealand study abroad program that aims to develop entrepreneurial skills by having students create a business plan that provides solutions to the most pressing challenges faced by vulnerable communities in Tarong (Philippines). The program illustrates how Western market principles are often presented as universal solutions to address and improve social issues in poor communities (Stein et al., 2016). In reality, what may be perceived as a universally positive service initiative in one context may clash with local values or inadvertently contribute to the erosion of indigenous knowledge systems in another. The "21 Day International Challenge" offers an example of how institutional strategies that promote the internationalization of service often prioritize the program's commercial return on investment and potential income generated by the creation of marketable activities that can be provided to the students studying abroad, rather than on the local communities hosting the program (Jones et al., 2021).

Through social cartography, Pashby and Andreotti (2016) describe how a neoliberal discursive orientation has penetrated higher education's tripartite mission. The authors explain how international service programs are often framed to benefit the internal academic community by commodifying international activities, enabling students to gain credentials in soft skills like intercultural competence and teamwork. This perspective highlights the power dynamics controlling the international service mission in higher education. Cleaver (2012) addresses the difficulties of transferring democratic values into non-democratic host contexts, particularly the challenging dynamics of local governance and the limitations of community collective decision-making processes. As a whole, critical scholars emphasize the need for a comprehensive examination of power dynamics, cultural complexities, and the potential neocolonial influences that shape the direction of international service initiatives. Institutions from economically privileged regions often wield significant control in international venues, drawing on influence that stems directly from legacies of colonialism and the resulting history of economic disparity. Ultimately, unequal power relations may lead to initiatives that prioritize institutional interests and reputation over genuine collaboration and mutual benefit.

It is naïve to suggest that the mechanisms that HEIs use to engage internationally are neutral or benign. An institution's third mission and its resulting service activities are deeply intertwined with power dynamics and cultural complexities—as we note with the U.S. CES model's links to nationalism. The internationalization of service involves navigating a landscape of diverse world views, historical legacies, and socio-political contexts. Assuming that service programs function neutrally ignores the underlying power structures in global interactions. Critical reflection on the process of internationalization must include consideration of how institutions implement their international service agendas because the act of providing service may come with negative impacts, not least in the level of administrative burden potential beneficiaries may face in attempting to access said service (Burden et al., 2012; Herd & Moynihan, 2019).

HEIs engaged in international service must consider the same three questions we ask in this chapter: who is in control, who benefits, and what accountability mechanisms exist—and they must also consider the implications these questions have for research and practice. Following our reading of critical scholarship above, Figure 7.2 attempts to capture the most common features found in international service models that are active today, allowing us to respond to these three questions.

Current practice in the internationalization of service often focuses on benefits for student participants through the provision of intercultural credentials. Control of an institution's third mission activities typically involves a dynamic relationship between internal structural units within the university, including global offices, with its external international partners promoting service activities *vis a vis* study abroad programming. These offices often partner with international companies that serve as logistics operators in different locations. Such companies generally work with local NGOs who provide access to local communities and serve as cultural brokers in the service experience. In some other cases, these companies are responsible for the whole experience and partner with universities to allow students to get academic credentials upon completion. Often, individual HEIs will establish an academic point person who leads the student group abroad and is responsible for any pedagogical service-learning components. These academic leaders, often faculty, establish contact with local HEI partners as local hosts for their activities, though collaboration rarely includes students from both institutions, perpetuating global systems of inequity.

Who Benefits?

Using current practices, the main beneficiaries of service activities visualized in Figure 7.2 are the students who pay to take part in these programs. The fees paid by students to participate in such programs are usually used to cover university fees and travel costs, rather than being invested in the needs of local communities. In contrast, local communities take on the role of local hosts and function as instrumental actors in achieving the academic goals of international students.

Who Is in Control?

Control over these programs is held by the institutions that are involved in the design and implementation of international service activities. As shown in Figure 7.2, these institutions are commonly based in the Global North, which generally set program goals, and include the participation of institutions and organizations from the Global South as academic hosts and cultural brokers. Unlike the robust network of extension agents present in the CES model, international service programs do not necessarily involve an

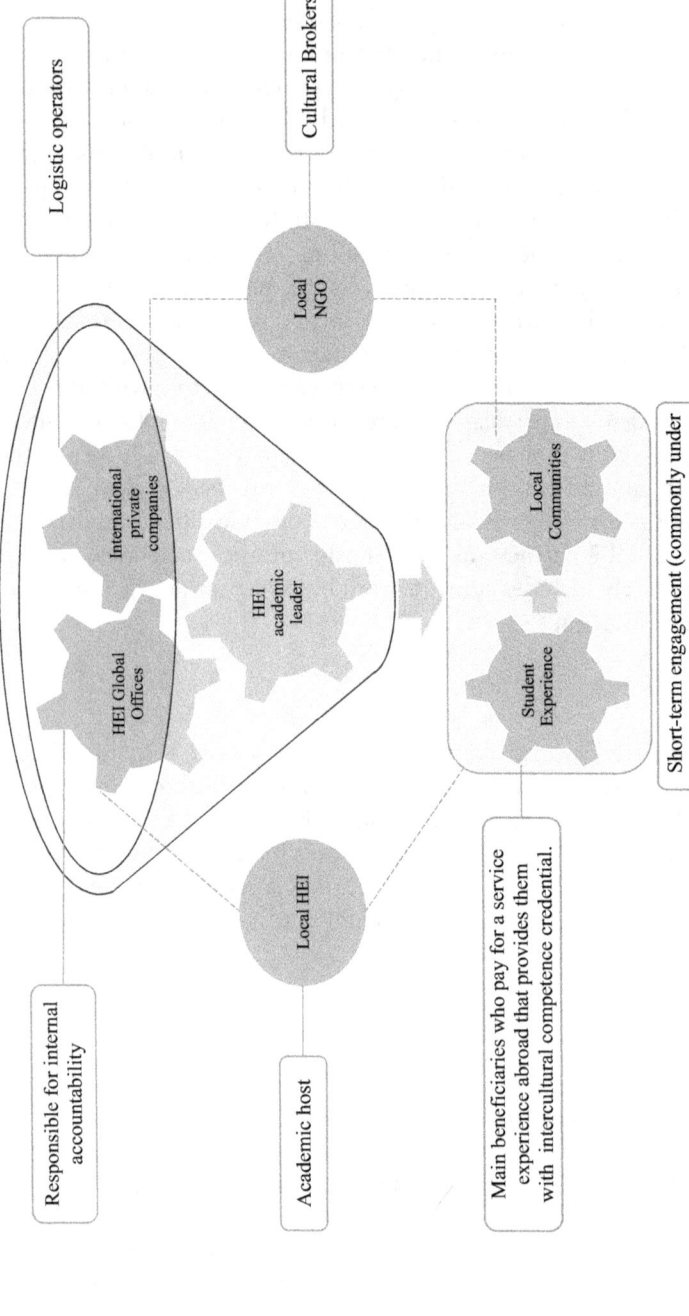

FIGURE 7.2 Visualizing the International Third Mission Today. Image produced by authors.

interdisciplinary team that engages researchers, extensionists, and community leaders to identify the needs and the scope of the service program.

What Accountability Mechanisms Exist?

The overall structure of Figure 7.2 limits the feasibility of developing a sound accountability system based on qualitative and quantitative methods that allow beneficiaries and program managers to track progress and implement improvements and prioritize responsiveness to student claims. Such processes face further limitations because of the lack of long-term engagement of these programs with a singular community. Thus, host institutions and local communities are once again inequitably served within the structural and cultural relational aspects of the internal organization and external environment.

Visualizing the current practices of international service programs and responding to who is in control, who benefits, and the existing accountability structures helps illuminate the non-benign nature of service programs, which should prompt institutions to approach their service agendas from an ethical perspective, steering away from self-serving motivations toward fostering a more inclusive and equitable collaboration that respects the autonomy of local communities.

An International Community-Centered University Service (ICCUS) Model

As highlighted in the Cultural Readiness for Internationalization (Agnew & VanBalkom, 2009) change model outlined in Chapter 1, international service missions must recognize the need for context-specific adaptations and avoid a one-size-fits-all approach. The risk of perpetuating power imbalances and neo-colonial structures in Global North development strategies underscores the importance of genuine collaboration and the empowerment of local communities. This may mean that those in positions of power will need to adjust or modify the scope of benefits to them while thoughtfully planning for more equitable and fair practices to better serve local communities, a central idea of the third mission. Biases, assumptions, and the potential for dependency must be critically examined to ensure that development initiatives respect the diverse realities and histories of Global South countries.

Insights drawn from the U.S. Cooperative Extension System have the potential to inform international service programs. We recognize, however, that any discussion of translating local practice into global standards requires an investigation of power. To address this challenge, we have critically analyzed the structural aspects of international development that have the potential to perpetuate patterns of global inequity, which represent a significant challenge facing the global higher education landscape today. In particular, discussions around neo-colonialism emphasize the need for careful consideration of contextual differences, acknowledging cultural sensitivities, and avoiding the imposition of Western-centric models.

Despite these limitations, we value the CES model for its community-centric approach and emphasis on two-way knowledge transfer, which prioritizes local engagement, cultural sensitivity, and adaptability to diverse contexts at local, state, and national levels. Its collaborative framework, emphasizing partnerships and capacity building, offers a holistic approach to addressing complex challenges in both rural and urban settings. The CES model offers an example of how to clarify the end beneficiaries of the programs, expand the decision-making process, and set up appropriate accountability mechanisms. Building on what we learn from the CES model, Figure 7.3 visualizes our proposed International Community-Centered University Service model (ICCUS).

The ICCUS model we advance addresses the same critical questions we engage with other models under review in this chapter.

Who Benefits?

Local communities occupy the heart of ICCUS model, which implies the direct involvement of local communities in the design and implementation of the entire program. To do so, HEIs should identify the local community leadership structure and develop a communication and negotiation mechanism that allows HEIs to identify the ongoing community processes and co-create the goals of the service program. Under this model, international and local students who engage in the service activities benefit equally by strengthening their intercultural competence and global citizenship skills. To support this process, it is important to engage with NGOs that work with partnering communities. Involving NGOs and local organizations will assist HEIs in articulating their efforts to support advancement in local processes. Similarly, the local HEI partners stand to benefit by strengthening their internationalization strategies through the reciprocal participation of their faculty and staff.

Who Is in Control?

Service programs should be implemented through formal institutional agreements allowing stakeholders to coalesce around collectively agreed-upon goals and implementation measures within a set timeframe,

International Development, HE's 3rd Mission & Service **151**

International Community-Centered University Service Model (ICCUS)

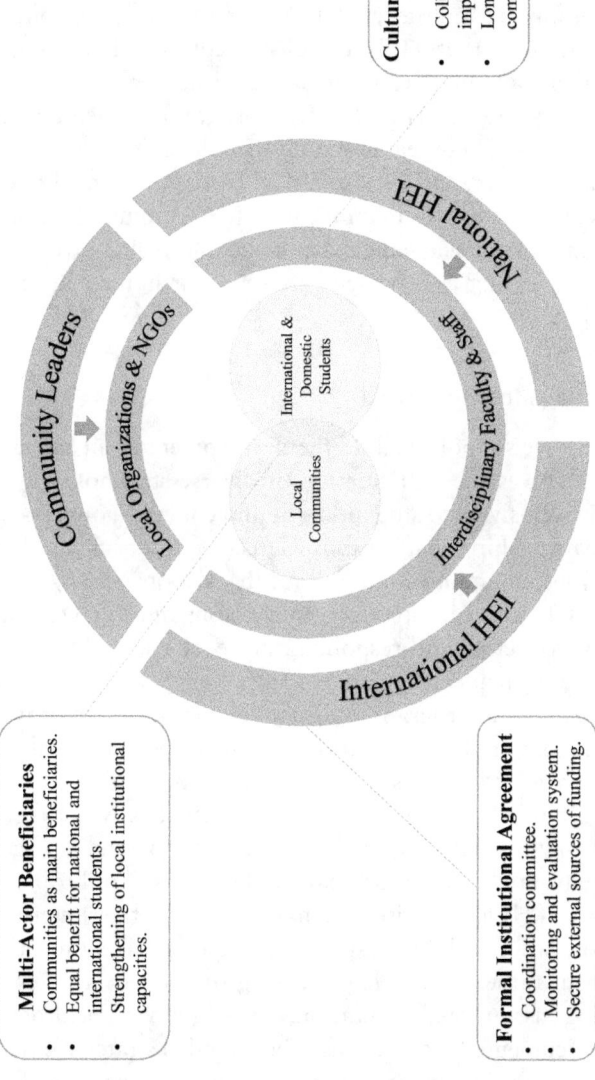

FIGURE 7.3 International Community-Centered University Service Model. Image produced by authors.

incorporating institutional monitoring systems. These institutional agreements should be promoted with local HEIs to enhance long-term engagement with the participation of community leaders' delegates and NGOs representatives. These partnerships can be based on holistic collaboration that integrates educational, research, and service components that link the expertise and strengths of both institutions with community engagement activities. The internal structure of these partnerships must support interdisciplinary collaboration, bringing together faculty from various departments to contribute to the service mission. Such an approach can help ensure that programs are multifaceted and address a range of community needs. It is paramount that HEIs establish dedicated interdisciplinary teams that focus on community engagement, ensuring that cultural competence and sensitivity are prioritized in the program's development and implementation stages. These teams should include staff with expertise in the local language, culture, and socio-political landscape to facilitate effective communication and collaboration with community partners. Particularly, scientific and academic diasporas could play a pivotal role in these programs by serving as a bridge between their home countries and international HEIs.

What Accountability Mechanisms Exist?

The ICCUS model we support enables the development of an accountability system that involves the participation of diverse stakeholders. Rather than responding exclusively to student needs and concerns, our model promotes formal partnerships that establish effective feedback mechanisms through continuous communication and feedback loops among all stakeholders, like the CES model. Internally, institutions must create transparent processes for collecting and responding to feedback from all partners involved. This could include regular meetings, surveys, and reports that track the progress of the program and highlight areas for improvement. Another element that could significantly transform power imbalances in international service activities is the diversification of funding sources. Instead of being funded by student fees, these activities would benefit if they were externally funded by a third party such as government agencies, multilateral organizations, international NGOs, or philanthropic initiatives. In this sense, if HEIs can raise external funding for their international service programs, accountability systems will be more likely to prioritize community benefit rather than solely focusing on student academic outcomes, improving institutional reputation, meeting government demands, and other well-documented motivations. The intended strategic outcome is that, by enhancing existing accountability measures, international service activities will expand beyond their connotation as a commodity within an institution's study abroad portfolio.

A variety of structural and cultural barriers in Global North HEIs complicate equitable service work. Entrenched institutional hierarchies often prioritize research output and academic prestige over community engagement (Hübner & King, 2023). This disconnect, driven by the perception of academic as an ivory tower (Chantler, 2016), hinders effective engagement with community needs. Additionally, HEIs in the Global North must grapple with legacies of colonialism and systemic inequities, which can influence their approach to service, sometimes perpetuating paternalistic attitudes. Competitive funding environments favor projects with immediate outcomes over long-term community engagement, making it difficult to sustain impactful service initiatives that direct aid from the Global North to the Global South.

To achieve the goals outlined in the ICCUS model, it is crucial for HEIs to shift from a top-down to a bottom-up approach in their international service missions. This shift requires embracing collaborative frameworks, prioritizing cultural sensitivity, and ensuring that local communities are at the center of all service activities. By doing so, HEIs can foster genuine partnerships, mitigate power imbalances, and promote sustainable development that is truly responsive to local needs. The integration of these principles into the fabric of institutional operations can lead to more impactful and ethical international service initiatives, ultimately enhancing the global higher education landscape.

Applying a Community-Centered Model of International Service through the Lens of CRI Model

The CRI model is particularly relevant to the framework we propose, enhancing local community engagement through a collaborative and decentralized approach. Our proposed model centers on the interplay between international HEIs, local communities, and national governments, facilitated through official peer-to-peer institutional agreements and interdisciplinary service teams. In doing so, our ICCUS model aligns closely with the principles of the CRI framework, offering practical applications for overcoming resistance and building capacity for change in the context of international service (see Table 7.1 for a comparison of the three models addressed in this chapter).

The CRI framework's emphasis on understanding and addressing sources of resistance is reflected in our model through the involvement of local communities in setting program goals. By engaging local community organizations and NGOs, we ensure that initiatives are culturally

TABLE 7.1 Comparative Table of the Cooperative Extension System, Current Practice, and ICCUS Models.

	CES Model	Current International Service Model	International Community-Centered University Service Model (ICCUS)
Who Benefits?	• Agricultural Communities (Farmers and producers) • Rural communities. • Youth.	• Students who enroll in international service programs. • Universities through academic fees. • Communities as local hosts.	• Local communities. • NGOs that work for community development. • Local HEIs that strengthen their internationalization strategies. • International and local students.
Who is in control?	• LGIs. • Extension professionals. • Local communities. • State and Federal Agencies. • Industry partners. • Funding Organizations.	• Universities in the Global North that design and implement international service programs. • Institutions in the Global South as academic hosts and cultural brokers.	• Community leaders. • Partnering HEIs. • Local NGOs. • Funding agencies and organizations.
What accountability mechanisms exist?	• Participatory needs assessment. • Advisory Boards and committees. • Regular monitoring and impact assessment. • Reporting mechanisms.	• Accountability mechanisms based on student academic outcomes. • Absence of interdisciplinary long-term engagement.	• Partnering HEIs coordination committee. • Participatory monitoring and impact assessment structure. • Reporting to external funders.

appropriate and responsive to local needs. This approach fosters mutual accountability and strengthens local processes, as advocated by the CRI model. Decentralized decision-making is key, and in our model, occurs through collaborative design and the engagement of interdisciplinary service teams from international and local universities. Involving a diverse range of stakeholders promotes inclusivity and mitigates the top-down decision-making that often leads to resistance.

Enhancing local accountability and community engagement, as highlighted by the CRI model, is further supported in the ICCUS model through regular consultations, participatory decision-making processes, and transparent evaluation. These practices build trust and ensure that services are responsive to local needs. The CRI model's emphasis on qualitative impacts over quantitative metrics is also integrated into our proposed model. By valuing alternative development pathways and promoting mutual learning, our model captures the social, cultural, and relational outcomes of service initiatives, moving away from purely numerical measures.

Fostering cultural competence and collaborative leadership, as suggested by the CRI model, is vital for building capacity for change. The ICCUS model supports capacity-building initiatives that equip stakeholders with the skills and knowledge needed to support equitable practices. By creating spaces for intercultural dialogue and embracing collaborative leadership, we promote a more inclusive and participatory institutional culture. In sum, the CRI model informs and enriches our proposed community-centered service model by providing a comprehensive framework for overcoming resistance and building capacity for change. This alignment enhances international service initiatives, fostering a more inclusive, equitable, and impactful approach to the higher education service mission.

Conclusion

Critical scholarship in the realm of international higher education provides a profound lens through which we can understand the complex dynamics of global engagement. The collective insights coalesce around fundamental questions that reveal who truly benefits from these initiatives, often exposing potential unequal power relations and cultural imperialism. At the same time, critical scholars scrutinize issues of control, highlighting the dominant influence of economically privileged institutions and nations, which makes fostering genuine collaboration challenging. Equally significant is the emphasis on accountability mechanisms, advocating for transparent participatory processes that involve local communities and stakeholders in decision-making and learning.

By intertwining these critical discussions, a transformative discourse emerges—one that shifts away from tokenism and the market-driven success metrics that define White saviorism and capitalism. Instead, the focus turns toward ethical, inclusive collaborations that prioritize community needs, cultural sensitivity, and a commitment to dismantling power imbalances. In this way, critical scholarship guides international higher education practitioners toward a more just, equitable, and ethical global engagement paradigm.

Exploring the confluence of international development, higher education's third mission, and critical scholarship on the internationalization of service reveals crucial insights, particularly in addressing overarching questions of who benefits, who is in control, what accountability mechanisms exist, and implications for practice. Though it is situated within a unique U.S. national content, lessons can be drawn from the Cooperative Extension System, particularly its focus on the importance of ethical and community-centered service.

Our proposed ICCUS model builds on the CES framework by emphasizing the need to approach international service initiatives with careful consideration for the local communities involved. The ICCUS model advocates for genuine, equitable partnerships where local voices are central to decision-making processes, thus ensuring that service initiatives are not only effective but also ethically grounded and responsive to community needs.

Critical investigation of international service initiatives prompts a fundamental reevaluation of the goals and motivations that drive much of the global postsecondary service mission today. By challenging assumptions of neutrality and benign intent, critical scholars urge a nuanced understanding of the power dynamics inherent in global interactions. The central questions—who benefits, who is in control, and what accountability mechanisms exist—offer profound implications for improving collective practice.

The intersection of these elements highlights a shared imperative: international service is crucial, but its execution demands ethical considerations. Ethical in this context means ensuring that individuals and communities are served more equally and fairly, emphasizing partnerships where decision-making is inclusive and considers the impacts on all stakeholders rather than self-serving interests. Ethical international service involves creating frameworks where local communities have an equal voice in decision-making processes, ensuring that the benefits of such initiatives are equally distributed, and prioritizing long-term, sustainable outcomes over short-term gains. This collective understanding points toward a transformative discourse that guides institutions in international higher education toward a more just, inclusive, and ethically grounded global engagement paradigm.

In summary, our approach to international service through the ICCUS model ensures a dynamic exchange of knowledge and practices that benefit both universities and the communities they serve on a global scale. This alignment not only enhances the effectiveness of international service initiatives, but also fosters a more inclusive, equitable, and impactful approach to the higher education service mission.

Implications for Ethical Policies and Practices

1 *Power Imbalances*: Acknowledge and address the inherent power imbalances between the Global North and the Global South. Strive to mitigate these effects by promoting equitable collaborations and partnerships based on formal agreements with local HEIs.
2 *Inclusivity and Local Agency*: Ensure the inclusion of local perspectives and respect the agency of communities involved in internationalization projects. Avoid top-down approaches and foster collaborative decision-making with local stakeholders to address their priorities and needs.
3 *Accountability and Transparency*: Maintain robust accountability mechanisms to ensure ethical and transparent conduct of projects. Communicate goals, methodologies, and outcomes clearly to all stakeholders, including local communities and funding organizations.
4 *Cultural Sensitivity*: Be culturally sensitive and aware of diverse contexts in which operations occur. Understand and respect local customs, traditions, and values, and incorporate these considerations into research design and implementation. Scientific and academic diaspora could play a pivotal role in these programs serving as a bridge with their home countries.
5 *Equitable Benefit Sharing*: Ensure that benefits are equitably distributed among all stakeholders, particularly marginalized groups. Develop international strategies to address disparities and prioritize the needs of underserved populations.
6 *Avoiding Neo-Colonial Practices*: Critically examine and alter practices that may impose external modes of development without considering local contexts and capacities. Avoid perpetuating neo-colonial dynamics through internationalization efforts.
7 *Collaborative Engagement*: Build relationships based on trust, mutual respect, and shared goals with local partners. Ensure that local partners are actively involved in all stages of project development and implementation.
8 *Continuous Improvement*: Establish mechanisms for continuous evaluation and improvement. Regularly assess the impact of internationalization initiatives, solicit feedback from all stakeholders, and make necessary adjustments to enhance effectiveness and relevance. Continuous improvement depends on long-term institutional engagement with a particular community to avoid establishing isolated, one-off programs.

References

Adamuti-Trache, M., & Schuetze, H. (2008). Editorial: University continuing education: Third mission or first? *Journal of Adult and Continuing Education, 14*(2), 105–111. https://doi.org/10.7227/JACE.14.2.1

Agnew, M., & VanBalkom, W. D. (2009). Cultural readiness for internationalization (CRI): A model for planned change. In S. Majhanovich, & M. Geo-Jaj (Eds.), *Education, language, and economics: Growing national and global dilemmas* (pp. 141–154). Sense Pub.

Alfonsi, A., Blok, V., Braun, R., Colonnello, C., Popa, E., Gerhardus, A., de Ruyter, C., Starkbaum, J., Walizer, M., & Wesselink, R. (2021). *Quadruple helix collaborations in practice: Stakeholder interaction, responsibility and governance* (788047). Riconfigure. https://riconfigure.eu/wp-content/uploads/2021/06/D6.4-Quadruple-Helix-Collaborations-in-Practice-1.pdf

Association for Public Land-Grant Universities. (n.d.). *Cooperative extension section (CES)*. APLU. Retrieved March 9, 2024, from https://www.aplu.org/food-environment-and-renewable-resources/board-on-agriculture-assembly/cooperative-extension-section/

Bamberger, A., Morris, P., & Yemini, M. (2019). Neoliberalism, internationalisation and higher education: Connections, contradictions and alternatives. *Discourse: Studies in the Cultural Politics of Education, 40*(2), 203–216. https://doi.org/10.1080/01596306.2019.1569879

Berry, H. A., & Chisholm, L. A. (1999). *Service-learning in higher education around the world: An initial look*. International Partnership for Service-Learning. https://files.eric.ed.gov/fulltext/ED439654.pdf

Bickell, E. G. (2024). *The agricultural cooperative extension system: An overview* (R48071). Congressional Research Service.

Blanco Ramírez, G. (2014). Trading quality across borders: Colonial discourse and international quality assurance policies in higher education. *Tertiary Education and Management, 20*(2), 121–134. https://doi.org/10.1080/13583883.2014.896025

Bogdan, M., Ferencz, I., Mitić, M., Rodríguez Somlyay, E. M., & Brandenburg, U. (2021). *The internationalisation in higher education for society. Mapping report.* Palacky University Olomouc. https://ihes.upol.cz/results/ihes-mapping-report/

Borron, A., Lamm, K., Darbisi, C., & Randall, N. (2019). Social impact assessment in the cooperative extension system: Revitalizing the community capitals framework in measurement and approach. *Journal of International Agricultural and Extension Education, 26*(2), 75–88. https://doi.org/10.5191/jiaee.2019.26206

Boschini, A., & Olofsgård, A. (2007). Foreign aid: An instrument for fighting communism? *The Journal of Development Studies, 43*(4), 622–648. https://doi.org/10.1080/00220380701259707

Brandenburg, U., de Wit, H., Jones, E., Leask, B., & Drobner, A. (2020). *Internationalisation in higher education for society (IHES). Concept, current research and examples of good practice* [(DAAD Studies)]. DAAD. chrome-extension://efaidnbmnnnibpcajpcglclefindmkaj/https://static.daad.de/media/daad.de/pdfs_nicht_barrierefrei/der-daad/analysen-studien/daad_s15_studien_ihes_web.pdf

Bringle, R., Hatcher, J., & Jones, S. (Eds.). (2012). *International service learning: Conceptual frameworks and research* (Vol. 1). Stylus Publishing, LLC.

Burden, B. C., Canon, D. T., Mayer, K. R., & Moynihan, D. P. (2012). The effect of administrative burden on bureaucratic perception of policies: Evidence from election administration. *Public Administration Review, 72*(5), 741–751. https://doi.org/10.1111/j.1540-6210.2012.02600.x

Caballero, P., & Londoño, P. (2022). *Redefining developpment: The extraordinary genesis of the sustainable development goals*. Lynne Rienner Publishers, Inc.

Chantler, A. (2016). The ivory tower revisited. *Discourse: Studies in the Cultural Politics of Education, 37*(2), 215–229. https://doi.org/10.1080/01596306.2014.963517

Chapman, R., Blench, R., Kranjac-Berisavljevic', G., & Zakariah, A. B. T. (2003). Rural radio in agricultural extension: The example of vernacular radio programmes on soil and water conservation in n. Ghana. *The agricultural research and extension network, network paper no. 127.* https://odi.org/en/publications/rural-radio-in-agricultural-extension-the-example-of-vernacular-radio-programmes-on-soil-and-water-conservation-in-n-ghana/

Christy, R. D., & Williamson, L. (Eds.). (1992). *A century of service: Land-grant colleges and universities, 1890–1990*. Transaction Publishers.

Cleaver, F. (2012). *Development through bricolage: Rethinking institutions for natural resource management*. Routledge.

Davis, K., Swanson, B., Amudavi, D., Mekonnen, D. A., Flohrs, A., Riese, J., Lamb, C., & Zerfu, E. (2010). In-depth assessment of the public agricultural extension system of Ethiopia and recommendations for improvement. *International Food Policy Research Institute, IFPRI Discussion Paper* (01041). https://www.ifpri.org/publication/depth-assessment-public-agricultural-extension-system-ethiopia-and-recommendations

De Wit, H., & Altbach, P. G. (2021). Internationalization in higher education: Global trends and recommendations for its future. *Policy Reviews in Higher Education, 5*(1), 28–46. https://doi.org/10.1080/23322969.2020.1820898

De Wit, H., Hunter, F., Howard, L., & Egron-Polak, E. (2015). *Internationalisation of higher education*. Publications Office. https://data.europa.eu/doi/10.2861/444393

Deardorff, D. K., & Van Gaalen, A. (2022). Assessing internationalization outcomes. In *The handbook of international higher education* (2nd ed., pp. 147–164). Association of International Education Administration.

DiMaggio, P. J., & Powell, W. W. (1983). The iron cage revisited: Institutional isomorphism and collective rationality in organizational fields. *American Sociological Review, 48*(2), 147–160.

Duara, P. (2019). Nationalism and development. In D. Nayyar (Ed.), *Asian transformations: An inquiry into the development of nations* (1st ed., pp. 346–372). Oxford University Press. https://doi.org/10.1093/oso/9780198844938.003.0014

Duttweiler, M. W. (2008). The value of evaluation in cooperative extension. *New Directions for Evaluation, 2008*(120), 87–100. https://doi.org/10.1002/ev.278

E3M. (2010). *Needs and constraints analysis of the three dimensions of third mission activities*. E3M. https://www.researchgate.net/publication/338194431_Benchmarking_Higher_Education_System_Performance

Eddy, E. D. (1957). *Colleges for our land and time: The land-grant idea in American education*. Harper & Brothers.

Eriksen, T. H. (2001). Between universalism and relativism: A critique of the UNESCO concept of culture. In J. K. Cowan, M.-B. Dembour, & R. A. Wilson (Eds.), *Culture and rights: Anthropological perspectives* (pp. 127–148). Cambridge University Press. https://doi.org/10.1017/CBO9780511804687.008

Escobar, A. (1995). *Encountering development: The making and unmaking of the third world*. Princeton University Press.

Ferroni, M., & Zhou, Y. (2012). Achievements and challenges in agricultural extension in India. *Global Journal of Emerging Market Economies, 4*(3), 319–346. https://doi.org/10.1177/0974910112460435

Finkielkraut, A. (1987). *La défaite de la pensée*. Gallimard. https://www.librairie-gallimard.com/livre/9782070709458-la-defaite-de-la-pensee-alain-finkielkraut/

Fleischer, G., Waibel, H., & Walter-Echols, G. (2002). Transforming top-down agricultural extension to a participatory system: A study of costs and prospective benefits in Egypt. *Public Administration and Development*, 22(4), 309–322. https://doi.org/10.1002/pad.233

Fraunhofer-Gesellschaft. (2022). *Fraunhofer-Gesellschaft 2022 annual report. Political sovereignty through economic competitiveness.* Fraunhofer-Gesellschaft. https://www.fraunhofer.de/content/dam/zv/en/publications/annual-report/2022/Fraunhofer-Annual-Report-2022.pdf

Geiger, R. L. (2015). Land-Grant colleges and the pre-modern era of American higher education, 1850–1890. In A. I. Marcus (Ed.), *Science as service: Establishing and reformulating american land-grant universities, 1865–1930*. University of Alabama Press.

George Mwangi, C. A., Jung-Hau, C., & Pempho, C. (2021). Exploring the geopolitics in U.S. campus internationalization plans. In J. J. Lee (Ed.), *U.S. power in international higher education*. Rutgers University Press.

Goetz, S. J., & Davlasheridze, M. (2017). State-level cooperative extension spending and farmer exits. *Applied Economic Perspectives and Policy*, 39(1), 65–86. https://doi.org/10.1093/aepp/ppw007

Gómez, L., Pujols, A., Alvarado, Y., & Vargas, L. (2018). Social responsibility in higher educational institutions: An exploratory study. In D. Crowther, S. Seifi, & A. Moyeen (Eds.), *The goals of sustainable development* (pp. 215–230). Springer Singapore. https://doi.org/10.1007/978-981-10-5047-3_13

Haj Taieb, S. (2024). Measuring the third mission of European Universities: A systematic literature review. *Society and Economy*. https://doi.org/10.1556/204.2023.00030

Haslam, P. A., Schaffer, J., & Beaudet, P. (2017). *Introduction to international development: Approaches, actors, issues, and practice* (3rd ed.). Oxford University Press Canada.

Hazelkorn, E. (2016). Contemporary debates part 2: Initiatives, and governance and organisational structures. In J. Goddard, E. Hazelkorn, L. Kempton, & P. Vallance (Eds.), *The civic university: The policy and leadership challenges*. Edward Elgar Publishing.

Hellin, J. (2012). Agricultural extension, collective action and innovation systems: Lessons on network brokering from Peru and Mexico. *The Journal of Agricultural Education and Extension*, 18(2), 141–159. https://doi.org/10.1080/1389224X.2012.655967

Herd, P., & Moynihan, D. P. (2019). *Administrative burden: Policymaking by other means* (1st ed.). Russell Sage Foundation.

Hübner, K., & King, C. (2023). Global knowledge flows, institutional hierarchies, and the roles of nation states. In N. Inamdar, & P. Kirloskar (Eds.), *Reimagining border in cross-border education*. Routledge.

Izadi, B., Hosseini, S. M., Asadi, A., & Alambaigi, A. (2020). The third mission of university beyond technology transfer: A critique of economic approaches in agricultural college's engagement with society in Iran. *Journal of Entrepreneurship in Agriculture*, 6(4). https://doi.org/10.22069/jead.2021.18678.1442

Jaeger, A., & Kopper, J. (2014). Third mission potential in higher education: Measuring the regional focus of different types of HEIs. *Review of Regional Research*, 34(2), 95–118. https://doi.org/10.1007/s10037-014-0091-3

Jones, E., Leask, B., Brandenburg, U., & de Wit, H. (2021). Global social responsibility and the internationalisation of higher education for society. *Journal of Studies in International Education*, 25(4), 330–347. https://doi.org/10.1177/10283153211031679

Kellogg Commission. (1999). *Returning to our roots the engaged institution* (3; Kellogg commission on the future of state and land-grant universities). https://www.aplu.org/wp-content/uploads/returning-to-our-roots-the-engaged-institution.pdf

Knowles, M. S., Holton, E. F., & Swanson, R. A. (2015). *The adult learner: The definitive classic in adult education and human resource development* (8th ed.). Routledge.

Krčmářová, J. (2011). The third mission of higher education institutions: Conceptual framework and application in the Czech Republic. *European Journal of Higher Education*, *1*(4), 315–331. https://doi.org/10.1080/21568235.2012.662835

Larrán Jorge, M., & Andrades Peña, F. J. (2017). Analysing the literature on university social responsibility: A review of selected higher education journals. *Higher Education Quarterly*, *71*(4), 302–319. https://doi.org/10.1111/hequ.12122

Lee, J. J. (2021). *U.S. power in international higher education*. Rutgers University Press.

Lee, R., Ahtone, T., Pearce, M., Goodluck, K., McGhee, G., Leff, C., Lanpher, K., & Salinas, T. (n.d.). *Land-grab universities: A high country news investigation*. https://Www.Landgrabu.Org Retrieved March 9, 2024, from https://www.landgrabu.org/

Lioutas, E. D., Charatsari, C., Černič Istenič, M., La Rocca, G., & De Rosa, M. (2019). The challenges of setting up the evaluation of extension systems by using a systems approach: The case of Greece, Italy and Slovenia. *The Journal of Agricultural Education and Extension*, *25*(2), 139–160. https://doi.org/10.1080/1389224X.2019.1583818

Mora, J.-G., Serra, M. A., & Vieira, M.-J. (2018). Social engagement in Latin American universities. *Higher Education Policy*, *31*(4), 513–534. https://doi.org/10.1057/s41307-017-0069-1

Nabaho, L., Turyasingura, W., Twinomuhwezi, I., & Nabukenya, M. (2022). The third mission of universities on the African continent: Conceptualisation and operationalisation. *Higher Learning Research Communications*, *12*(1). https://doi.org/10.18870/hlrc.v12i1.1298

Nandy, A. (2000). Recovery of indigenous knowledge and dissenting futures of the university. In S. Inayatullah, & Jennifer Gidley (Eds.), *The university in transformation: Global perspectives on the futures of the university*. Bergin & Garvey.

National Education Association. (2022). *A looming crisis for HBCUs? An analysis of funding sources for land grant universities*. National Education Association.

National Institute of Food and Agriculture. (n.d.). *Cooperative extension history | NIFA*. Cooperative Extension History | NIFA. Retrieved March 9, 2024, from https://www.nifa.usda.gov/about-nifa/how-we-work/extension/cooperative-extension-history

Nevins, A. (1962). *The state universities and democracy*. Iowa State University Press.

OECD. (2019). *Benchmarking higher education system performance*. OECD. https://doi.org/10.1787/be5514d7-en

OECD. (n.d.). *The 0.7% ODA/GNI target—A history—OECD*. Retrieved February 12, 2024, from https://www.oecd.org/dac/financing-sustainable-development/development-finance-standards/the07odagnitarget-ahistory.htm

Ohio Cooperative Extension Service. (1986). *4-H future focus: 1986–1996: Future directions for the 4-H education program of the cooperative extension system*. Ohio State University.

Pardello, R., & Michaels, C. (2020). The United States cooperative extension system: Contributing to a partnership system. *Interdisciplinary Journal of Partnership Studies*, 7(2), 1. https://doi.org/10.24926/ijps.v7i2.3507

Pashby, K., Da Costa, M., Stein, S., & Andreotti, V. (2020). A meta-review of typologies of global citizenship education. *Comparative Education*, 56(2), 144–164. https://doi.org/10.1080/03050068.2020.1723352

Pashby, K., & De Oliveira Andreotti, V. (2016). Ethical internationalisation in higher education: Interfaces with international development and sustainability. *Environmental Education Research*, 22(6), 771–787. https://doi.org/10.1080/13504622.2016.1201789

Pinheiro, R., Langa, P. V., & Pausits, A. (2015). One and two equals three? The third mission of higher education institutions. *European Journal of Higher Education*, 5(3), 233–249. https://doi.org/10.1080/21568235.2015.1044552

Preece, J. (2011). Higher education and community service: Developing the National University of Lesotho's third mission. *Journal of Adult and Continuing Education*, 17(1), 81–97. https://doi.org/10.7227/JACE.17.1.7

Raditloaneng, N. (2013). Impact of implementing the third mission of Universities in Africa (ITMUA) collaborative research project, 2010–2011. *International Journal of Peace and Development Studies*, 4(5), 90–99. https://doi.org/10.5897/IJPDS12.017

Rasmussen, W. D. (1989). *Taking the university to the people: Seventy-five years of cooperative extension* (1st ed.). Iowa State University Press.

Robertson, G. P., Allen, V. G., Boody, G., Boose, E. R., Creamer, N. G., Drinkwater, L. E., Gosz, J. R., Lynch, L., Havlin, J. L., Jackson, L. E., Pickett, S. T. A., Pitelka, L., Randall, A., Reed, A. S., Seastedt, T. R., Waide, R. B., & Wall, D. H. (2008). Long-term agricultural research: A research, education, and extension imperative. *BioScience*, 58(7), 640–645. https://doi.org/10.1641/B580711

Ross, E. D. (1942). *Democracy's college: The land-grant movement in the formative stage*. Iowa State College Press.

Sant, E., Davies, I., Pashby, K., & Shultz, L. (2018). *Global citizenship education: A critical introduction to key concepts and debates*. Bloomsbury Academic, an imprint of Bloomsbury Publishing Plc.

Sataøen, H. L. (2018). Transforming the "third mission" in Norwegian higher education institutions: A boundary object theory approach. *Scandinavian Journal of Educational Research*, 62(1), 52–67. https://doi.org/10.1080/00313831.2016.1212253

Schaffer, J., Haslam, P. A., & Beaudet, P. (2017). Meaning, measurement, and morality in international development. In P. A. Haslam, J. Schafer, & P. Beaudet (Eds.), *Introduction to international development: Approaches, actors, issues, and practice* (3rd ed.). Oxford University Press Canada.

Schnurbus, V., & Edvardsson, I. R. (2022). The third mission among Nordic universities: A systematic literature review. *Scandinavian Journal of Educational Research*, 66(2), 238–260. https://doi.org/10.1080/00313831.2020.1816577

Sengupta, E., Blessinger, P., & Mahoney, C. (2020). Introduction to Civil Society and Social Responsibility in Higher Education: International Perspectives on University–Community Partnerships. In E. Sengupta, P. Blessinger, & C. Mahoney (Eds.), *Innovations in Higher Education Teaching and Learning* (pp. 3–14). Emerald Publishing Limited. https://doi.org/10.1108/S2055-36412020 0000023001

Silva, D. F. da. (2015). Globality. *Critical Ethnic Studies*, 1(1), 33–38. https://doi.org/10.5749/jcritethnstud.1.1.0033

Smith, D. N. (2013). Academics, the 'cultural third mission' and the BBC: Forgotten histories of knowledge creation, transformation and impact. *Studies in Higher Education, 38*(5), 663–677. https://doi.org/10.1080/03075079.2011.594502

Springett, D., & Redclift, M. (2015). Sustainable development history and evolution of the concept. In *Routledge international handbook of sustainable development* (1st ed.). Routledge. https://doi.org/10.4324/9780203785300

SQW. (2023). *Final report. Knowledge transfer partnerships evaluation.*

Stein, S. (2015). Mapping global citizenship. *Journal of College and Character, 16*(4), 242–252. https://doi.org/10.1080/2194587X.2015.1091361

Stein, S., Ahenakew, C., Jimmy, E., & Andreotti, V. (2021). *Developing stamina for decolonizing higher education: A workbook for non-indigenous people.*

Stein, S., Andreotti, V., Bruce, J., & Suša, R. (2016). Towards different conversations about the internationalization of higher education. *Comparative and International Education, 45*(1). https://doi.org/10.5206/cie-eci.v45i1.9281

Symaco, L. P., & Tee, M. Y. (2019). Social responsibility and engagement in higher education: Case of the ASEAN. *International Journal of Educational Development, 66*, 184–192. https://doi.org/10.1016/j.ijedudev.2018.10.001

Taffet, J. F. (2007). *Foreign aid as foreign policy: The Alliance for Progress in Latin America.* Routledge.

Tannock, S. (2007). To keep America number 1: Confronting the deep nationalism of US higher education. *Globalisation, Societies and Education, 5*(2), 257–272. https://doi.org/10.1080/14767720701427186

Thorn, K., & Soo, M. (2006). *Latin American universities and the third mission: Trends, challenges, and policy options.* The World Bank. https://doi.org/10.1596/1813-9450-4002

Tonelli, D. F., & Gibson, D. (2023). Financial decentralization and third-Mission outputs: A comparative study of Higher Education contexts in Brazil and the United States. *Industry and Higher Education*, 09504222231208438. https://doi.org/10.1177/09504222231208438

Truman, H. S. (1949). *Harry S. Truman inaugural address.* Collection at Bartleby. Com. https://www.bartleby.com/lit-hub/inaugural-addresses-of-the-presidents-of-the-united-states/harry-s.-truman-inaugural-address/

U.S. Department of Agriculture. (n.d.). *A condensed history of American agriculture 1776–1999.* Retrieved March 9, 2024, from https://www.usda.gov/sites/default/files/documents/history-american-agriculture.pdf

UNESCO. (2017). *Education for sustainable development goals.* UNESCO.

UNESCO. (2019). *Global convention on the recognition of qualifications concerning higher education.* UNESCO.

UNESCO. (n.d.). *UNESCO chair in community based research and social responsibility in higher education.* Retrieved March 9, 2024, from https://www.unescochair-cbrsr.org/

United Nations. (2023). *The sustainable development goals report 2023. Special edition. Towards a rescue plan for people and planet.* United Nations. https://unstats.un.org/sdgs/report/2023/

Wang, S. L. (2014). Cooperative extension system: Trends and economic impacts on U.S. agriculture. *Choices, 29*(1), 1–8.

Warner, P. D., & Christenson, J. A. (1984). *The cooperative extension service: A national assessment.* Westview Press.

Williams, K. L., & Davis, B. L. (2019). *Public and private investments and divestments in historically black colleges and universities.* American Council on Education, Minority-serving institutions series.

Woldegiyorgis, A. A., Proctor, D., & de Wit, H. (2022). Internationalization of research. In *The handbook of international higher education* (2nd ed., pp. 343–359). Routledge.

Workman, J., & Scheer, S. (2012). Evidence of impact: Examination of evaluation studies published in the journal of extension. *Journal of Extension*, 50(2). https://doi.org/10.34068/joe.50.02.57

Yitayew, A., Abdulai, A., Yigezu, Y. A., Deneke, T. T., & Kassie, G. T. (2021). Impact of agricultural extension services on the adoption of improved wheat variety in Ethiopia: A cluster randomized controlled trial. *World Development*, 146, 105605. https://doi.org/10.1016/j.worlddev.2021.105605

Zahavi, H., & Friedman, Y. (2019). The Bologna Process: An international higher education regime. *European Journal of Higher Education*, 9(1), 23–39. https://doi.org/10.1080/21568235.2018.1561314

Zawdie, G. (2010). *Special Issue*: Knowledge exchange and the third mission of universities: Introduction: The triple helix and the third mission – Schumpeter revisited. *Industry and Higher Education*, 24(3), 151–155. https://doi.org/10.5367/000000010791657437

Zuti, B., & Lukovics, M. (2014). *How to Measure the Local Economic Impact of the Universities' Third Mission Activities?* https://www.ssoar.info/ssoar/handle/document/54499

8
COLLABORATIVE PARTNERSHIPS

Epistemic Fluency, Transcultural Competence and the Sustainability of Identity

Anne Carr,
(co-ordinating author) Gabriela B. Bonilla Chumbi, Matias Abad, Patricia Tineo, Pilar Constanzo, Antonina Bulyna, Jorge R. Lemos Shlotter, Athena Alchazidu, Katerina Chudova, William A. Booth, Olena Yasynetska, Oleh Shlapakov, Bahar Aksu, and Oguzhan Yilmaz, The authors wish to acknowledge the support of: Olena Krut, Liudmyla Sukhovetska, and Myroslava Lendel

Introduction

Students in Higher Education, as a subset of the millions of people on the move around the world, are arguably experiencing an increased fragmentation of identity. They no longer perceive themselves as having a single, fixed identity but instead recognize multiple, overlapping, and sometimes contradictory identities constructed through discourse, power relations, and cultural contexts.

For various reasons, whether generational, demographic, social, or climate-related, students have been displaced or forced to move internally or across continents and cultures for their studies. In our era of ambivalence and uncertainty, features of solid institutions like family, community, and the state have become fluid. We have been inspired by Miranda Fricker's (2007) notion of epistemic injustice and Zygmunt Bauman's (2000) neologism 'glocal' to indicate the involvement of values that belong to the local in a transnational perspective, impacting daily life concretely.

In 2021, the University of Azuay's International Studies Program initiated a research investigation based on previous transdisciplinary projects. This involved inviting four professors and their students from universities in the Global South and North to participate in a series of virtual meetings. These meetings aimed to explore and present the multiple threads that connect the local expression and negotiation of student identity to broader social contexts and ontologies.

The joint virtual sessions provided a unique platform for exchanging ideas, methodologies, and knowledge between teachers and students, transcending the limitations of traditional academic discourse and serving as a dynamic space for intellectual exchange. These sessions contributed to a nuanced understanding of the multifaceted challenges and opportunities faced by students (and teachers) in different cultural contexts, navigating the complex dynamics of identity formation within global and local spheres. Despite facing the fluidity of modernity and identity, there are aspirations for sustainability. The sustainability of identity is scarcely possible without cultivating humanity.

Our Process

The values of intentional inclusion, reciprocity, and students as partners help us with relational accountability and show what and why we are doing from Global South to Global North and Global East to Global West. The University of Toronto Scarborough provides a Partnership and Engagement Framework[1] (Tull & Blackman, 2023) that acts as a guide of bridging relationships among its partners. The framework exemplifies fluidity and interconnectedness in that it operates continuously and simultaneously as the partnership progresses. The framework is designed with eight stages that are dynamic and process- and relationship-oriented. Thus, it is possible for any one or more individuals to be working in multiple stages and steps simultaneously, as was the case in our partnership project.

The Partnership and Engagement Framework Stages include:

1. Values: Where it asks partners to share guiding beliefs and principles that inform the partnership's decisions and activities.
2. Understanding: Understanding is about establishing the purpose of coming together and what the relationship is hoping to accomplish based on each other's priorities.
3. Self-Determination: Self-determination revolves around partners choosing and setting their own goals, making decisions, self-advocating, and then working together to reach those goals.
4. Shared Interests: Shared interests are partnerships that embed mutual benefit, contribution of expertise, and dedication of time and energy.
5. Coordination: Coordination focuses on organizational independence. It's where self-interests and resources are defined.

6 Collaboration: Collaboration is when partners work together on a specific project to reach a common goal and innovative ideas are presented to meet a common priority.
7 Collective Interests: Collective Action is a multisector coalition toward a common goal with an aim of holistically improving conditions for a group of people, neighborhood, or region.
8 Revisit, Rethink, and Evolve: Revisit, rethink, and evolve, decisions and actions are subject to regular oversight and evaluation of the agreed to values, while principles and objectives are met and benefit the external committee as intended (Tull & Blackman, 2023).

This framework is used here to describe our project's process as it organically unfolded, reflecting the dynamic nature of relationships and processes with the complex network of partners.

Nests of Possibility

Following is a discussion of an interdisciplinary, transcultural collaboration project involving students and faculty from multiple universities across different countries, focusing on issues of global migration, identity, and epistemic justice.

Institutional

As indicated by Agnew & Carvan in Chapter 11, the macro mission of higher education is in a constant struggle to redefine itself and maintain autonomy amidst shifting ideologies and policies.

Historically, one mission has been focused on local engagement with little service-oriented work for the global context. However, global issues know no boundaries and require global policies. In the Czech language, *průkopník* means pioneer. Being educational pioneers in service-oriented work across continents in the Global North and Global South, and cultures from Latin America to Asia brings advantages – educational innovation and progress, learning and growth, inspiration, support, and collaboration for a shared purpose among like-minded individuals. However, as *pioneros* (Spanish), differently motivated, we may also have lacked some institutional or technological resources, as our innovations can be met with skepticism. Carrying the burden of high expectations, our innovations may be impatient with or even disrupt existing institutional cultures that are in the process of developing coordination and integration for internationalization practices.

For example, some of our institutions include the word 'international' in their mission statements; their 'ways of doing things' may be variously described as 'structured and bureaucratic', located within context-dependent cultural values. Yet location is also a signifier for statements about diverse faculty and students who may suffer from natural and military disasters within a particular continental space. Additional phrases stress innovative technology to train people at a local, national, and international level and sustainable management of resources with a view to permanent growth. These mission statements mention aligning innovation with respect for tradition and diversity; engaging with the wider world and committing to changing it for the better; being recognized for radical and critical thinking and its widespread influence; as well as seeking to promote internationalization by encouraging the learning of languages such as English and facilitating opportunities for study and work abroad.

At the time of writing this chapter in June 2024, the authors are now from eight culturally, linguistically, and contextually diverse universities. For example, in response to the adaptability of our institutional procedures – 'ways of doing things' – the additional factors of secular, religious affiliation, and private and/or public funding play significantly into themes such as: a culture that uses productivity and efficiency as the basic criteria of success to achieve a certain goal with a directive and goal-oriented leadership style; an accessible, publicly engaged organization that fosters a life-long community; and being responsive to all types of demands arising from society, government policies, and organizational-related ones in higher education. Additionally, the closeness of borders with several countries can impact how a university seeks to employ the experience of internationalization and strengthen diversity and inclusion by responding to challenges due to pandemic, natural, and military emergencies.

Drawing on the Cultural Readiness for Internationalization (CRI)[2] model, the clarity of our institutional aims and goals, coordinated among the three levels of internal stakeholder engagement—macro (senior leadership), meso (deans or department-level management), and micro (faculty), impact the implementation of stated aims and values. In consideration of stage five of the framework, for example, the meso (deans) layer of the hierarchy is very thick, various initiatives at the micro (faculty) level can chafe against one another, or university management may even overrule the academic board and wider public opinion concerning existing or new programs.

With initiatives that fit closely with stated aims, there can be productive engagement up a hierarchical chain even if decision-making can seem rather capricious. For example, our project, in the context of Sustainable Development Goal #17, emphasizes interconnectedness and shared responsibility transcending national borders to involve understanding diverse worldviews and perspectives to effectively address political, environmental, social, and economic issues that constitute Global Citizenship. Even though global issues know no boundaries and require global approaches, there appears to be little service-oriented work globally, but because of 'good governance' approaches in the pursuit of 'integrity', funding for our transdisciplinary transcultural collaboration has been fragile.

Our Process Narrative

Evidence, often illuminated in critical reflections and/or because of critically reflective interactions, illustrates the meanings and practices of how people experience themselves in their worlds – in other words, their identities (Freire, 1972). For example, in 2017, with our university students, we listened to the narratives of young children aged 9–11 years, from a small coastal community in Ecuador, recounting the everydayness of being prepared for the next earthquake. These contained distressing descriptions of their previous disaster experiences 18 months earlier in April 2016: evacuation decisions, risk of separation from parents, witnessing injury and death of family members and peers in the 7.8 earthquake that took the lives of 63 members of their community and 675 in the general area (Carr et al., 2019).

In 2021, we listened to the experiences and perceptions of students compared to their teachers' perceptions of them, regarding modes of distance learning and remote classes during the COVID-19 pandemic. Our investigation found statistically significant preferences by students for social media sites for academic learning in contrast with the perceptions of their teachers (Carr, 2023).

To take another example, by June 2022 Ecuador had hosted an estimated 500,000 Venezuelans migrating from the economic and health impacts of the COVID-19 pandemic when the government-initiated provision of legal protection, social stability, and training opportunities, for example, car mechanics, seam-stressing and hospitality skills, delivered by universities. This also offered us the opportunity to highlight and disrupt how both historical and contemporary power structures of geopolitics impact marginalized populations, such as migrants and refugees.

Before proceeding further, in summation of our feelings and thoughts and as reflexive intermediate step, we listened to Gloria Anzaldúa, a Chicana cultural theorist born in the United States who was exiled for her political views. Her 1987 poem, To Live in The Borderlands, summarizes that exile, that is to live in the Borderlands, you must live 'sin fronteras', or without borders. You must be a 'crossroad-like person' to survive.

Tull and Blackman's (2023) stage four of the partnership framework, shared interests, situates our collective desire for an educational crossroad, that is, 'Epistemic (In)justice: Whose Voices Count? Listening to Migrants and Students' (2023) was finally developed through an information ethics perspective of the 'dilemma of culturality' (Wimmer, 2007). No longer merely a comparative or dialogical project, it was now polylogical where different traditions and inter-epistemic dialogues about global migration might take place digitally. This notion aligns with the research of Miranda Fricker (2013) who argued that it is probable that well-founded theories of epistemic (in) justice) have developed in more than one cultural tradition. After a slow passage through meso (faculty) and macro (senior leadership) levels of our university, the proposal was accepted and transdisciplinary-oriented colleagues from law, history, philosophy, linguistics, psychology, and tourism from Caribbean, Czech, and British universities, and later through international connections like COIL (Argentina) and EU projects (Ukraine and Turkey) welcomed the online opportunities for their students to polylogue in English.

Although De Sousa Santos (2014) argues in *Epistemologies of the South* that no single type of knowledge/language can account for all possible interventions in the world, most of the participating faculty in the project are multilingual. However, we propose that this project, enacted in English, is a step in the process for students to join and engage with multiple subject positions in a vibrant network of our global knowledge societies. In fact, during breakout activities, students did switch to their mother tongues for clarifications that, while also helpful in terms of achieving the project goals, advocates for linguistic justice through multilingualism.

Transcultural Interdisciplinary Collaboration

The project has gathered students majoring in various areas, as well as teachers who are experts in diverse fields. Both teachers and students come from numerous backgrounds, turning universities into venues where cultures are introduced not only theoretically through academic disciplines but also practically through living people and culture bearers. According to Jose Ortega y Gasset (1999), one of the fundamental pillars of the university mission, in addition to teaching and research, is the creation and dissemination of culture as it embodies the vital system of ideas, traditions, and customs of any age. Universities, as main social institutions operating in every society, act as levers in the process of enculturation (socialization) through which culture is instilled and acquired, be it national or universal human culture. Our virtual sessions, involving eight different universities, guarantee the growth of cultural contacts (Safronova & Michshenko, 2023). Representatives of each culture, being carriers of a certain national culture and sense of identity, share the qualities of consciousness shaped by their cultural development.

Communication is a complex and multifaceted process that functions both as an interaction between individuals and as an expression of their attitudes toward each other, mutual influence, empathy, and understanding. As self-described *Öncüleri* (the Turkish word for pioneers), we recognize that innovation, knowledgeable action, and actionable knowledge, as identified as stage seven in the partnership framework, involve understanding different 'epistemic spaces' such as formal education, workplace practices, and collaborative networks (stage six, collaboration) formed intentionally or randomly, as well as through personal experiences. Learning about interdisciplinary and ultimately transdisciplinary matters as faculty or students requires adapting previous knowledge to align with current educational tasks (Ivanitskaya et al., 2002). This becomes particularly challenging in fields of study that are strongly interdisciplinary, such as transcultural studies (involving many continents) or at the boundary of human and engineering sciences.

To develop common ground through shared interests (stage four) for interdisciplinary learning, it is important to specify and comprehend different learning objectives, such as what engineering students should know about human-related considerations and what human science students should know about technology.

Epistemic fluency, the ability to navigate and integrate diverse forms of knowledge through effective synthesis to address complex problems, is context-dependent, recognizing that what works in one situation may not be applicable elsewhere.

This flexibility can help in discovering innovative solutions and forming stronger, more effective partnerships by creating intentional space for reflection and honest conversation, as described in stage eight.

For example, during our 2021–2022 virtual sessions among students from universities in the Czech Republic, Dominican Republic, United Kingdom, and Ecuador, we learned how participating students began to navigate new experiential knowledge (Carr et al., 2023). Migration, whether forced, voluntary, or due to internal displacement, affects the world we all live in: Venezuelans migrating to Ecuador, Colombians, Cubans, and Bolivians to Argentina, Haitians to the Dominican Republic, refugees and migrants crossing the perilous Channel from France to England, Ukrainians seeking safety internally or in the Czech Republic, and Afghans and Iraqis journeying to Turkey.

A student documented their experience, stating:

> By being able to talk with students from other parts of the world, I was able to understand how many times the situations that we live daily are transferred to other contexts and have similar shareholders. We do not

see them in the same way, that is, we think that what happens in our country is the worst, or that in other places they handle these issues better, but the reality is not like that.

(Dominican Republic student)

The discussion with students from the Dominican Republic regarding the situation in Haiti during 2022 was particularly eye-opening. This is because it is a situation with profound effects on both Haitian and Dominican people, yet there is very little information about it in Europe. This is an example of global epistemic injustice, where knowledge about a certain part of the world is minimized and reduced, meaning that their voices are not heard.

(United Kingdom student)

The breakout discussions helped me realize the magnitude of the problem. Unless one knows the world, one remains only in one's own little shell with one's own problems and does not care about other people and their problems. Especially here in the Czech Republic, we are used to solving our own problems and not helping others. Unfortunately, this is a consequence of communism, when people did not have much and were afraid of losing what little they had. They protected their property, their close people, and did not care about others. Exchanging our narratives about refugees and migrants with students in other countries helped me realize that there are countries that deal with much worse problems than we do in the Czech Republic, and that they encounter these problems daily.

(Czech Republic student)

The atmosphere of the group discussions allowed me to open my heart and speak my mind. The most touching part was the commonality, rather than the difference, in the views of students from different countries. I found that despite the very different social realities we were exposed to, when it came to issues of principles and the morality of immigration, there was a consistent tendency to oppose all forms of discrimination and to encourage ordinary people to speak out for disadvantaged groups.

(Ecuadorian student)

In designing our 2022–2023 virtual series, we again took creating space for the partnership to take pause and reflect on and evaluate our previous work, an important dimension of the partnership framework. Based on the previous narratives of student experiences, we focused our systematic research on migrant narratives of identity negotiation by individual interdisciplinary university teams in eight countries. The students carried out this research under the guidance of their professors, learning about ethical issues, interview skills, design of PowerPoint content and presentations, as well as strategies for opening, maintaining, and closing breakout sessions. The evidence was presented in virtual sessions to their peers who live in different cultural and social contexts, which allowed them to critically examine the same phenomena from new perspectives, becoming more culturally sensitive.

Using the metaphor of a suitcase as a place where migrants might share experiences through an object, students could contemporaneously access a complex theoretical framework from different perspectives of method, discipline, epistemology, ontology, and culture. Each object is a storyteller that reflects a unique experience. These objects transcend their material nature and embody the stories of the people who have chosen them, thus becoming a vehicle for migrant identity. The Migrant Suitcase becomes a specific biography that encompasses diverse narratives of displacement, injustice, and the desire for stability in the migrants' often involuntary and/or forced journey. Factual knowledge and logic alone will not suffice for comprehending the complex world around us (Nussbaum, 2010; Southworth, 2022). The suitcase metaphor contributes to evolving the narrative imagination, which builds empathetic understanding of many different human experiences. Our interactions are pivotal in enabling democracies to tackle current problems responsibly. Distant lives are real lives, and distance is no longer an excuse for ignorance; our Zoom sessions make them visible.

In addition to comparing quantitative data from students' completion of pre- and post-surveys of empathy and transcultural competence, our methodological roadmap followed a six-step inductive thematic analysis (Naeem et al., 2023). Aligning to the seventh stage in the partnership framework, our collective action toward a common goal culminating in the development of a conceptual model that encapsulated our findings:

1 **Transcription** of students navigating new experiential knowledge with the Migrants' 'Suitcase Stories' and selection of quotations.
2 **Selection of keywords** that encapsulate their experiences and perceptions directly derived from the data.
3 **Coding** short phrases or words using keywords to identify elements related to our research.
4 **Theme development** involves organizing codes into meaningful groups to identify patterns and relationships.

5 **Conceptualization** through interpretation of keywords, codes, and themes to identify social patterns.
6 **Writing the 'storyline'** of the data collected enabled us to collectively and collaboratively identify gaps in our developing theory (6) about:

- Creating a virtual context for transdisciplinary learning about migration.
- Practicing epistemic fluency.
- Connections to the sustainability of identity.

Future Transcultural Planning (2024–25)

Whilst the 'hard skills' of digital technology have simplified the communication process and expanded potential interactive communication opportunities, live interaction on academic sites such as Zoom, creates the possibility of manifesting the authenticity of participatory 'soft skills'. Transcultural participation requires epistemic fluency and resourcefulness involving a set of capabilities, or 'soft skills' for students to develop a critical appreciation of situations with peers, recognizing actions that are systematically desirable and culturally feasible.

The European Commission (2024) has designated the '4Cs in education: communication, collaboration, critical thinking and creativity' as essential 21st-century skills. In today's rapidly evolving transcultural educational landscape, students must be adept at combining different kinds of specialized and context-dependent knowledge and at reconfiguring their work environment to see problems and solutions anew. However, for making conceptual knowledge actionable, students becoming professionals need far more than just abstract concepts and far more than just the skills involving actions. They need epistemic resourcefulness to make concepts for and through action; to develop a critical appreciation of situations with others, recognizing what actions are systemically desirable and culturally feasible. Hence, academic endeavors within the project are intended in such a way as to raise retrospective and perspective awareness of traditionality and contemporaneity which might consequently anticipate and avert dark scenarios of our immediate future.

From our ongoing research since 2021, as facilitators we have come to experientially understand from and with students that epistemic fluency involves a set of capabilities that allow people to recognize and participate in different ways of knowing initially about migration. Our strong and ongoing value of shared interest defined in stage four as partnerships that embed mutual benefit, mutual contribution of expertise, and mutual dedication of time and energy have contributed to our research process in 2024/25 to implement a comparative and thematic analysis of a transcultural transdisciplinary collaborative module with asynchronous and synchronous components to support epistemic fluency skills of Higher Education undergraduate students across continents and cultures about several themes.

From a matrix of four broad themes – culture and language, education and society, migration and global issues – teachers and their undergraduate student teams of ten participants in each university (which may be constituted from various disciplines) will identify a research topic that has as its focus both changing local and glocal identity. The teacher leading each team will have two tasks: to initially apply an interdisciplinary as well as a communication skills questionnaire and a Hofstede country profile (Hofstede Insights, n.d.). Additionally, teachers will prepare an asynchronous component of the module with their contextual topic using a variety of media. Before the eight virtual synchronous sessions, hosted by each university, all students will access the related asynchronous component. Process data, during their presentations and breakouts, will be recorded by students using a Shared Google and later content analyzed for individual and team contextual epistemic resourcefulness. The skills questionnaires will be repeated and compared across all teams. All data, both quantitative and qualitative will be comparatively evaluated and overall content from all contexts will be thematically analyzed.

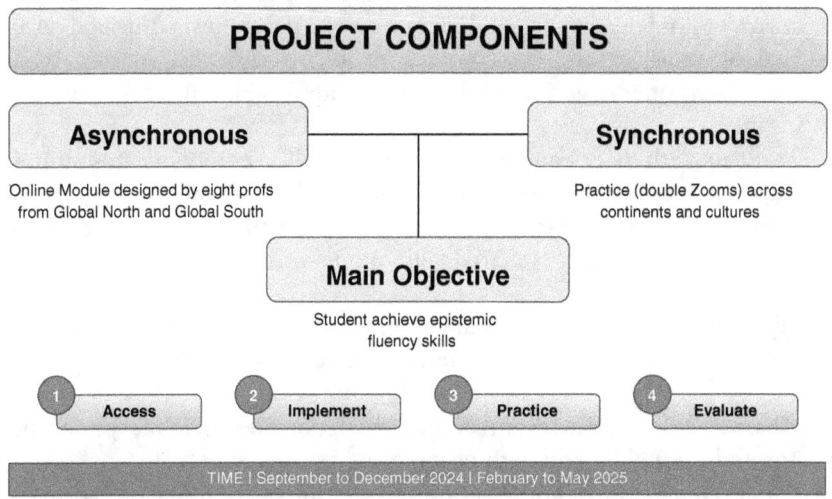

Note: Designed by the authors.

FIGURE 8.1   Project Components.

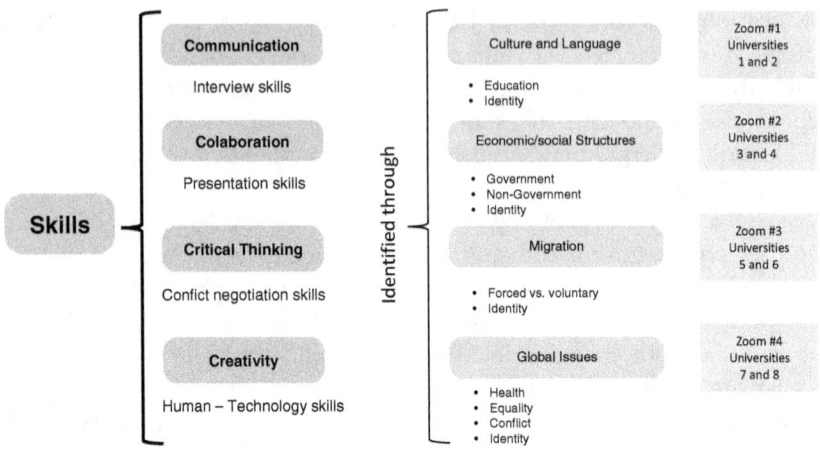

Note: Designed by the authors.

FIGURE 8.2 Skills.

We will establish whether this design helps:

1 **Students with strategies to define their disciplinary insights** and combine each other's insights to create a more comprehensive and interdisciplinary understanding of their chosen thematic research question.
2 **Students demonstrating their understanding is culturally context-dependent** and involves the ability to navigate and integrate diverse forms of knowledge – scientific, practical, or theoretical – through effective blending to address complex problems, recognizing that what works in one situation may not be applicable in other cultural contexts.
3 **Students with theory and practice using the 4Cs:** communication (interview skills), collaboration (presentation skills), critical thinking (negotiation skills), and creativity through human-virtual interaction to share knowledge and create a shared team model of identity.

Additionally, we seek to collect and analyze data concerning opportunities the synchronous virtual session can provide for students:

- **To practice epistemic resourcefulness** to make interdisciplinary concepts for and through action with peers.
- **To develop a critical appreciation of situations with others**, recognizing what actions are systemically desirable and culturally feasible related to the research theme.

In our times of Liquid Modernity (Bauman, 2000), 'liquid identities', according to Brandao (2021), reflect risks and contingencies of social and cultural processes and influence the formation of abstract or vague identities. Despite facing liquid modernity and liquid identity, there are aspirations for sustainability. Live and virtual interaction creates the possibility of manifesting the authenticity of individuals, having an elicitation effect on the participants, and preventing the danger and temptation of losing identities.

Since 2021, we have been examining the multiple threads that connect local expression and negotiation of the identity of students to wider social contexts and ontologies. The joint virtual sessions have provided a unique platform for the exchange of ideas, methodologies, and knowledge between teachers and students, transcending the limitations of traditional academic discourse and serving as a dynamic space for intellectual exchange. The sessions contribute to a nuanced understanding of the multifaceted challenges and opportunities faced by students (and teachers) in different cultural contexts, navigating the complex dynamics of identity formation within global and local spheres.

On Transdisciplinary Collaboration, Partnership, and Identity

When asked what makes a good partnership, we, from across continents, cultures, genders, languages, and ages, respond: epistemic fluency!

Relative to migration, whether forced or voluntary – culture and language, economic structures, or the myriad of current global issues – we are interested in situated-identity phenomena. This includes how students (and faculty) accomplish, construct, or establish a sense of self, and how identities develop in real-time. How do new self-representations become introduced, and how are 'old' self-representations left behind? How do new narrative stories become prominent narratives where we are not tied to our birthplace, past, or societal convention?

Bauman (2000) describes our identities, or rather the process of identification, as not static; in his words, they are 'never-ending' and always incomplete, a dynamic force shaped by the interplay of globalizing and individualizing pressures on our capabilities. He stresses the ability to be constantly ready and willing to change and adapt to transforming environments rapidly. The digital age has enabled virtual connections that transcend physical boundaries, allowing us to communicate with individuals across continents and cultures while, according to Bauman, being completely disconnected from one's immediate surroundings.

In our era of ambivalence and uncertainty, features of solid institutions like family, community, and the state have become liquid. With lives marked by globalization, heightened individualization, and preferred new social media information landscapes, 'young students' as well as 'old teachers' are continually forming or contributing to their identities and perspectives within a transcultural context (Harris, 2013, p. 145).

It is in the public sphere that our **shared characteristics** become visible across continents and cultures, whether students or faculty. According to Hannah Arendt (1958), our human identity emerges primarily through public action and speech. For example, in one university's virtual team PowerPoint presentation, using the metaphor of a suitcase, a Ukrainian student's present reality and identity became visible to students in seven other countries.

> After sitting in a cold pipe basement under the civil dormitory without any food, surviving a Russian genocidal permanent bloody bombardment of my beloved home city and brave country, Ukraine, I realized you should not be attached to material possessions. Instead, you should take care of your own physical and mental health first because this is the only thing that cannot be taken away from you by anyone.
> *(Ukrainian student, March 30, 2024)*

Our process of collaboration and **equitable partnerships** is both transcultural and transdisciplinary. Our **educational aims**, necessary to ensure ethical global engagement, remain at the forefront of our project. These exist in what Agnew (2024) describes in the first chapter of this book as the 'enabling environment.' Foundational to our reflexive, inclusive, and decolonial approach to knowledge – and for its importance to democratic life, deliberation, and participation in international Higher Education – is whose voices are enabled, who gets to tell their stories, and who is heard and listened to (Walker et al., 2020). This is crucial whether we are situated in previously colonizing or colonized territories.

The basic challenge posed by a specifically epistemic form of justice is how some students – and not others – may be advantaged in influencing and contributing to public discourse, whether at the micro (faculty), meso (deans), or macro (senior leadership) level, and in contributing to our multilingual pluri-verse. Moreover, what occurs through our joint endeavors is the incorporation of the tensions between the individual and the collective, the local and the global, and the homogeneous and the diverse. This leads to a true paradigm shift in terms of becoming responsible autonomous societal actors during the project, upon the completion of participation, and after the project itself is over.

Being engaged in **peer research** as a collective – where communicative openness, dialogue, critical reflexivity, horizontality, care, and attention to power relations exist – is a practice that can support four capabilities:

to be, to do, to advocate, and to transform epistemic barriers that students (and we teachers) face with internationalization in person or virtual campus contexts. For example, in our new project (2024–2025), teachers showcase how their dialogical and participatory transdisciplinary transcultural collaboration is crucial in bringing the realities of their participating universities into a **shared epistemic production** space to navigate the ethical dimensions of knowledge practices – the asynchronous component. To practice and strengthen their epistemic resourcefulness, Higher Education students participate in synchronous virtual engagement with their peers.

(Leivas et al., 2022)

What Makes Our 'Epistemic Partnership' Work?

Stage eight of the partnership framework is defined as

> revisiting, reflecting, and evolving where decisions and actions are subject to regular oversight and evaluation of the agreed values and principles. Objectives are met and benefit the external community as intended. Emphasis is on the importance of ethical behavior and accountability to strengthen the relationships and work.

We reflect on our process that through connectivity, our Higher Education students (and faculty) in the Global South and North are exposed to the current politics and economics of how nation-states maintain societal order by policing geographical boundaries and operationalizing categories and hierarchies of humanity (citizens, refugees, and migrants) in the tension to ensure system continuity and potential progress.

From different onto-epistemological localities, the focus of our transcultural 'assemblage' has been, and continues to be, on de-centering and reframing our knowledge traditions as we address Sustainable Development Goal #17 for Partnerships. We are a DeleuzoGuattarian collection of 'pioneers' with expressive capacities to affect and be affected by each other and by other assemblages themselves produced through their relations or connectivity (Deleuze & Guattari, 1988) The only unity in assemblage is that of the co-functioning of living parts in the social world that is unstable, mobile, and inseparable, always becoming rather than parts that are fixed or hierarchical. Our assemblage works the way it does despite and because of our differences.

The development of our project, then, took on an organic character. While of course we planned and developed our program thoughtfully and consciously, we did not adhere to a strictly prescribed roadmap. Indeed, we did not foresee the growth of the project to encompass eight universities in seven countries, which has occurred in a rhizomic fashion. At this pivot between the establishment of a regular series of collaborative seminars – the project's past – and its expansion and associated publications – the project's future – it behooves us to pause and think about whether our work fits into an existing theoretical model or whether it represents something new and different.

Conclusions

Re-examining the University of Toronto Framework we find the four core values – intentional inclusion, reciprocity, students as partners, and relational accountability – are profoundly important to our aims and motivations. Yet because our project is focused on the meeting points of northern, eastern, southern, and western epistemologies, our project looks rather different to many of the existing models for international collaboration. There are echoes of COIL, for instance, in our student-led breakout rooms, but these do not lead to formal outputs, as in our view the conversation depends on its free-flowing and organic nature. Similarly, although the layering of student narratives might resemble story circles in some ways, this is not by design – we have found that if we are too prescriptive or directive, the sessions are likely to be less generative overall. There are similar conclusions to be drawn from our own collaboration as educators. From the outset we have worked in an egalitarian and informal way, by necessity as our institutional settings and frameworks are so different.

We will continue to listen, question, and plan, based on the results of our research, hoping to contribute to a kind of transnational education that invites students, as becoming global citizens, to interrupt the reproduction of colonial futures and deepen their sense of social justice responsibility in the present.

Implications for Ethical Policies and Practices

1 *Connect and Amplify Voices across Continents and Cultures*: The need to amplify diverse voices and perspectives, especially those from the Global South, to counter epistemic injustice and dominant narratives. This involves intentionally creating spaces and opportunities for marginalized communities to share their knowledge and lived experiences.
2 *Collaborations*: The importance of transdisciplinary, transcultural collaborations that bridge different knowledge traditions and promote mutual understanding. Such collaborations can lead to more comprehensive and nuanced understandings of complex global issues by drawing on diverse disciplinary and cultural insights.

9
ASSESSING RISKS AND MONITORING INTERNATIONAL STUDENT RECRUITMENT PARTNERS

Toward Ethical Engagement with Education Agents

Pii-Tuulia Nikula

Introduction

Internationalization of higher education includes partnerships and contractual arrangements with other educational institutions and various public and private entities. Pursuing ethical internationalization requires higher education institutions (HEIs) to have an evidence-based understanding of the risks that their arrangements might pose, and how to monitor the behavior of actors involved in these partnerships. This has been known to be particularly challenging in cross-country and cross-cultural contexts, both within and beyond higher education (Filatotchev & Wright, 2011; Fladmoe-Lindquist & Jacque, 1995; Mazzarol et al., 2003).

Prior research has highlighted how countries and HEIs have various rationales for recruiting international students, such as diplomacy, capacity building, skilled migration, reputation/rankings, and revenue generation/economic benefits, of which the latter – and the underlying financial pressures – are often now among the key rationales (Kim, 2023; Knight, 2004; Lomer, 2017). As part of this commercialization trend and due to the financial pressures to intensify international student recruitment, a diverse range of commercial actors has emerged, offering their services to HEIs in their pursuit of fee-paying international students.

Contracting third parties might appear an attractive strategy, but it also leads to new risks and ethical issues. Therein lies the challenge. Situated within the Cultural Readiness for Internationalization (CRI) Model[1] (Agnew & VanBalkom, 2009), the organizational culture and internal readiness of institutions should align with the external environment. The basis of this

DOI: 10.4324/9781315623337-11

alignment is a solid understanding of all actors that institutions decide to collaborate with, as well as an understanding of the wider external environment, such as relevant government policies. Pursuing ethical internationalization is challenging if HEIs lack the required capabilities and resources to assess risks and conduct monitoring of their partners and contracted third parties.

This chapter focuses on a specific area of internationalization, namely the use of for-profit third-party education agents that assist HEIs in recruiting international students. While focusing on this particular case many of the issues and solutions are applicable to a range of international higher education partnerships. All internationalization modes should include an assessment of the institution's readiness to engage in them as well as discussions about how to assess risks and monitor performance.

In this chapter *education agents* or *international student recruitment agents* are defined as actors that have formal relationships with HEIs to recruit international students in exchange for (typically financial) compensation paid by the client institution. This differentiates education agents from other actors, such as fully student-contracted counselors or independent agents, who have no formal relationships with institutions, but are, instead, contracted by students (Roy, 2017). The use of both types of actors is widespread across the globe when prospective students seek information about international study opportunities (Nikula et al., 2023; Roy, 2017).

HEIs can choose to recruit international students directly, but many have decided to contract agents due to the perceived benefits of this recruitment mode (BUILA & Universities UK International, 2021; Kim, 2023; Parliament of Australia, 2023). This practice, and its support and acceptance by many HEIs and governments, can be seen to align with the internationalization for a 'Global Knowledge Economy narrative', which focuses on economic benefits, competition, and education as an investment (Stein et al., 2016). The critical question is whether the pursuit of these external opportunities aligns with the internal readiness of HEIs to pursue ethical internationalization.

Despite the popularity of agent use, the risks associated with agent engagement and/or how HEIs can best work with these commercial actors have not always been well understood (Huang et al., 2016). Higher education commercialization, including agent-based student recruitment, can be problematic from the perspective of ethical internationalization. Unwanted behavior by agents, maybe driven by short-term commercial interests, can breach the interests of international students, HEIs, and other key stakeholders. Examples of agent misbehavior include distributing inaccurate and misleading information, limited transparency, financial fraud, document fraud, human trafficking, and multiple other issues (Coco, 2015; Fittante, 2023; Ghosh & Garrison, 2024; Huang et al., 2016; McKenzie & Bachelard, 2023; Migration Advisory Committee, 2024; Nikula & Kivistö, 2020; Parliament of Australia, 2023).

Therefore, HEIs wanting to pursue ethical internationalization must have the skills to assess risks as well as a technical understanding of how to work with agents. Moreover, HEIs subscribing to ethical international student recruitment need effective monitoring practices to reduce information asymmetries between them and their agents, ensuring that their contracted agents don't engage in unwanted behaviors. A critical review of the capabilities of HEIs to assess risks and monitor third parties allows for an examination of potential gaps and the identification of solutions that can help institutions improve their current practices to pursue more thoughtful and ethical internationalization.

This chapter begins by exploring risks associated with the practice of using education agents. It then asks whether, and to what extent, HEIs can mitigate these risks, including problems to do with adverse selection when choosing new agents. After that, the abilities of HEIs to monitor their agents are evaluated. By engaging in critical analysis of this common practice in the internationalization of higher education, this chapter contributes to a better understanding of the ethicality, and its limits, of HEIs when pursuing internationalization via third parties. Some of the issues and solutions discussed in this chapter can also be extended to other international higher education partnerships.

The Remits of Ethical Agent-Based Internationalization

The practice of contracting for-profit education agents to enhance institutional international student recruitment activities can be seen as a result of the marketized system of higher education where institutions compete with each other to recruit fee-paying students (Cerna & Chou, 2023; Chen, 2023; Komljenovic, 2017, 2019; Naidoo & Williams, 2015). In many countries and institutional contexts, international education is now considered an export *industry*, and the role many HEIs play in this system is similar to private businesses engaging in international business opportunities. Some institutions in countries such as the UK, Canada, and Australia, have become highly reliant on this income, and hence, are likely to feel pressures to remain competitive in the international student *marketplace* to ensure their own survival (Ghosh & Garrison, 2024; Migration Advisory Committee, 2024; Parliament of Australia, 2023).

This desire for a growing number of international full fee-paying students has created the business of education agents. As part of the exploration of ethical agent-based recruitment and related risks, it is important to consider how the arrangements of this agent-based model take into account the interests of various stakeholders, such as HEIs, students, and governments. The commercial and contractual relationship is between HEIs and their agents, incentivizing agents for their work if they fulfill the needs of HEIs to acquire new students. Usually, HEIs compensate agents' services on a commission basis (e.g., specific percentage of the first-year tuition fee) as well as other kick-backs, such as marketing fees, bonuses etc (BUILA & Universities UK International, 2021; Parliament of Australia, 2023). Hence, it can be argued that this model is built on the prioritization of agents' and HEIs' interests. This issue is further pronounced by the fact that there is limited transparency about HEI–agent arrangements, many students and other stakeholders, have limited knowledge and understanding of these relationships, or the terms underlying this representation (Chen, 2023; Coco, 2015; Migration Advisory Committee, 2024; Nikula et al., 2023)

The extent to which other interests, such as those of students, are considered by agents, can be influenced by multiple factors. For instance, in certain countries it is common for students to pay service fees and to have formal contracts with agents, which might incentivize agents to prioritize students' interests as it creates a principal–agent relationship between these two parties (Feng & Horta, 2021). In addition, it can be argued that it is in the best interests of good agents to take into account the interests of the students to ensure the long-term sustainability of agency operations (BUILA & Universities UK International, 2021; Nikula et al., 2023). Also, other stakeholders and their interests need to be considered. For instance, governments in both destination countries, and the countries students frequently depart from for overseas study opportunities have been interested in influencing and regulating the agent space (Nikula et al., 2023).

A relevant theme is the question of who is served and for what purpose. It is evident that international students' interests are not the only consideration in internationalization of higher education. For instance, HEIs' admission practices and government policies exclude many candidates interested in studying in a specific institution/destination. Also, some agent-related policies and practices are there to protect the interests of governments and/or HEIs, rather than students (Nikula, 2022). However, at the very minimum, prospective students using the services of agents should be entitled to receive correct and up-to-date information, free of issues such as financial fraud, unprofessional service, discrimination, and limited transparency.

It would be reasonable to expect that all HEIs exercise scrutiny when working with agents to ensure that the risks to themselves and prospective students are minimized. This is a key requirement for ethical use of education agents. However, the global evidence available from the past decade does not inspire much confidence that this is always the case (Coco, 2015; Commonwealth Ombudsman, 2018; Ghosh & Garrison, 2024; Huang et al., 2016; Joint Standing Committee on Migration, 2019; McKenzie & Bachelard, 2023; Migration Advisory Committee, 2024; Ministry of Education, 2015; Nikula & Kivistö, 2020; Parliament of Australia, 2023; Visentin, 2015; Worthington et al., 2019).

The assessment of HEIs' abilities to evaluate risks and monitor them lends itself to the consideration of issues identified in agency theory (Jensen & Meckling, 1976). Agency theory posits that there are often potential goal incongruences between principals (such as HEIs) and their agents (such as contracted education agents) and that these relationships are affected by information asymmetries which make it difficult for principals to assess their agents (Jensen & Meckling, 1976). Information asymmetries and practices to mitigate them can be highly challenging or costly in cross-country situations: organizations need sufficient resources and competencies to detect the behavior of their overseas partners (Filatotchev & Wright, 2011; Fladmoe-Lindquist & Jacque, 1995).

In this chapter the agency theory lens is used to discuss information asymmetries when HEIs contract agents as well as the abilities of HEIs to identify risks and monitor their agents' behaviors. It is important to note that this lens does not imply that prospective students don't have agency. Some prospective students pursue roles where they are critical users of education agent services (Nikula et al., 2023). However, many examples also point in the opposite direction (Ghosh & Garrison, 2024; Migration Advisory Committee, 2024). Therefore, HEIs committed to ethical recruitment practices should have proper measures in place to identify risks and reduce the likelihood of agent misbehavior that might breach international students' interests.

The next two sections explore HEIs' abilities to identify and manage risks associated with agent engagement, and the extent to which HEIs can effectively monitor their agents. These questions are critical when considering the ethicality of agent-based international student recruitment.

Engaging Agents – A Risky Business?

All internationalization modes carry a degree of risk. Higher education internationalization modes, such as international branch campuses, study centers, and acquisitions/mergers carry the highest risk, followed by medium-risk activities, such as affiliations, double degrees, and franchising, while the lowest risks are associated with activities to do with student/faculty exchange, online delivery, or internationalization at home (Beecher & Streitwieser, 2019; Healey, 2015; Wilkins & Huisman, 2012).

Risks can be further categorized into different types of risk. The key risks can involve physical harm/human well-being, resource/financial risks, and reputational/brand risks (Beecher, 2016; Healey 2015). Agent use could be considered as an 'affiliation', carrying risks associated with prospective students' well-being (physical, mental, financial) and/or reputational risks to the HEIs (Fittante, 2023; Ghosh & Garrison, 2024; Huang et al., 2016, 2022; Migration Advisory Committee, 2024; Parliament of Australia, 2023). Usually, HEIs do not make notable upfront investments in agency operations, but mitigate financial risks by the use of outcome-based contracts, where agents receive commission payments based on the number of students recruited (BUILA & Universities UK International, 2021; Parliament of Australia, 2023). However, in some instances, such as in cross-ownership situations, financial risks may be relevant. Furthermore, other resource-related risks, such as investments required in internal operations to facilitate and manage agent-based recruitment (e.g., software, staff training, other costs), should be considered.

Risk assessment in agent use can be linked to wider institutional strategies, policies, and due diligence practices. First, all relevant risks should be part of discussions when HEIs consider whether they should, or should not, work with agents. Similarly, to other international modes (Mazzarol et al., 2003), HEIs interested in contracting agents, should first engage in comprehensive analysis of risks associated with this recruitment mode and the markets in which they are planning to engage agents. With reference to the CRI model, the internal 'risk appetite' (Huang et al., 2016) should be coupled with a discussion of institutional beliefs, values, and underlying assumptions, and the extent to which the use of agents aligns with these risks.

HEIs must also acknowledge how risks are dependent on the level of institutional resourcing available for agent management, including training, support, due diligence, and monitoring of agents. A low-risk endeavor with insufficient resourcing might end up a high-risk undertaking. The level of risk can also be mitigated by decisions on how much authority agents are allocated, for instance, whether agents are authorized to translate and verify documents, or sub-contract. Or whether agents are allowed to pursue other activities on behalf of their client institutions, such as marketing and parts of the admissions process. Other decisions that impact risk, include the size of the agent network and the countries in which agents are used (BUILA & Universities UK International, 2021). Aligning the internal with the external is important. For instance, the number of staff available for agent oversight should align with the number of agents contracted. There may also be need for staff to have an understanding of different cultures and language skills to work with agents across the globe. If conducted in an ethical manner, agent management requires sufficient resourcing.

How due diligence is conducted is an example of how HEIs assess risks associated with individual education agents. In agency theory, adverse selection refers to principals' difficulties to identify whether or not the agent meets their criteria and expectations (Eisenhardt, 1989). Education agents may decide to misrepresent themselves to win a contract with an institution (Huang et al., 2016; Ott, 2016). Hence, HEIs as principals have to screen agents by conducting careful due diligence before agents are accepted as formal recruitment partners.

Due diligence should not be a quick 'tick-box' exercise as this might mean that institutions appear to possess evidence, but the validity and reliability of this evidence might be questionable, and not necessarily revealing the true nature of the agent. For instance, typically the due diligence process has involved asking agents to fill in a form and provide references (BUILA & Universities UK International, 2021; NACAC, 2021; New Zealand Qualifications Authority, n.d.; Queensland Government, 2009; Raimo et al., 2015). In the form agents are asked to provide information about their operations, business licences, and a business plans/targets (BUILA & Universities UK International, 2021; Huang et al., 2016; NACAC, 2021). While useful for other reasons, this information is unlikely to offer sufficient information about the ethical behavior of these actors. Also reference checking can provide limited value, as often agents are allowed to self-appoint referees – a practice that may lead to bias (Hedricks et al., 2018). It is also unclear how HEIs verify that the referee is who they purport to be to avoid fake/paid references and to identify conflicts of interests. Therefore, any evidence collected when referees are self-appointed should be approached with caution.

This section discussed the importance of risk assessment when deciding whether or not to engage with agents as well as provided some examples of issues associated with adverse selection when choosing agent partners. HEIs should consider introducing a mix of information collection methods, including a comprehensive review of a range of publicly available information, office visits, in-person (/online) interviews, knowledge tests, mystery shopping, and careful background checking, before deciding on new agent partnerships. Ethical agent engagement requires that HEIs conduct a careful due diligence to minimize the likelihood of engaging with unethical agents. However, even then, they are unlikely to detect all issues, and hence, a degree of risk will always be inherent in the process of selecting new agent partners.

Monitoring Agent Behavior

After deciding to work with agents or other partners to pursue internationalization, HEIs need to monitor these arrangements to ensure that all contract terms and other criteria are being met. Monitoring refers to the continuous process of collecting data. In ethical internationalization this includes monitoring techniques that help ensure that international students' interests are protected.

Agency theory highlights how information asymmetries can make effective monitoring challenging and costly (Jensen & Meckling, 1976). Agents have more information about their own behavior than HEIs, and there are multiple aspects of agent behavior that HEIs are unlikely to detect easily (Nikula & Kivistö, 2020). Effective monitoring requires resource allocation, including financial resources as well as technical and language and cultural competencies of the staff involved.

Several entities have provided guidance to HEIs on how to effectively monitor their agents (e.g., BUILA & Universities UK International, 2021; New Zealand Qualifications Authority, n.d.; Queensland Government, 2009). Unfortunately, most guidelines and commonly used practices by HEIs cover only a limited range of monitoring techniques, hence not necessarily allowing HEI to detect the true behavior of education agents (Nikula & Kivistö, 2020). For instance, many HEIs use automatically available data to monitor trends, such as offer-acceptance conversions and visa approval rates. However, this should be extended to a more comprehensive analysis of differences between agent and non-agent recruited students, including factors such as longitudinal outcomes and academic performance, to monitor the actual success of agent-based recruitment (Nikula & Kivistö, 2020).

Furthermore, much value is placed on student feedback as an indicator of agent behavior, without critically considering its many limitations. First, most international students are not in the position to critically evaluate the truthfulness of all information provided by agents (e.g., whether there would have been a better-suited institutions/country, or agent claims about future employment prospects). Second, there are issues to do with timing of student feedback (e.g., recall bias); collection methods (e.g., surveys rather than interviews) as well as the way questions are asked, including issues to do with language skills (Coco, 2015; Nikula & Kivistö, 2020). Third, in certain situations the interests of the student and the agent might align (e.g., in a situation where an agent has helped student to fabricate documentation), and hence, it is unlikely that student feedback would help institutions to collect reliable information. Finally, due to a plethora of cultural, language, and visa considerations, international students may feel uncomfortable making formal complaints or not even be aware of their ability to report issues (Ghosh & Garrison, 2024; Hart & Coates, 2010; Ramia et al., 2013). Hence, putting the onus on students to identify issues is highly problematic and likely to lead to under-reporting.

HEIs need a range of monitoring techniques to assess their agents. This requires significant resources. These costs should have been considered when the initial decision to engage agents was made. A systematic approach to monitoring would require HEIs to draw a matrix consisting of the range of issues that may be present (such as misinformation, disinformation, financial fraud, document fraud, and unprofessional service), and a list of suitable monitoring tools against each issue to detect the (non-)existence of each issue.

Some of the effective monitoring solutions would include regular scans of agent websites and/or social media pages and other communications methods to evaluate whether agents provide accurate and up-to-date information about the study destination. Another approach that has great potential, but is largely under-utilized, is mystery shopping which would help HEIs to monitor the verbal guidance offered to applicants, including the ability to monitor the guidance offered to those who decide to study elsewhere as well as the way student applications are processed (Nikula & Kivistö, 2020).

The move toward more ethical agent engagement requires that HEIs conduct systematic and comprehensive monitoring. This requires sufficient resourcing. Nevertheless, similarly to risk assessment, HEIs must accept that – even when following best practices – they are unlikely to eliminate all information asymmetries, and hence, contracting third parties comes with inherent risks that must be accepted if this recruitment mode is chosen.

Discussion

This chapter explores the risks associated with agent use and whether agent behavior can be reliably detected to ensure ethical agent-based recruitment. Unfortunately, various issues in the way institution-contracted agents behave are regularly reported across the globe. This indicates that many HEIs have not been able to reliably assess risks when choosing which agents to work with. Also, HEIs' abilities to conduct effective monitoring have been questioned (Nikula & Kivistö, 2020). This can leave prospective students in a vulnerable position.

The agency theory lens points out that the HEI–education agent arrangement favors the interests of these two parties over the interests of international students. It also highlights how information asymmetries that exist between HEIs and their agents can be difficult to eliminate. When making a commitment to ethical internationalization, HEIs have a choice of conducting student recruitment without agents, or resourcing and modifying their agent management practices, so that the risks and information asymmetries are minimized. This highlights the importance of the CRI model and assessing the match between the internal culture/readiness and external opportunities.

A large part of the agent-facilitated mobility directs student flows from low-income to high-income contexts. Hence, any unethical practices by agents are disproportionately impacting people and communities in the Global South, whilst the benefits are mainly incurred by HEIs in high(er)-income countries – reinforcing global injustices. These injustices are further reinforced by other issues related to this mobility, such as brain drain and neo-colonialism (Stein, 2021; Stein et al., 2016). Education agents contribute to these developments as part of their role in the marketized system of international higher education. Moreover, it is important to note that agents and other intermediaries have been found to reproduce social inequalities: different types of services and sources are used depending on the socioeconomic status of prospective students and the guidance and recommendations on destination/institutions may depend on prospective students' social and financial status (Feng & Horta, 2021; Ghosh & Garrison, 2024; Kim, 2023; Tuxen & Robertson, 2019; Ying & Wright, 2023). It was beyond the scope of this chapter to provide a comprehensive critique of these wider structural issues associated with agent-facilitated mobility, but these questions warrant the future attention of critical internationalization studies scholars.

We can also ask whether the discontinuation of agent-use by HEIs would lead to better outcomes? Stein (2021) warns against our tendencies to seek simple stories and solutions. This also applies to the discussion about ethical risks associated with agent-based recruitment. Deciding not to contract agents wouldn't automatically remove problems that prospective students face, but might actually increase risks and further complicate international students' pathways. Good agents have expertise and knowledge which is known to be valued by students as it reduces information asymmetries and barriers that prospective students face when seeking information about overseas study opportunities and/or the application process (Chen, 2023; Jafar & Legusov, 2021; Kim, 2023; Liu-Farrer & Tran, 2019; Yang et al., 2023; Zhang et al., 2023).

Also, if HEIs decided not to contract agents, an increasing number of students might decide to contract independent counsellors. This would mean that HEIs lost all control of the guidance provided to prospective students. Hence, while removing agents would remove the problematic conflict of interest underlying HEI–agent relationships, it is less clear whether the discontinuation of agent use would lead to more ethical recruitment or better outcomes for students.

Implications for Ethical Policies and Practices

1 *Need to Critically Self-Assess*: HEIs play a key role and need to critically assess their own practices around agent engagement, moving beyond financial considerations to prioritize ethical factors.
2 *Ongoing Risk Assessment*: Effective risk assessment, due diligence, and implementation of best practices are crucial before and during agent engagement.
3 *Transparency*: Institutions should enhance transparency by informing prospective students about their relationships with agents.
4 *Regulate for Accountability*: Government regulation requiring minimum standards for agent management could help increase accountability, especially for institutions primarily driven by financial incentives.
5 *Future Research*: Continue to explore the structural issues associated with agent-facilitated mobility, including the actions of HEIs in this context, and how agent-use can perpetuate global injustices and/or reproduce social inequalities.

Note

1 See Chapter 1 for a more detailed explanation of the CRI Model.

References

Agnew, M., & VanBalkom, W. D. (2009). Cultural readiness for internationalization (CRI): A model for planned change. In S. Majhanovich, & M. Geo-JaJa (Eds.), *Education, language, and economics: Growing national and global dilemmas* (pp. 141–154). Sense Pub.
Beecher, B. (2016). Internationalization Through the International Branch Campus: Identifying Opportunities and Risks [Doctoral Dissertation, The George Washington University]. https://www.proquest.com/docview/1807962232
Beecher, B., & Streitwieser, B. (2019). A risk management approach for the internationalization of higher education. *Journal of the Knowledge Economy, 10*(4), 1404–1426. https://doi.org/10.1007/s13132-017-0468-y
BUILA, & Universities UK International. (2021). *The good practice guide for providers using education agents. A modular guide*. British Universities' International Liaison Association and Universities UK International.
Cerna, L., & Chou, M.-H. (2023). Politics of internationalisation and the migration-higher education nexus. *Globalisation, Societies and Education, 21*(2), 222–235. https://doi.org/10.1080/14767724.2022.2073975
Chen, K. H. (2023). Pipelines of schooling: Pathways to the United States and rent-seeking practices by education agents. *International Journal of Educational Development, 97*, 102714. https://doi.org/10.1016/j.ijedudev.2022.102714
Coco, L. (2015). *Capturing a global student market for colleges and universities: The use of private third party agents in international student recruitment* [Doctoral dissertation]. The University of Georgia.

Commonwealth Ombudsman. (2018). *Issues in the administration of the international student protection framework identified through the investigation of complaints about an education agent*. Parliament of Australia.
Eisenhardt, K. M. (1989). Agency Theory: An Assessment and Review. *The Academy of Management Review*, 14(1), 57–74. https://doi.org/10.2307/258191
Feng, S., & Horta, H. (2021). Brokers of international student mobility: The roles and processes of education agents in China. *European Journal of Education*, 56(2), 248–264. https://doi.org/10.1111/ejed.12442
Filatotchev, I., & Wright, M. (2011). Agency perspectives on corporate governance of multinational enterprises. *Journal of Management Studies*, 48(2), 471–486. https://doi.org/10.1111/j.1467-6486.2010.00921.x
Fittante, D. (2023). Beyond brokering for recruitment: Education agents in Armenia. *Population, Space and Place*, 29(1), e2622. https://doi.org/10.1002/psp.2622
Fladmoe-Lindquist, K., & Jacque, L. L. (1995). Control modes in international service operations: The propensity to franchise. *Management Science*, 41(7), 1238–1249.
Ghosh, S., & Garrison, R. M. (2024). "To whom should I complain"?: Exploring the obfuscated role of state and non-state agencies in Indian international student recruitment by GTA colleges. *India Migration Report 2023*. Routledge India. doi https://doi.org/10.4324/9781003490234
Hart, D. J., & Coates, N. F. (2010). International student complaint behaviour: How do East Asian students complain to their university? *Journal of Further and Higher Education*, 34(3), 303–319. https://doi.org/10.1080/0309877X.2010.484051
Healey, N. M. (2015). Towards a risk-based typology for transnational education. *Higher Education*, 69(1), 1–18. https://doi.org/10.1007/s10734-014-9757-6
Hedricks, C., Rupayana, D., Puchalski, L., & Robie, C. (2018). Content of qualitative feedback provided during structured, confidential reference checks. *Personnel Assessment and Decisions*, 4(1). https://doi.org/10.25035/pad.2018.004
Huang, I. Y., Raimo, V., & Humfrey, C. (2016). Power and control: Managing agents for international student recruitment in higher education. *Studies in Higher Education*, 41(8), 1333–1354. https://doi.org/10.1080/03075079.2014.968543
Huang, I. Y., Williamson, D., Lynch-Wood, G., Raimo, V., Rayner, C., Addington, L., & West, E. (2022). Governance of agents in the recruitment of international students: A typology of contractual management approaches in higher education. *Studies in Higher Education*, 47(6), 1150–1170. https://doi.org/10.1080/03075079.2020.1861595
Jafar, H., & Legusov, O. (2021). Understanding the decision-making process of college-bound international students: A case study of greater toronto area colleges of applied arts and technology. *Community College Journal of Research and Practice*, 45(7), 463–478. https://doi.org/10.1080/10668926.2020.1723740
Jensen, M. C., & Meckling, W. H. (1976). Theory of the firm: Managerial behavior, agency costs and ownership structure. *Journal of Financial Economics*, 3(4), 305–360. https://doi.org/10.1016/0304-405X(76)90026-X
Joint Standing Committee on Migration. (2019). *Report of the inquiry into efficacy of current regulation of Australian migration and education agents*. Commonwealth of Australia. https://www.aph.gov.au/Parliamentary_Business/Committees/Joint/Migration/Migrationagentregulatio/Report

Kim, S. K. (2023). *Constructing student mobility: How universities recruit students and shape pathways between Berkeley and Seoul*. The MIT Press. https://doi.org/10.7551/mitpress/13955.001.0001

Knight, J. (2004). Internationalization remodeled: Definition, approaches, and rationales. *Journal of Studies in International Education*, *8*(1), 5–31. https://doi.org/10.1177/1028315303260832

Komljenovic, J. (2017). Market ordering as a device for market-making: The case of the emerging students' recruitment industry. *Globalisation, Societies and Education*, *15*(3), 367–380. https://doi.org/10.1080/14767724.2017.1330136

Komljenovic, J. (2019). Making higher education markets: Trust-building strategies of private companies to enter the public sector. *Higher Education*, *78*(1), 51–66. https://doi.org/10.1007/s10734-018-0330-6

Liu-Farrer, G., & Tran, A. H. (2019). Bridging the institutional gaps: International education as a migration industry. *International Migration*, *57*(3), 235–249. https://doi.org/10.1111/imig.12543

Lomer, S. (2017). *Recruiting International Students in Higher Education: Representations and Rationales in British Policy*. Springer International Publishing. https://doi.org/10.1007/978-3-319-51073-6

Mazzarol, T., Norman Soutar, G., & Sim Yaw Seng, M. (2003). The third wave: Future trends in international education. *International Journal of Educational Management*, *17*(3), 90–99. https://doi.org/10.1108/09513540310467778

McKenzie, M., & Bachelard, N. (2023, May 15). Fake schools, fake students: Criminals make mockery of education visas. *The Age*. https://www.theage.com.au/politics/federal/fake-schools-fake-students-criminals-make-mockery-of-education-visas-20230419-p5d1mw.html

Migration Advisory Committee. (2024). *Graduate route: Rapid Review*. Migration Advisory Committee. https://assets.publishing.service.gov.uk/media/6641e1fbbd01f5ed32793992/MAC+Rapid+Review+of+Graduate+Route.pdf

Ministry of Education. (2015). *Consultation on the draft code of practice for the pastoral care of international students. Summary of written submissions*. New Zealand Ministry of Education.

NACAC. (2021). *Part 3: Vetting and external training*. National Association for College Admission Counseling. https://www.nacacnet.org/knowledge-center/international/Commisioned_agent_series/

Naidoo, R., & Williams, J. (2015). The neoliberal regime in English higher education: Charters, consumers and the erosion of the public good. *Critical Studies in Education*, *56*(2), 208–223. https://doi.org/10.1080/17508487.2014.939098

New Zealand Qualifications Authority. (n.d.). *Outcome 2: Managing and monitoring agents*. Retrieved from October 4, 2024, https://www2.nzqa.govt.nz/tertiary/the-code/the-code-for-education-providers/guide-to-managing-education-agents/

Nikula, P.-T. (2022). Education agent standards in Australia and New Zealand–government's role in agent-based international student recruitment. *Studies in Higher Education*, *47*, 831–846. https://doi.org/10.1080/03075079.2020.1811219

Nikula, P.-T., & Kivistö, J. (2020). Monitoring of education agents engaged in international student recruitment: Perspectives from agency theory. *Journal of Studies in International Education*, *24*(2), 212–231. https://doi.org/10.1177/1028315318825338

Nikula, P.-T., Raimo, V., & West, E. (Eds.). (2023). *Student recruitment agents in international higher education: A multi-stakeholder perspective on challenges and best practices*. Routledge.

Ott, P. (2016). *Agencies, third-party vendors, and the grooming of the college applicant in China* [Doctoral dissertation]. University of Pennsylvania.
Parliament of Australia. (2023). *Inquiry into Australia's tourism and international education sectors: "Quality and Integrity—The Quest for Sustainable Growth": Interim Report*. Parliament of Australia.
Queensland Government. (2009). *International education agent management. A best practice guide for the Queensland VET Sector*. Department of Education and Training.
Raimo, V., Humfrey, C., & Huang, I. Y. (2015). *Managing international student recruitment agents. Approaches, benefits and challenges*. https://www.britishcouncil.org/sites/default/files/managing_education_agents_report_for_bc_2.pdf
Ramia, G., Marginson, S., & Sawir, E. (2013). *Regulating international students' wellbeing*. The Policy Press.
Roy, M. (2017, June 6). Decoding International Students' Experiences with Education Agents: Insights for U.S. Institutions. WENR, https://wenr.wes.org/2017/06/decoding-international-students-experiences-with-education-agents-insights-for-u-s-institutions
Stein, S. (2021). Critical internationalization studies at an impasse: Making space for complexity, uncertainty, and complicity in a time of global challenges. *Studies in Higher Education, 46*(9), 1771–1784. https://doi.org/10.1080/03075079.2019.1704722
Stein, S., Andreotti, V., Bruce, J., & Suša, R. (2016). Towards different conversations about the internationalization of higher education. *Comparative and International Education, 45*(1), Article 1. https://doi.org/10.5206/cie-eci.v45i1.9281
Tuxen, N., & Robertson, S. (2019). Brokering international education and (re)producing class in Mumbai. *International Migration, 57*(3), 280–294. https://doi.org/10.1111/imig.12516
Visentin, L. (2015, April 23). Sydney University to continue relationship with suspect education agent. *The Sydney Morning Herald*. https://www.smh.com.au/national/nsw/sydney-university-to-continue-relationship-with-suspect-education-agent-20150422-1mqf73.html
Wilkins, S., & Huisman, J. (2012). The international branch campus as transnational strategy in higher education. *Higher Education, 64*(5), 627–645.
Worthington, E., O'Neill, S., & Selvaratnam, N. (2019, May 6). When large numbers of students started failing, alarm bells began ringing for academics. *ABC News*. https://www.abc.net.au/news/2019-05-06/uni-academics-risk-jobs-to-speak-about-international-students/11082640
Yang, Y., Lomer, S., Mittelmeier, J., & Lim, M. A. (2023). Giving voices to Chinese international students using interpretative phenomenological analysis (IPA): The application experiences to UK universities via education agents in uncertainty. In V. Raimo, C. Humfrey, & Y. Huang (Eds.), *Student recruitment agents in international higher education* (pp. 164–183). Routledge.
Ying, M., & Wright, E. (2023). Outsourced concerted cultivation: International schooling and educational consulting in China. *International Studies in Sociology of Education, 32*(3), 799–821. https://doi.org/10.1080/09620214.2021.1927143
Zhang, Y. L., Xiao, M., & Hagedorn, L. S. (2023). Pursuing higher education dreams in the US: Portraits of Chinese families assisted by an education agent. In *Student recruitment agents in international higher education* (pp. 151–163). Routledge.

10
BEYOND METRICS

A Critical Framework for Evaluating Higher Education Internationalization

Melanie Agnew, Christopher Fuglestad, and Megan Lochhead

Introduction

This chapter introduces an innovative evaluation model for the internationalization of higher education situated within a critical framework. Specifically, it focuses on the tensions between higher education's educational missions and market-driven approaches to internationalization.

The authors draw on two existing frameworks: 1) Stein et al.'s (2016) four articulations of internationalization[1] and 2) Agnew and Van Balkom's (2009) Cultural Readiness for Internationalization (CRI) Change Model.[2] It is also guided by Buckner & Stein's (2020) discussion on "encountering difference." This critical evaluation framework seeks to reverse "internationalization drift," a phenomenon in which market-oriented objectives overshadow higher education's foundational education and societal purposes like cultural exchange, global citizenship, and mutual understanding. Internationalization has become disconnected from its anchor to its educational mission and social responsibility. "Traditional values such as cooperation, peace and mutual understanding, human capital development, and solidarity, have been moved to the sidelines as universities strive for competition, revenues, and reputation/branding" (De Wit & Altbach, 2021, p. 35). In the process, dominant market forces fuel the perpetuation of inequities and power imbalances that continue to reinforce harmful historical patterns of global engagement.

The question posed by Biesta (2009) concerning "whether we are indeed measuring what we value, or whether we are just measuring what we can easily measure and thus end up valuing what we (can) measure" (p. 35) is

DOI: 10.4324/9781315623337-12

the genesis for this chapter. It encapsulates a core tension in higher education internationalization—namely, how market-driven metrics and measurements have overshadowed longstanding educational and societal values that *should* guide international initiatives and thus *should* be measured.

The marketization of internationalization has led to increased institutional branding, revenue generation, and competitive advantages while stifling efforts to prioritize long-established educational aims (De Wit & Altbach, 2021; Stein et al., 2016; Tomàs-Folch, 2015; Pashby & De Oliveira Andreotti, 2016). However, understanding the extent to which market-driven practices exist within internationalization may be more present than currently realized. Because multiple ideologies operate simultaneously at any given time, it is possible to legitimize predominantly economic activities under the guise of academic purposes. This is what Schein (1993) refers to as espoused values—what we say we do versus enacted values—what we do. Oftentimes, there are discrepancies between what an institution of higher education espouses (e.g., mission) and what is enacted (practices). Therefore, it can be assumed that market forces are more prevalent in internationalization than otherwise thought, indicating that strong measures are needed to ensure educational aims of higher education are the priority.

There have been numerous internationalization evaluation models developed over the past several decades (Altinay et al., 2019; Deardorff & Van Gaalen, 2012, 2021; De Wit, 1999; Hudzik & Stohl, 2009; Knight, 2008), each contributing important insights to understanding how institutions can effectively assess and improve their internationalization efforts. These models range from broad process-oriented approaches to more detailed frameworks focusing on specific aspects such as intercultural competence, strategic management, and ethical considerations. However, there is a call for more attention to the *qualitative* dimension of internationalization (De Wit & Altbach, 2021) and more holistic and nuanced approaches that can address the complex motivations and potential pitfalls of internationalization.

Internationalization for Achieving Sustainable Development Goals

Higher education's three core missions—teaching, research, and service—evolved in distinct historical phases, each shaped by different philosophical approaches (Scott, 2006). Teaching emerged first (12th–15th century) during the pre-nation period, guided by Scholasticism. The research and service missions developed during the nation-state era (16th–20th century), influenced by Humanism. In the 21st century, internationalization has emerged as a fourth mission[3] during the globalization phase, characterized by postmodernist philosophy uniquely positioned to address the complexity of today's global challenges. The challenge, however, remains in higher education's capacity and agency to temper market forces.

The purpose of internationalization is gaining prominence as a strategy to address the United Nations Sustainable Development Goals (Cai & Leask, 2024; De Wit & Altbach, 2021; Marinoni & Cardona, 2024), a strategy that higher education institutions are uniquely positioned to execute (Pashby & de Oliveira Andreotti, 2016). The United Nations' SDGs offer a globally recognized framework for addressing pressing social, economic, and environmental challenges. They are an essential benchmark for ethical practices in higher education internationalization. By aligning the SDGs with each of Stein et al.'s (2016) four articulations, institutions can create a more globally equitable framework for evaluating their global engagement strategies.

The four articulations of internationalization present distinct approaches to global higher education (Stein, et al., 2016). Internationalization for the Global Knowledge Economy frames higher education as essential for success in a competitive global market. It prioritizes STEM fields and income-generating research while selectively valuing non-Western knowledge. Internationalization as a Global Public Good focuses on democratizing access to higher education worldwide. It views higher education as necessary for producing such concepts as democracy, prosperity, and knowledge. Anti-Oppressive Internationalization advocates for systemic change to achieve greater social justice. It specifically critiques the previous approaches for their uncritical support of capitalism and questions the definitions of "public" and "good." Finally, Relational Translocalism challenges the foundations of the modern/colonial global imaginary, acknowledging higher education's complicity in its harmful systems. It seeks to nurture alternative ways of knowing and being, emphasizing the need to unlearn existing attachments and experiment with rearranging modern desires.

The SDGs, which emphasize interconnected social, economic, and environmental goals, serve as a valuable benchmark for assessing higher education's contributions to these global challenges. The SDGs can be integrated with Stein et al.'s (2016) four articulations of internationalization, as depicted in Table 10.1, This integration aligns the SDGs with various underlying aims and outcomes of internationalization. Cai & Leask (2024) argue this alignment is best accomplished through an 'outside-in' perspective, which emphasizes higher education's opportunities to better align with external societal needs.

The outside-in perspective parallels what Agnew (2012, 2021) and Agnew & Van Balkom (2009) referred to as the external or enabling

TABLE 10.1 Examples of SDGs Aligned to Stein et al.'s (2016) Four Articulations of Internationalization: Critiques and Limitations

Articulations of Internationalization of Higher Education	Example SDGs	Key Principles	Critiques & Limitation
Global Knowledge Economy	• SDG 8: Decent Work & Economic Growth • SDG 9: Industry, Innovation & Infrastructure	• Market imperatives • Economic competiveness • Knowledge as a commodity • Prestige through local rankings & metrics	• Reinforces neoliberal paradigms • Perpetuates western dominance • Overlooks local context • Prioritizes profit over social impact • Risk of brain drain
Global Public Good	• SDG 3: Good Health and Well-Being • SDG 4: Quality Education • SDG 13: Climate Action	• Democratizing access to education • Shared benefits • Globally minded outcomes	• Often Western-centric • Highlights existing structural inequities
Anti-Oppressive	• SDG 5: Gender Equality • SDG 10: Reduced Inequalities • SDG 16: Peace, Justice, and Strong Institutions	• Deep systemic change • Challenges colonial legacies • Amplifying marginalized voices	• Often too extreme for preferred political neutrality
Relational Translocalism	• SDG 17: Partnerships for the Goals	• Reciprocal context-aware, localized focus • Values collaboration longevity	• Limited resources • Varied institutional capacity levels

environment. The external environment consists of major stakeholder groups including international networks and partnerships, local business communities, and state/national governments, with students' families and alumni embedded within these stakeholder groups. These external stakeholders offer insightful and necessary perspectives on internationalization practices.

The Global Knowledge Economy articulation, for example, primarily engages with SDG 8 (i.e., Decent Work and Economic Growth) and SDG 9 (Industry, Innovation, and Infrastructure). This framework drives educational initiatives that align with market demands, emphasizing competitiveness, knowledge commodification, and institutional prestige (Hazelkorn, 2015). However, a critical analysis reveals significant concerns as the approach perpetuates Western-centric norms, risks causing brain drain from non-Western regions (Marginson, 2016) and tends to overlook local diversities because economic return is often prioritized over social or environmental sustainability.

In contrast, the Global Public Good articulation engages with SDGs that emphasize social welfare and sustainability, specifically SDG 3 (Good Health and Well-Being), SDG 4 (Quality Education), and SDG 13 (Climate Action). This framework takes a more positive stance, reflecting an effort to democratize access to higher education and emphasize collective benefits that underscore its responsibility in producing globally beneficial outcomes. Yet, this approach is not without its limitations. It often fails to critically assess the Western dominance and structural inequities in higher education; by failing to critically address systemic inequities efforts toward SDGs risk perpetuating rather than mitigating global injustices (Pashby & De Oliveira Andreotti, 2016).

The Anti-Oppressive approach aligns closely with SDG 5 (Gender Equality), SDG 10 (Reduced Inequalities) and SDG 16 (Peace, Justice, and Strong Institutions) by advocating for deep systemic change that challenges colonial legacies and prioritizes marginalized voices. Internationalization approaches that confront entrenched power structures within higher education can dismantle what Mignolo (2011) refers to as the "colonial matrix of power" that perpetuates systemic inequities. While these perspectives underscore the transformative potential of internationalization when it actively disrupts oppressive systems and advances equity on a global scale, it often faces resistance from traditional institutions that prefer conventional, politically neutral approaches.

The Relational Translocalism articulation, for example, aligns with SDG 17 (Partnerships for the Goals) by fostering reciprocal, context-aware, and localized partnerships that transcend borders. Intentional collaborations are positioned to create reciprocal, context-sensitive work that respects diverse ways of knowing and fosters sustainability beyond dominant narratives. However, resource constraints and varying levels of institutional capacity will likely emerge as challenges to consistent engagement and, therefore, to becoming complicit when power imbalances emerge.

Each of Stein et al.'s (2016) articulations present unique potential and limitations for implementing the SDGs effectively within higher education's internationalization efforts. To operationalize these approaches, a recent case study highlights the importance of leadership and governance in enabling the alignment of institutional goals with the SDGs: partnerships such as the Global Challenges University Alliance (CGUA 2030)—a network of universities that share a vision of contributing to the SDGs—demonstrate how institutions can collaboratively address SDG 13 (Climate Action) and promote SDG 4 (Quality Education) through open-access knowledge sharing while continuing to navigate the pressures of global competition. Whether acting as strategic tools for advancement, frameworks for expanding access, or as a means of advocating for fundamental change, internationalization efforts are enhanced through the deliberate inclusion of the SDGs. As Cai & Leask (2024) argue, new paradigms in the internationalization of higher education are not only possible but necessary.[4]

The economic—education paradox strengthens the argument for a critical stance on internationalization. The field may be more profoundly shaped by market forces than is commonly acknowledged, potentially reproducing, or exacerbating global inequities (Stier, 2004; Beck, 2021; Buckner & Stein, 2020; Stein et al., 2016; Pashby & De Oliveira Andreotti, 2016). Critical internationalization advocates a fundamental reevaluation, challenging institutions to realign their global engagement with the original intent of promoting peace and mutual understanding, rather than primarily pursuing economic priorities (De Wit & Altbach, 2021; Boni & Walker, 2013, 2016). Given the urgency for a critical evaluation of internationalization of higher education considering the paradox between economic and educational priorities, it is important to examine the existing models used to assess and evaluate internationalization efforts.

Existing Evaluation Models of the Internationalization of Higher Education

The current landscape of internationalization is characterized by a variety of evaluation models and frameworks that have been developed to measure the processes, outcomes, and impacts of these initiatives. Understanding the strengths and limitations of existing approaches is vital to developing a more critical perspective on internationalization.

Over the past several decades, numerous scholars have contributed significant models and frameworks for evaluating internationalization. De Wit (1999), Knight (2008), Hudzik and Stohl (2009), Deardorff and Van Gaalen (2012, 2021), Altinay et al. (2019), and others have all contributed important aspects to this phenomenon. These models generally recognize the need to integrate internationalization into the core functions of higher education while emphasizing strategic planning, leadership, and collaborative partnerships.

Important differences in these models are discerned here. Knight's (2008) model is broad and process-oriented, while Hudzik and Stohl's (2009) model offers a more detailed and institution-wide approach. Deardorff and van Gaalen's (2012) model uniquely centers on intercultural competence, while Rudzki's (1995) emphasizes strategic management and continuous improvement. More critical perspectives on internationalization, like Stein et al.'s (2016) articulations, consider global inequities and power dynamics, and Altinay et al.'s (2019) model emphasize entrepreneurial and market-oriented strategies designed to encourage innovation and adaptability.

Evaluating the evolving field of internationalization remains an ongoing challenge. A flexible, context-sensitive, and culturally situated evaluation model is needed to empower institutions to decide what internationalization means for their own culture, context, and internationalization priorities. This is increasingly important as institutions navigate complex economic, ideological, and educational pressures. While existing models provide valuable frameworks, there is an urgency for a more critical and adaptive approach that addresses internationalization of higher education's drift toward market-oriented approaches, which draws away from its primary educational aims.

Organizational Development Phases and Multilevel Indicators of Internationalization

For higher education institutions advancing a mission of internationalization, disrupting conventional academic work may involve an ideological shift from "an ethnocentric" focus on education to one with a "transnational" focus. Culture change or adaptation can be viewed as an organization's movement through historical phases, with each phase representing unique characteristics of internationalization of higher education.

Bartell (2003) analyzes the evolution of internationalization in higher education, drawing parallels with the globalization of business. He describes internationalization as a spectrum, ranging from basic activities like funding study abroad programs to comprehensive processes that transform entire institutions. He identifies four organizational developmental phases:

1 the ethnocentric phase, prevalent in the post-World War II era, where universities maintain a domestic focus with a home-country orientation,
2 the multidomestic phase, characterized by the study abroad movement, where institutions begin to engage with international markets separately,
3 the multinational phase, emerging in the 1980s, marked by bilateral models, increased sensitivity to global pricing, and the establishment of international branch campuses, and
4 the transnational phase, where institutions prioritize high-quality, cost-effective education with cultural adaptability and form global alliances.

Bartell's phases are used here to provide a model for which critical internationalization indicators can be identified across specific dimensions and organized by the university's micro (faculty), meso (deans), and macro (senior leadership) levels inherent in the CRI change model.

Critical internationalization in higher education can be measured across three levels of analysis—micro, meso, and macro. Agnew and VanBalkom's CRI model (2009) provides a framework for assessing an institution's cultural readiness for internationalization at various levels.[5] This assessment then informs the strategic planning process to advance internationalization in alignment with the institution's unique culture and context. When evaluating internationalization, various indicators—assessed as outcomes—can be used to measure progress across the primary functional dimensions of internationalization policies and practices.

Micro-Level (Faculty) Indicators

The most visible and promoted aspects of internationalization include how curricula incorporate global perspectives and how students and faculty engage in intercultural experiences. Scholars emphasize the importance of student and faculty mobility for developing global competencies (Knight, 2012; Rumbley & De Wit, 2017) and global citizenship (Rhoads & Szelényi, 2011). The CRI model suggests that intentional institutional cultures that invite internationalization can more easily embed global perspectives into their curricula and provide opportunities for intercultural research and study.

Another key indicator Gao (2019) identified is participation in international research projects. This aligns with Agnew and VanBalkom's notion of organizational rationality, which stresses the importance of aligning institutional goals such as global research impact with international partnerships. Universities that prioritize and engage in high levels of international collaboration demonstrate a clear commitment to global knowledge production, a strategic approach to enhancing academic excellence on a global scale.

Concerning internationalization at home (IaH), Gao (2019) proposes analyzing the proportion of international staff and students, which connects to the organizational culture dimension from the CRI model. A higher proportion of international students and staff can lead to a more multicultural and inclusive campus environment. While it can reflect an institution's commitment to diversity and the cross-pollination of cultural perspectives, it can also highlight an institution's commitment to the global knowledge economy by means of benefiting from international student tuition. Often, it is both.

Further, the internationalization of curriculum (IoC) is a recognized indicator in broader literature (Agnew, 2012; Bulnes & de Louw, 2022; Eftekhari et al., 2025; Knight, 2004). Santos (2014, 2018, 2024) posits that to dutifully provide the tools to study and engage with global challenges critically, the curriculum must include and feature non-Western epistemologies, challenging dominant paradigms and promoting equitable knowledge exchange. Embedding international and intercultural dimensions within the curriculum can also fall under organizational rationality in Agnew and VanBalkom's model, as it strategically integrates global competencies into the university's educational mission. Without this intention and critical engagement, internationalization risks reinforcing established global hierarchies and perpetuating exclusionary practices in higher education.

Meso-Level (Deans) Indicators

Agnew and VanBalkom's CRI model places institutional leadership and governance at the academic unit level (e.g., Faculty/School) as critical elements at the meso level, an organizational level that also necessitates an institutional commitment. De Wit (2012) emphasizes that governance structures should be designed to foster broad stakeholder engagement and allocate resources strategically for internationalization. Similarly, George S. Yip (1989, 2001), a business scholar whose work has been adapted to higher education, highlights that institutions must develop coherent internationalization strategies, especially in resource management and leadership.

Institutions with adaptive structures and strategic power can better respond to global changes and foster an environment conducive to internationalization. Knight's (2001) Internationalization Quality Review Process (IQRP) advocates internal assessment systems that track the integration of internationalization into governance and leadership practices. Institutions that fail to adapt their governance systems will remain stuck in a resistive culture with a rigid structure, unable to fully engage with global opportunities.

In line with Stein's critical lens, governance models must not simply adopt global trends without questioning their ethical implications, especially regarding equity and power dynamics in international collaborations. Effective internationalization at the meso level requires institutional commitment, strategic resource allocation, and adaptive governance structures that engage diverse stakeholders and integrate internationalization into core practices.

Macro-Level (Senior Leadership) Indicators

At the macro level, internationalization is driven by overarching global policies and international partnerships that shape the educational landscape. As Stein et al. (2016) consistently point out, this approach to internationalization inherently engages with power dynamics and questions embedded in global higher education policies. Scholars such as Jane Knight (2008, 2015) and Ulrich Teichler (2012, 2017) focus on how institutions navigate global agreements such as the Bologna Process and the growing concern of global rankings. Knight, notably, has emphasized that internationalization is not merely a reaction to globalization but a strategic process that embeds an international dimension into institutional strategies (2008). Philip Altbach (2015), along with Reisberg and Rumbley (2009) and Salmi (2011), contributes by critiquing how Western-centric models dominate these global trends, thus often marginalizing the perspectives and participation of Global South institutions.

In Agnew and VanBalkom's CRI model, the macro-level indicators include cross-border partnerships and policies, aligning with Bartell's (2003) typology of transnational partnerships. Institutions with organizational cultures that invite internationalization will form sustained multilateral collaborations and base their decisions on multicultural perspectives, reflecting openness to diverse global influences. Stein et al.'s (2016) analysis notes that, at the macro level, institutions should challenge Western-centric international policies to prevent reinforcing inequities and promote a more equitable global knowledge exchange. More recently, global university rankings have emerged as a measure of internationalization (Yudkevich et al., 2016; De Wit & Altbach, 2021). However, these rankings require scrutiny, as they can reveal institutions that prioritize their own interests over the equitable development of universities worldwide.

Integrating Equity and Reflection in the Evaluation of Internationalization

Stein's et al. (2016) critique of internationalization as reinforcing global inequities serves as an important reminder for institutions to address the perpetuation patterns of global inequities. The CRI model's focus on an institution's readiness for internationalization aligns with Stein's argument, provided institutions approach internationalization with critical self-reflection at all organizational levels. Stein's caution underscores the risk that when internationalization is driven solely by economic motives or the pursuit of global prestige, it can foster ethnocentrism, as described by Sumner (1906), rather than achieving the educational goals that the CRI model ideally supports.

Jane Knight (2004) contributes a nuanced perspective by distinguishing between "internationalization at home" and "internationalization abroad." While many indicators, such as student and staff mobility, focus on the latter, Knight emphasizes that curriculum change and internal policies—aligned with Agnew and VanBalkom's view of organizational culture—are equally essential for embedding internationalization into the institution's DNA.

Similarly, De Wit (2002) advocates for a comprehensive approach integrating mobility-focused indicators with internal cultural reforms. This perspective aligns with Agnew and VanBalkom's comprehensive approach in the CRI model, emphasizing that isolated metrics, such as student mobility are insufficient indicators for genuine internationalization. Instead, De Wit and Knight argue for a cohesive strategy that includes governance, curriculum development, and partnerships, resonating with Agnew and VanBalkom's strategic outlook. This approach also echoes Stein's (2017) critique: institutions must go beyond quantifiable metrics like the number of partnerships or programs and critically evaluate whose knowledge is being valued and prioritized.

Stein's critique reinforces the idea that moving from a resistive to an inviting culture is a two-way process, requiring institutions to embrace global engagement while questioning whose interests this engagement serves. Together, the CRI model (2009) and Stein et al.'s work (2016) provide a robust framework for evaluating higher education internationalization across micro (faculty), meso (deans), and macro (senior leadership) levels of the university. By assessing the primary functional domains of internationalization, such as global partnerships, national policies, institutional governance, leadership, and curricula, universities can work toward internationalization strategies that promote cultural readiness, equity, and inclusivity in their internationalization policies and practices.

A Critical Integrated Framework for Evaluation of Internationalization of Higher Education

A critical framework that combines multiple perspectives is needed to evaluate higher education internationalization. The proposed approach integrates Stein et al.'s (2016) four articulations of internationalization with Agnew and VanBalkom's Cultural Readiness model, highlighting indicators at the micro (faculty), meso (deans), and macro (senior leadership) levels. Buckner & Stein's (2020) notable article "What Counts as Internationalization" contributes to this framework, particularly their analysis of how internationalization is discussed by the three largest professional associations in international education: NAFSA, the International Association of Universities (IAU), and the European Association for International Education (EAIE). Their research revealed a concerning pattern—these organizations tend to frame internationalization as "apolitical and largely divorced from broader discussions of historical or geopolitical inequities, ethical responsibilities, and alternative possibilities for engaging with and across difference" (Buckner & Stein, 2020, p. 152). In response to these limitations, they propose a more nuanced understanding of internationalization as an approach to encountering difference:

> We argue that internationalization should be understood as an approach to "encountering difference" and perhaps, as a way to "encounter difference *differently*," that opens up possibilities for examining and re-examining biases, stereotypes, and hegemonic assumptions about ways of being and knowing. In line with this argument, we would ask administrators to reflect on questions such as the following: What are you measuring? What assumptions and investments are reflected in those measurements? To what extent are the outcomes of internationalization framed in terms of "acquiring" knowledges about places and peoples, rather than "deconstructing" assumed knowledge, and "opening up" new possibilities for relating to ourselves and the world in ways that account for our differences *and* interdependencies?
>
> (Buckner & Stein, p. 164)

The Cultural Readiness for Internationalization (CRI) model integrates with Buckner and Stein's approach to internationalization as a means of "encountering difference" and their call for critical reflection. This approach manifests through four key dimensions. First, it examines how different stakeholder groups (faculty, deans, senior leadership) understand and value internationalization, including their beliefs, values, and underlying assumptions. Second, it analyzes leadership and governance across three organizational levels. Third, it places institutional context and culture at the center of analysis. Finally, it explores the dynamic reciprocity of influence between the internal operations and external forces. Through these dimensions, the CRI model provides a comprehensive framework for understanding an institution's readiness for meaningful internationalization to specific institutions in preparation for future planning.

The CRI model helps institutions analyze their approach to Stein et al.'s (2016) four distinct articulations of internationalization—global knowledge economy, global public good, anti-oppressive, and relational transnationalism. By examining internationalization through these lenses, institutions can critically evaluate their assumptions, values, and beliefs that directly inform their practices. The model's focus on transforming organizational culture enables institutions to "deconstruct" their existing approaches and explore new possibilities for critical internationalization. This aligns with Buckner and Stein's (2020) call for more reflective engagement with internationalization practices. The CRI model provides a structured framework for institutions to undertake this critical self-examination.

Primary functional areas are provided as examples at each institutional level of analysis. At the micro level, faculty members implement internationalization directly through their teaching, research, and service work. They facilitate student and staff mobility programs, develop internationalized curricula, and create inter- and multi-cultural experiences for students. At the meso level, academic deans are responsible for leadership and management at the academic unit level. For example, they guide research and academic activities, engage in strategic planning, provide leadership and governance within their units, and manage budget and human resources. At the macro level, senior leadership focuses on broad institutional priorities. They have responsibility for campus-wide leadership and governance, lead strategic planning and resource allocation, oversee institutional assessment systems, and develop both local and global partnerships. This tiered structure ensures that internationalization efforts are coordinated collectively from institutional-level strategy through to classroom teaching and learning.

In the remainder of this section, functional domains are provided for each of the three organizational levels of analysis—micro, meso, and macro—which align with Stein et al.'s (2016) four articulations of internationalization.

Micro-level functional domains are the most visible indicators expressed by Stein et al.'s (2016) four articulations of internationalization (Table 10.2). These domains, such as mobility, program content and structure, and cultural engagement at home and abroad, visibly indicate an institutional commitment to internationalization to external observers. Within a Global Knowledge Economy framework, faculty, students, and staff

TABLE 10.2 Micro-Level Functional Domains with Sample Evaluative Questions

Micro-Level Analysis

Global Knowledge Economy (GKE), Global Public Good (GPG), Anti-oppressive (AO), Relational Translocalism (RT)

Functional Domains	Sample Framing Questions To what extent is the focus of internationalization activities on:
Mobility (students and staff)	• mobility that enhances institutional prestige and student/staff marketability? (GKE) • mobility as a means of promoting global understanding and shared knowledge creation? (GPG) • addressing inequalities in access to mobility opportunities? (AO) • fostering *long-term*, reciprocal mobility program? (RT)
Program Structure and Content	• programs that meet global market demands & enhancing employability? (GKE) • curriculum design that promotes international cooperation? (GPG) • Western-centric curricula and promoting diverse knowledge systems and perspectives? (AO) • collaborative program development with international partners, integrating multiple cultural perspectives? (RT)
Cultural Engagement	• intercultural skills as a competitive advantage in the global job market? (GKE) • cultural engagement as a means of promoting global citizenship and mutual understanding? (GPG) • cultural dominance and promoting equal valuation of diverse cultural perspectives in education? (AO) • deep, reciprocal cultural exchanges that transform educational practices and perspectives? (RT)

mobility initiatives enhance competitive advantage, global prestige, and marketability. In contrast, Global Public Good approaches aim to foster a global community. This is accomplished through programming that promotes mutual understanding, supports shared knowledge creation, and inclusively addresses global challenges. The third articulation, Anti-Oppressive Internationalization, addresses power dynamics and examines

TABLE 10.3 Meso-Level Functional Domains with Sample Evaluative Questions

Meso-Level Analysis	
Global Knowledge Economy (GKE), Global Public Good (GPG), Anti-oppressive (AO), Relational Translocalism (RT)	
Functional Domains	**Sample Framing Questions** To what extent is the focus of internationalization activities on:
Research and Academic Activities	• research to enhance prestige in rankings? (GKE) • research to promote open access and knowledge sharing? (GPG) • research that addresses power imbalances? (AO) • research that prioritizes marginalized voices and perspectives? (RT)
Strategic Planning and Governance	• aimed at attracting international talent and resources? (GKE) • creating inclusive governance structures that promote collaborative decision-making? (GPG) • implementing planning and governance approaches that actively promote transparency? (AO) • design governance structures that reflect complex global interconnections and diverse cultural perspectives? (RT)
Leadership and Human Resources	• recruiting and developing faculty with strong international reputations to boost institutional competitiveness? (GKE) • developing leadership and faculty with a global orientation? (GPG) • prioritizing diverse leadership and faculty recruitment? (AO) • nurturing leaders and faculty capable of building and sustaining complex global relationships? (RT)

how mobility programs, for example, address inequities and access at home and abroad. The final articulation, Relational Translocalism, advocates for centering interdependence to expand imaginaries of existence beyond what is currently possible. At the individual level for example, this articulation of internationalization aims for disillusionment and disenchantment with existing imaginaries, relationships, and existence which bring about internationalization practices that are yet to be imagined.

At the meso level, Stein et al.'s (2016) four articulations of internationalization focus on the academic unit (Table 10.3). The Global Knowledge Economy articulation prioritizes significant research and development initiatives, such as developing faculty and leaders with global reputations. This commitment often guides strategic planning toward competitive, revenue-generating fields, with leadership and human resources policies incentivizing productivity and global rankings. By improving rankings and overall reputation, institutions can attract top international talent and thereby secure significant revenue.

Global Public Good articulation reorient governance to support research, for example, on broad social issues, such as climate change and health, with leadership promoting policies that balance global and local impact to foster equitable development. Examples include promoting open-access knowledge sharing and dedication to cross-cultural collaboration, especially for underserved groups.

Anti-Oppressive Internationalization critiques dominant models of internationalization by encouraging governance structures to dismantle inequitable practices and decolonize curricula and research, for example. This can be accomplished by recruiting faculty, staff, and leadership from diverse backgrounds and promoting transparent, inclusive communication practices.

Finally, the Relational Translocalism articulation redefines governance and leadership by emphasizing the centering of interdependence and reimaging new realities in which unlearning will destabilize organizational norms. In this way, marginalized knowledge will be revitalized. It promotes academic activities that prioritize relational knowledge-sharing and respect of local contexts over competitive gain. In other words, institutions should design strategic plans and internationalization efforts that center diverse perspectives and epistemologies.

At the macro level, Stein et al.'s (2016) four articulations of internationalization are expressed in the institution's organizational structure, including its leadership, governance, and strategic partnerships (Table 10.4). Global Knowledge Economy approaches leadership and governance toward resource allocation that maximizes economic return. In the case of partnerships, for example, this often favors agreements that align with broader institutional market-driven goals. Further, the assessment metrics institutions use focus intently on overall institutional impact, especially global rankings, and research outcomes.

The Global Public Good pillar highlights collective well-being, emphasizing knowledge-sharing, inclusive access, and aligning resources toward investments that benefit the community. Assessments under this pillar would focus on gauging the social impact of internationalization efforts. Anti-Oppressive Internationalization encourages leadership and governance to question the many inequities surrounding internationalization efforts, prioritizing partnerships that amplify marginalized voices or otherwise aim to decolonize institutional practices. Finally, Relational

TABLE 10.4 Macro-Level Functional Domains with Sample Evaluative Questions

Macro-Level Analysis

Global Knowledge Economy (GKE), Global Public Good (GPG), Anti-oppressive (AO), Relational Translocalism (RT)

Functional Domains	Sample Framing Questions To what extent is the focus of internationalization activities on:
Leadership & Governance	• a competitive market positioning of the institution? (GKE) • emphasizing cooperation and knowledge sharing? (GPG) • addressing systemic power imbalances? (AO) • centering interdependence? (RT)
Strategic Planning & Resource Allocation	• prioritizing economic advantage and rankings? (GKE) • expanding opportunities for social mobility? (GPG) • allocation of resources to address historical inequities? (AO) • allocate resources to trace patterns of systemic violence? (RT)
Institutional Assessment System	• metrics return on investment and employability? (GKE) • assessing contribution to global challenges (e.g., SDGs) (GPG) • incorporating diverse voices in assessment design? (AO) • assessing cultural competence of students and staff? (RT)
Local and International Partnerships (global community)	• partnerships that lead to commodification and innovation? (GKE) • partnerships that promote knowledge sharing? (GPG) • partnerships that address internal power imbalances & inequities? (AO) • partnerships that connect local institutional contexts to global narratives? (RT)

Translocalism directs governance to critically rethink strategic planning to value localized partnerships that foster global communities based on mutual respect rather than historical hierarchies. These macro-level indicators illustrate an institution's broader values in global education that ultimately maintain or reconfigure global dynamics.

This integrated framework offers a comprehensive, multilevel evaluation of an institution's internationalization strategies situated in the critiques of internationalization. In using this framework, institutions can align their international policies and practices, specific to their own organizational culture and context. Further, they can identify how and where their internationalization practices perpetuate or challenge existing global inequities and develop strategies to address them. Because multiple ideologies operate simultaneously, it is likely that individual and group responses reflecting internationalization activities will be represented in one or more of the articulations of internationalization.

Conclusion

The primary goals in creating this critical evaluation framework are to:

1 address the rising economic and political concerns in the practice of internationalization,
2 to ensure measurements of internationalization go beyond a simple inventory of activities,
3 to provide higher education leadership with a framework to guide more ethical practices of internationalization on their campuses and, importantly,
4 maintain higher education that serves in the betterment of society.

This chapter emphasized the necessity of adopting a critical approach to evaluating internationalization within higher education to uphold its long-standing educational mission amidst the challenges posed by market-driven forces. The pervasive influence of the market economy often obscures the foundational academic values of higher education institutions. By integrating critical perspectives like those articulated by Stein et al. (2016) with Agnew and VanBalkom's Cultural Readiness for Internationalization (CRI) model (2009), institutions are better equipped to temper market forces and contribute to a more equitable and inclusive global academic landscape.

Implications for Ethical Policies and Practices

1 *Rising Economic and Political Concerns*: Address the rising economic and political concerns in the practice of internationalization, ensuring that market-driven goals do not supersede the educational mission of higher education.
2 *Beyond Metrics*: Ensure measurements of internationalization go beyond a simple inventory of activities, and instead critically evaluate the underlying motivations and outcomes of these efforts.

3 *Empower Higher Education*: Develop a framework to guide more ethical practices of internationalization, empowering them to make informed decisions that prioritize academic values over economic interests.
4 *Internationalization as the Fourth Mission of Higher Education*: Maintain higher education's role in its fourth mission to serve in the betterment of society by aligning internationalization strategies with the United Nations Sustainable Development Goals.
5. *Temper Market Forces*: Prioritize educational mission and social responsibility over economic gains in internationalization, aligning global initiatives with the fundamental values of higher education.
6 *Take a Critical Stance*: Critically evaluate an institution's underlying assumptions, values, and beliefs (systems) that inform internationalization practices, identifying potential biases that perpetuate the reproduction of harmful ongoing global patterns of educational engagement.
7 *Self-reflexivity*: Promote critical self-examination of existing internationalization approaches and practices, encouraging institutions to unlearn harmful attachments and experiment with alternative ways of engaging globally.
8 *Impacts of Internationalization*: Examine how internationalization perpetuates or challenges global inequities, with a focus on power dynamics, marginalized perspectives, and the decolonization of knowledge production.

Notes

1 See Chapters 1 and 2 for deeper discussion of Stein et al.'s (2016) four articulations of internationalization.
2 See Chapter 1 for deeper discussion of the Cultural Readiness for Internationalization (CRI) change model.
3 See Chapter 11 on an in-depth discussion on internationalization as the emerging fourth macro mission of higher education.
4 See Chapter 11 for deeper discussion of postmodernism and higher education.
5 See Chapter 1 for a deeper discussion of the Cultural Readiness for Internationalization (CRI) change model.

References

Agnew, M (2012). Strategic planning: An examination of the role of the disciplines in sustaining internationalization of the university. *Journal of Studies in Internationalization*, 17(2),183–202.
Agnew, M. (2021). *In conversation with Melanie Agnew*. Internationalization for All: Distributed Leadership in International Education. European Association for International Education. Fall Forum (Invited).
Agnew, M. & Van Balkom, W. D. (2009). Internationalization of the university: Factors impacting cultural readiness for organizational change. *Intercultural Education*, 20(5), 451–462.

Altbach, P. G. (2015). The Carnegie classification of American higher education: More—and less—Than meets the eye. *International Higher Education*, 80, 21–23. https://doi.org/10.6017/ihe.2015.80.6127

Altbach, P. G., Reisberg, L. and Rumbley, L. E. (2009). Trends in global higher education: Tracking an academic revolution. *UNESCO 2009 World Conference on Higher Education*, Paris, 5–8 July 2009.

Altbach, P. G., & Salmi, J. (Eds.). (2011). The road to academic excellence: The making of world-class research universities. Direction in development; human development. World Bank. http://hdl.handle.net/10986/2357 License: CC BY 3.0 IGO.

Altinay, F., Basari, G., Altinay, M., Dagli, G., & Altinay, Z. (2019). An evaluation of strategies and policies in higher education management in internationalization process: New pedagogy. *Revista Romaneasca pentru Educatie Multidimensionala*, 11(4), 304–320. https://doi.org/10.18662/rrem/171

Bartell, M. (2003). Internationalization of universities: A university culture-based framework. *Higher Education*, 45, 43–70.

Beck, K. (2021). Beyond internationalization: Lessons from post-development. *Journal of International Studies*, 11(S1), 133–151.

Biesta, G. (2009). Good education in an age of measurement: on the need to reconnect with the question of purpose in education. *Educational Assessment, Evaluation and Accountability*, 21, 33–46. https://doi.org/10.1007/s11092-008-9064-9

Boni, A., & Walker, M. (2013). *Human development and capabilities: Re-imagining the university of the twenty-first century*. Taylor & Francis.

Boni, A., & Walker, M. (2016). *Universities and global human development: Theoretical and empirical insights for social change*. Taylor & Francis.

Buckner, E., & Stein, S. (2020). What counts as internationalization? Deconstructing the internationalization imperative. *Journal of Studies in International Education*, 24(2), 151–166.

Bulnes, C., & de Louw, E. (2022). Towards a typology of internationalisation at home activities in academic disciplines: A study conducted at a Dutch university of applied sciences. *Compare: A Journal of Comparative and International Education*, 52 1–20.

Cai, Y., & Leask, B. (2024). Rethinking internationalization of higher education for society from an outside-in perspective. *Journal of Asian Public Policy*, 1–19. https://doi.org/10.1080/17516234.2024.2406093

De Wit, H. (1999). Changing rationales for the internationalization of higher education. *International Higher Education*, 15. https://doi.org/10.6017/ihe.1999.15.6477

De Wit, H. (2002). *Internationalization of higher education in the United States of America and Europe: A historical, comparative, and conceptual analysis*, Greenwood Press.

De Wit, H. (2012). Student mobility between Europe and the rest of the world: Trends, issues and challenges. In A. Curaj, P. Scott, L. Vlasceanu, & L. Wilson (Eds.), *European higher education at the crossroads*. Springer. https://doi.org/10.1007/978-94-007-3937-6_24

De Wit, H., & Altbach, P. G. (2021). Internationalization in higher education: Global trends and recommendations for its future. *Policy Reviews in Higher Education*, 5(1), 28–46. https://doi.org/10.1080/23322969.2020.1820898

Deardorff, D. K., & van Gaalen, A. (2012). Outcomes assessment in international higher education. In D. K. Deardorff, H. de Wit, J. D. Heyl, & T. Adams (Eds.), *The Sage handbook of international higher education* SAGE Publications. .

Deardorff, D. K., & van Gaalen, A. (2021). Assessing internationalization outcomes. In D. Deardorff, H. de Wit, B. Leask, & H. Charles (Eds.), *Handbook of International Higher Education* (2nd ed.). Stylus.

Eftekhari, P., Coelen, R., & Yousefzadeh, S. (2025, in press). *Internationalization of the curriculum at home (IoCaH): Why academic disciplines matter.* Journal of Studies in International Education. Manuscript under review. https://doi.org/10.1177/10283153241307967

Gao, C. Y. (2019). *Measuring university internationalization: Indicators across national contexts.* Springer International Publishing.

Hazelkorn, E. (2015). *Rankings and the reshaping of higher education: The battle for world-class excellence*Palgrave Macmillan.

Hudzik, J., & Stohl, M. (2009). Modelling assessment of the outcomes and impacts of internationalisation. In H. de Wit (Ed.), *Measuring success in the internationalisation of higher education* (pp. 9–21). European Association for International Education.

Knight, J. (2001). Monitoring quality and progress of internationalization. *Journal of Studies in International Education, 5*(3), 228–243.

Knight, J. (2004). Internationalization remodeled: Rationales, strategies and approaches. *Journal for Studies in International Education, 8*(1), 5–31.

Knight, J. (2008). The internationalization of higher education in the 21 century: New realities and complexities. In *Higher education in Turmoil: The changing world of internationalization.* https://doi.org/10.1163/9789087905224_002

Knight, J. (2012). Student mobility and internationalization: Trends and tribulations. *Research in Comparative and International Education, 7*(1), 20–33. https://doi.org/10.2304/rcie.2012.7.1.20

Knight, J. (2015). International universities: Misunderstandings and emerging models? *Journal of Studies in International Education, 19*(2), 107–121. https://doi.org/10.1177/1028315315572899

Marginson, S. (2016). *Higher education and the common good.* Melbourne University Publishing.

Marinoni, G., & Cardona, S. (2024). *Internationalization of higher education: Current trends and future scenarios.* 6th IAU Global Survey Report. UNESCO House.

Mignolo, W. (2011). *The darker side of western modernity: Global futures, decolonial options.* Duke University Press.

Pashby, K., & De Oliveira Andreotti, V. (2016). Ethical internationalisation in higher education: Interfaces with international development and sustainability. *Environmental Education Research, 22*(6), 771–787. https://doi.org/10.1080/13504622.2016.1201789

Rhoads, R., & Szelényi, K. (2011). *Global citizenship and the university: Advancing social life and relations in an interdependent world.* Stanford University Press.

Rudzki, R. E. J. (1995). The application of a strategic management model to the internationalization of higher education institutions. *Higher Education, 29*(4), 421–441. https://doi.org/10.1007/BF01383961

Rumbley, L. E., & de Wit, H. (2017). International faculty mobility: Crucial and understudied. *International Higher Education,* 88 6–8.

Santos, B. D. S. (2014). *Epistemologies of the south: Justice against epistemicide* (1st ed.). Routledge. https://doi.org/10.4324/9781315634876

Santos, B. D. S. (2018). *The end of the cognitive empire: The coming of age of epistemologies of the south.* Duke University Press.

Santos, B. D. S. (2024). The epistemologies of the south and the future of the university. *Journal of Philosophy of Education, 58*(2–3), 166–188, https://doi.org/10.1093/jopedu/qhad038

Schein, E. (1993). Defining organizational culture. In J. M. Shafritz, S. Ott, & Y. S. Jang (Eds.), *Classics of organization theory* (pp. 360–367). Thomson Wadsworth.

Scott, J. C. (2006). The mission of the university: Medieval to postmodern transformations. *The Journal of Higher Education*, 77(1), 1–39. https://doi.org/10.1080/00221546.2006.11778917

Stein, S. (2017). Internationalization for an uncertain future: Tensions, paradoxes, and possibilities. *The Review of Higher Education*, 41(1), 3–32. https://doi.org/10.1353/rhe.2017.0031

Stein, S., Andreotti, V., Bruce, J., & Suša, R. (2016). Towards different conversations about the internationalization of higher education. *Comparative and International Education*, 45(1). 1–18

Stier, J. (2004). Taking a critical stance toward internationalization ideologies in higher education: Idealism, instrumentalism and educationalism. *Globalisation, Societies and Education*, 2(1), 1–28. https://doi.org/10.1080/1476772042000177069

Sumner, W. G. (1906). *Folkways: A study of the sociological importance of usages, manners, customs, mores, and morals*. Ginn & Company.

Teichler, U. (2012). International student mobility and the bologna process. *Research in Comparative and International Education*, 7(1), 34–49. https://doi.org/10.2304/rcie.2012.7.1.34

Teichler, U. (2017). Internationalization trends in higher education and the changing role of international student mobility. *Journal of International Mobility*, 4, 177–216.

Tomàs-Folch, M. (2015). Trends in higher education rankings. *Conference: The Twenty-First International Conference on Learning, The Learner.*

Yip, G. S. (1989). Global strategy … In a world of nations? *Sloan Management Review*, 31(1), 29–41.

Yip, G. S. (2001). *Total global strategy* (2nd ed.). Prentice Hall PTR.

Yudkevich, M., Altbach, P., & Rumbley, L. (Eds.). (2016). *The global academic rankings game: Changing institutional policy, practice, and academic life*. Routledge. https://doi.org/10.4324/9781315677170

11

LEADERSHIP

A Call to Action

Melanie Agnew and Moreen Carvan

Introduction: Universities Have Always Been an International Organization

The medieval university's organizational structure was unique, featuring groups called "nations" that included both students and professors. International students and professors historically possessed a special birthright within universities. In the earliest university environments, participants naturally grouped themselves according to their national or regional origins, which led to the formation of these "nations". As noted by Schachner (1938), "the origins and early development of these groups remained largely obscure, with even their fundamental constitution being a matter of scholarly debate until relatively recently" (p. 74).

While both students and professors belonged to "nations" (medieval university groupings), historians believe that masters mainly included scholars in these organized groups to keep them safe. The nations were especially important for protecting students. As Daley (1961) describes, a nation can be understood as "a subdivision within the 'university' of out-of-town students who have banded together for mutual protection, help, and collective security against local authorities" (p. 30). One of the oldest universities, the University of Bologna, for instance, had nations "composed of non-Bolognese students only, originating probably as voluntary organizations of students from the same districts, who would naturally tend to join together" (Daley, 1961, p. 33).

Each nation had an administrative leader—an elected proctor—who managed the group's financial affairs, university-related business, and most importantly, looked after its members' interests (Schachner, 1938). By virtue of "nations", universities have historically been an international organization (Agnew, 2008).

Internationalization Resurfacing to Center

Internationalization is evolving from a peripheral activity to a core strategic mission in higher education, once again. There are current trends, however, that reveal significant challenges. While student mobility is often prioritized, many institutions lack a comprehensive strategic approach to internationalization (De Wit & Altbach, 2021). The benefits of internationalization have largely privileged elite groups of students, faculty, and institutions, driven by economic interests and market forces (Buckner and Stein, 2020; Pashby & De Oliveira Andreotti, 2016; Stein et al., 2016; Stier, 2004). These forces are visibly expressed at the individual, institutional, regional, and national levels resulting in what Agnew terms *internationalization drift*.

Internationalization drift refers to how internationalization is deviating from its foundational educational and societal purposes (like cultural exchange, global citizenship, and mutual understandings) and privileging market goals. Internationalization of higher education has become disconnected from its "anchor" of educational mission and social responsibility, guided by external *market forces*. In the process, dominant market forces fuel the perpetuation of inequities and power imbalances that sustain harmful historical patterns of global engagement. This situation demands leaders with deep knowledge of higher education, internationalization, and transformative leadership to ensure higher education serves in the betterment of society.

Recent data underscores the need for leadership. The IAU 2024 Global Survey Report reveals that over four-fifths of institutions have increased their focus on international engagement in the past five years, with a third reporting substantial growth and half noting moderate increases in strategic importance (Marinoni & Cardona, 2024). Furthermore, the purpose of international engagement is gaining prominence as a strategy to address the United Nations Sustainable Development Goals (Cai & Leask, 2024; De Wit & Altbach, 2021; Marinoni & Cardona, 2024).

The increased growth in the global engagement of higher education and its focus on solving complex global problems further positions it as higher education's emerging fourth macro mission.

University Missions

Every society, in its own time, must study the complex questions concerning the purposes of education not once and for all, but as well and as conscientiously as it can for the benefit of its people, and for the earth, now and in the future (Noddings, 1995). The university as a social organization is continuously in construction in its response to the society in which it finds itself. A modern university must recreate itself on a regular basis to ensure the relevancy of its purpose (Frank & Gabler, 2006). The "re-creation" includes shifting its mission to internationalization as the fourth macro mission to ensure it remains relevant to its purpose of serving in the best interests of society, locally and globally.

The emergence of a new macro mission of education is a profound historical process that can span decades and even centuries. As history demonstrates, the transition between major educational philosophies—such as from scholasticism to humanism or from humanism to postmodernism—is not abrupt but very gradual. During this transition, multiple educational mission co-exists, with the emerging philosophy gaining societal acceptance while the previous mission continues to influence before eventually fading out.

The transition from the humanistic educational mission to postmodernism is similarly complex and time-dependent. While the exact duration of this transition cannot be precisely predicted, historical precedent (Scott, 2006) suggests that such a philosophy shift could take a century or more to fully manifest and be embraced by society. This pattern of transition is evident in our current historical moment.

The same holds true now.

Stages of Transformation of the University Mission

One of the greatest achievements of the Middle Ages was the organization of the university, complete with its traditions, studies, progress, and intellectual development, which had a profound influence on Europe and, indeed, the development of Western civilization (Agnew, 2008). The evolution of higher education's philosophical foundations can be traced through three distinct periods—scholasticism, humanism, and postmodernism, each characterized by its own intellectual philosophy. The first of these periods was shaped by Scholasticism, which emerged during the medieval era and laid the groundwork for formal university education (Scott, 2006) (Table 11.1).

Scholasticism

Scholasticism, the dominant philosophical approach from the 12th to 15th centuries, emerged as the medieval method of learning before the rise of nation-states. This approach was characterized by logical reasoning and

TABLE 11.1 Scott's (2006) Stages of Transformation of the University Mission

Stages	Pre-nation	Nation-state	Globalization
Time Period	12th–15th century	16th–20th century	21st century
Universities' Missions	Teaching	Teaching *Nationalism* *Democratization* *Public Service*	Teaching Nationalism Democratization Public Service *Internationalization*
Philosophy	Scholasticism	Humanism	Postmodernism

dialectical methods, the harmonization of classical philosophy (particularly Aristotle) with Christian theology, systematic organization of knowledge, and the use of formal debate and inquiry. The movement developed from a fundamental tension between two intellectual approaches: 1) Abelard's emphasis on reason and 2) Anselm's focus on mysticism. Abelard was a prominent French philosopher, theologian, and logician who was one of the most important intellectual figures of the early Medieval period. He is renowned for his emphasis on rational inquiry and dialectical reasoning (King & Arlig, 2022.). Anselm was a brilliant and controversial scholar who championed the power of reasoning in understanding theological concepts (Williams, 2023). As Rashdall (1936) notes, this conflict shaped early university education, "With Abelard the great scholastic movement reaches a point at which it begins to identify itself with what we may call the university movement" (p. 43).

When philosophical methodologies were incorporated into theological study, Aristotelian dialectic experienced a revival. This development marked a crucial shift. Reason began to stand alongside Authority as a legitimate source of understanding. Schachner (1938) describes Abelard's revolutionary approach. All things

> [Abelard] insisted, must prove amenable to the active processes of the mind, to the rigorous following of major premise, minor premise, and conclusion; event the sacrosanct articles of theology. Nothing was immune from his method; he must understand in order to believe.
> *(p. 33)*

This intellectual transformation, combining Scholastic methods with renewed Aristotelian dialectic, ultimately led to the establishment of the university system and to the systematic organization of knowledge and use of formal disputation and questioning.

Humanism

In the early modern period (16th–20th century), humanism was the dominant philosophy actuated, in part, by the Enlightenment period and consequentially, secularization. During the nation-state stage, universities emphasized nationalization (German origin) and democratization (American origin), in addition to the teaching mission. It had a focus on human potential and achievement, revival of classical learning and literature, emphasis on individual dignity and worth, and belief in education as a means of human development.

Humanism emerged as a philosophical framework with distinct views on the universe, human nature, and the resolution of human challenges. Its influence on higher education was significant. "During early modern times, humanism took root in the universities of Europe and Latin America. Later, following the doctrine of Wilhelm von Humboldt, the neo-humanist German university of the 19th century promoted original inquiry" (Scott, 2006, p. 3). The "modern" refers to strongly held assumptions both in and out of academia regarding the core values of the Enlightenment: the centrality of reason, the belief in progress, the virtues of individualism, and faith in the scientific method (Bloland, 2005, p. 122). The task of humanism is to "organize into a consistent and intelligible whole the chief elements of philosophical truth and to make that synthesis a powerful force and reality in the minds and actions of living persons" (LaMont, 1997, p.13). Humanists believe, among other things, in metaphysics, laws of science, the state of welfare of the community, they appreciate the aesthetics of nature and believe in a far-reaching social program of democracy and peace (Bloland, 2005; LaMont, 1997).

Postmodernism

The philosophy that *is* characterizing the globalization stage (21st century) is postmodernism. Postmodernism reflects skepticism toward grand narratives and universal truths recognition of multiple perspectives and relativism, questioning of traditional authority and knowledge structures, emphasis on diversity and plurality of viewpoints, and the critical approach to knowledge construction (Crişan, 2019; Nguyen, 2010; Wheatley, 2021).

The early 21st century marks a transformative period in education, characterized by several key developments: new debates about education's purpose and relevance in a global economy, emerging competitive markets that challenge institutional autonomy, threats to institutions' public service commitments, potential constraints on the free pursuit of knowledge, and opportunities for innovative educational approaches (Crişan, 2019;

Williams & Marsh, 2008). In this globalized context, internationalization is emerging as the defining macro mission of 21st-century education (Scott, 2006).

Scott (2006) identifies the 21st-century university as distinctly postmodern. Postmodernism functions as both an intellectual movement and a critical lens that challenges modernist assumptions, using structural analysis to reveal the scientific principles underlying social organization. Bloland (2005) describes this postmodern age as a period when "transformation is taking place that involves how we think, understand, and live in a knowledge-saturated society and in a changing culture" (p. 127).

Postmodernist scholars envision higher education evolving into a flexible, global network capable of adapting to rapid change (Scott, 2006). While postmodernists argue against grand narratives, higher education remains largely bound by traditional scientific and knowledge frameworks. However, the system faces increasing vulnerability: market pressures threaten institutional autonomy (Morrow, 2006) and potentially compromise universities' privilege and responsibility to serve the public interest.

The progression clearly demonstrates how universities' philosophical underpinnings have evolved from medieval religious-focused scholarship to human-centered learning, and finally to a more complex, multiperspective approach in the global era. The global era calls for the adoption of a new macro mission for higher education that is reflective of the postmodern philosophy—internationalization.

Internationalization as the Fourth Macro Mission of Higher Education

Internationalization as the emerging fourth macro mission of higher education (Scott, 2006; Agnew, 2008) requires institutions worldwide to undergo deep transformative change such that they untether from the pre-globalization philosophy (Agnew, 2008; Scott, 2006).

Crişan (2019) offers a comparative analysis between traditional or modern (pre-globalization) and postmodern (21st century) universities examining key organizational aspects such as structure, culture, power dynamics, and human resources. Christensen (2011) outlined distinctive characteristics of modern universities with corresponding recommendations for transformative change. De Wit and Altbach (2021) further contributed by suggesting recommendations to prepare internationalization for the "next phase". Together, these three frameworks illustrate the evolution of universities in the global context, from modern models to more adaptive, internationally and future-oriented postmodern universities (Table 11.2).

TABLE 11.2 Modern to Postmodern University Traits and Recommendations Framed in Bolman & Deal's Organizational Theory

	Structural	Political	Human Resources	Symbolic
Crisan (Modern)	Outdated specializations without market coverage Un-disciplinary scientific approach= Expository methods, one-sided communication expository Rigidity in approaching courses, disciplines that never change Learning outcomes: memorization and reproduction Rigid evaluation Centralization Technology	Government funding University as monopoly on market	Focus on the teacher Autocrat teacher The student as object of the educational act Individual work techniques	Multicultural orientation Finished studies, resulting in diploma Maintenance education University as ivory tower, hardly accessible Elite education, exclusive Isolated existence, split from social realities Undeniable quality of university education

(*Continued*)

TABLE 11.2 (Continued)

	Structural	Political	Human Resources	Symbolic
Crisan (Postmodern)	Specializations in line with labor market requirements Multi- and trans- and interdisciplinary scientific approach Interactive methods, bilateral communications Flexibility, organizations of courses on request Learning outcomes: competences of different levels (through activity and interactivity) Multicriteria evaluation, rigorous, based on recognized standards Decentralization Investment in technology and infrastructure	Financial autonomy; multiple sources of financing Focusing on the student Student as client The student as subject of the educational act Group work techniques, cultivating team spirit	Focusing on the student Student as client The student as subject of the educational act Group work techniques, cultivating team spirit	Global orientation Lifelong learning Education for change, orientation to the future University as a "social partner", open to all Mass education, inclusive University – satellite, up to date on everything; active participation in community life Education perceived as a service

Christensen (Postmodern)	Cross-disciplinary majors, with technical certificates and associate degrees nested within bachelor's degrees Strong graduate programs only Undergraduate student involvement in research	Funds used primarily in support of students, especially need-based aid	Interdependent faculty collaboration Heavyweight innovation teams Hiring with intent to train and retain Customized scholarship Minimized rank and salary distinctions Student mentoring Increased attention to values Increased attention to values	Institutional focus on mentoring students, especially undergraduates
De Wit & Altbach (Postmodern)	Stimulate global learning for all, by paying to internationalization of the curriculum, internationalizing teacher education, and foreign language education. Strive for a more comprehensive approach, integrating the different dimensions of internationalization	Reduce the over commercialization of internationalization Better regulate and control for-profit companies		Develop a more inclusive and social internationalization that addresses ethical concerns Future orientation

(Continued)

TABLE 11.2 (Continued)

Structural	Political	Human Resources	Symbolic
Diversify the international student body Stimulate and facilitate the participation of disadvantaged groups in mobility Strengthen the relationship between internationalization K-12 and tertiary education Collaborative Online International Learning			

The university is shifting from narrow, specialized disciplinary approaches to a more integrated, flexible academic model. This is indicative of the shift in rigid unchanging disciplines to cross-disciplinary and interdisciplinary approaches. There are more flexible course structures like technical certificates and associate degrees, expanding undergraduate research involvement and developing year-round operational capabilities.

There is a reimaging of pedagogy. The educational approach has shifted from a one-sided expository "sage-on-the-stage" to more interactive, bilateral, and group communication and discussion. This has resulted in less memorization-based learning to competence-driven outcomes and implementation of mixed learning models (face-to-face and online). The student-faculty relationship has also changed shifting from the student as a passive object to an active subject of the teaching and learning process. The faculty are prioritizing team collaboration and group work over individual work techniques.

There is an evolutionary change in technology and infrastructure. The university is becoming more technologically integrated and accessible in moving from a centralized to a decentralized structure, implementing collaborative online international learning platforms, and expanding capacity through digital and flexible learning options. There is significant investment in technological infrastructure across all administrative and academic functional areas.

There has been a fundamental shift in human resource approach from a teacher-centric to student-centric pedagogical model, with more individual student mentorship and personalized education. Interdependent faculty collaboration is emphasized and there are more flexible retention strategies.

The university financial model is undergoing significant changes. Once funded by governance funds as a public responsibility, it is increasingly generating new funding models with ties to market and financial autonomy shifting the university to a private enterprise. The future orientation includes reducing over-commercialization while maintaining financial stability.

While the physical campus is not represented in Table 11.2, the following can be surmised by the changes outlined. With the shift to more collaborative group work and inclusion of students in research, the traditional campus has given way to adaptable, multipurpose spaces that can be quickly reconfigured to accommodate changing needs, and the creation of spaces that blend physical and digital learning environments.

Technological infrastructure has demanded a redesign of spaces to support hybrid learning models, integrated spaces that facilitate both face-to-face and online learning, smart classrooms with flexible layouts, and space design that supports collaborative online international learning.

The emphasis of the postmodern university on accessibility and inclusivity also brings change to the physical campus. There are more welcoming and accessible spaces for diverse student populations, spaces that accommodate different learning styles and physical abilities, and the removal of physical barriers (e.g., ramps alongside stairs, inviting spaces) that once symbolized academic exclusivity.

The global community integration of the 21st century has emphasized community engagement and lifelong learning. This "community integration" has led to less isolation as universities are more connected to surrounding communities, both local and global. The postmodern emphasis on sustainability and future-oriented design places pressure on universities to create environmentally conscious building designs with spaces that reflect the university's commitment to future-oriented education. The physical campus is evolving from a traditional structure to a dynamic, postmodern structure designed around principles of adaptability, inclusivity, and technological integration through its teaching, research, and service missions.

The redistribution of power in international education, as it is unfolding, mirrors postmodern questioning of traditional hierarchies, advocating networks between systems, multidirectional student and faculty mobility, joint educational programming between the Global North and South, and international research collaborations. Internationalization further reflects postmodern emphasis on complexity and individualization through utilization of hybrid learning environments, transnational education programs, virtual mobility initiatives, and cross-border knowledge networks. However, the drive for these complex systems is still from the traditional hierarchy as humanism and postmodernism simultaneously remain as dominant philosophies.

Leading Internationalization in a Time of Drift

In the early 21st century, internationalization as a mission of higher education still retains echoes of its initial identification to build an international, educated workforce to support the goal of creating a globalized, non-state economy of markets as envisioned by multinational corporations. The point at which the practice of internationalization in higher education diverges most from the postmodernist framing of necessary change is in continuing to position internationalization as an economic rather than a non-economic mission, which is in large part contributing to the current state of internationalization *drift*.

The emerging critique of the scholarship and practice of internationalization (Agnew, 2008) presents internationalization drift as an outcome of both early definitions of the purpose of internationalization of higher education as a means of expanding the development of human capital, framing higher education as an economic enterprise rather than a unique and essential non-economic sector.

What Stein, et al. (2016) illuminates for the field of internationalization is the awareness that, collectively, internationalization is situated in a habitual dominant imaginary, by scholars and practitioners who sit uncomfortably on the boundary between the modernist market-driven system still driving decisions, and the emergent, postmodern global landscape of higher education.

Modernist Market: Higher Education's Role in Generating Human Capital

The modernist view of the purpose of internationalization is consistent with Friedman's (1955) statement on the role of government investment in individual education, and use of measures of return on investment as a proxy for its value. The influence of Friedman's (1955) economic philosophy in framing higher education as an industry is evident in the systems that govern higher education as an enterprise, particularly in the United States.

Expanding on Friedman's rationale for setting the value of higher education in society as the correct model for government investment in education, Gary S. Becker (1964) laid out his understanding of the development and management of people as a workforce in his book titled "Human Capital: A Theoretical and Empirical Analysis, with Special Reference to Education".

In his paper tracing the development of the concept of human capital, Adamson (2009) identifies "the human capital strategy" as establishing a market value for what Adam Smith (2017, p. 1776) had identified as "the acquired and useful abilities of all inhabitants or members of a society".

Becker proposed the term, human capital, to describe the means of measuring human contribution to corporate (not state) value as a form of fixed capital with an "asset value" and provided the mathematical construct by which to calculate this value. By 1989, the success of the approach was evident; the undergraduate academic degree had become a proxy for the valuation of people in the corporate labor market, translating the "immaterial, cognitive, and affective" (Christensen & Eyring, 2011) work of education into a commodity (Adamson, p. 271).

As Becker (1964) himself stated, he hesitated to use the term human capital, and it was originally criticized as "treating people like slaves or machines". He made that observation as he was celebrating, in 1989, the fact that the term had come to dominate understanding of human resource development and establish marginal value for human work within a labor market.

When the United States passed the Higher Education Act of 1965, it established an investment model approach for transforming higher education into an engine for producing human capital. The act created the federal student loan program, which is structured as a type of human capital contract, in which families and individuals enter a legal contract with the federal government or its designated contractors. The recipients gain the funds to pay the tuition associated with earning a degree at an accredited institution. In return, recipients take on a debt that cannot be discharged and that must be repaid through applying the complex of knowledge and skill acquired through that education in the workforce.

The government's investment is indirect, as proposed by Friedman, and higher education, formerly subsidized directly by states, becomes part of the human capital market with all its attendant forces. The value of the academic degree is now explicitly measured in economic terms, as a return on investment. Federal student loan recipients have effectively transferred ownership of a defined portion of their lifelong human capital value to the federal government and its privately owned proxies, as a return on investment in that person. This is seen as good in modernist perspectives, because it "enable[s] capital to flow wherever there is an opportunity to liberate value by investing in education. That should be the aim of policy makers around the globe" (Palacios Lleras, 2004).

This framing captures the essence of a modernist understanding of both globalization as a process and the role of higher education in that process. It reduces the purpose of higher education to create a fixed amount of measurable human capital in the form of the degree, and one that can be further capitalized. It ignores the indispensable and unique role of the higher education mission to educate people, create and disseminate knowledge, and promote individual and social well-being. And this understanding contributes to higher education's seeming inability to evolve to meet the opportunities of a postmodern, global society.

While higher education has played a unique role in developing modern thought and practice in all fields, it is also subject to the outcomes of its own practice. And, similar to the transformation from religious philosophies to humanist philosophies, the current need to transform and recreate higher education itself is driven by globalization and an emergent postmodern philosophy that future generations will continue to shape and ultimately name.

Furthermore, internationalization continues to be framed as an economic driver by governments, higher education as an enterprise, and by the field of internationalization practice. This framework drives decisions about the purpose of internationalization and therefore the scope and scale of its impact on programs, impact on students and their learning, and the value of service. Internationalization at the institutional level in higher education is seen as adding value in meeting market needs. Internationalization of higher education globally expands the human capital market.

Postmodern Perspectives on the Global Landscape and the Source of Action for Internationalization

In 2006, United States Secretary of Education Dr. Margaret Spellings asserted that "higher education has become what is, in the business world, a mature enterprise; increasingly risk-averse, at times self-satisfied, and unduly expensive" (U.S. Department of Education, 2006, p. xii). She noted that higher education as an enterprise had yet to successfully address "the fundamental issues of how academic programs and institutions must be transformed to serve the changing educational needs of a knowledge economy" (U.S. Department of Education, 2006, p. xii).

In 2011, Christensen and Eyring published "The Innovative University", a text in which they applied economic disruption theory to understanding the state of higher education. While they wrote in response to Secretary Spelling's address, Christensen and Eyring posed a counterpoint to her framing. Disruption theory, which they had developed, could be applied to higher education. However, higher education is not an industry that produces goods; its tripartite non-economic mission is itself indispensable to creating the future landscape of globalization. It is an enterprise that is unique in its ability to foster discovery, education and mentoring, and pluralistic well-being globally, for all humans (Christensen & Eyring, 2011).

Because their analysis indicated that higher education must adapt its understanding of itself to meet the opportunities and challenges of globalization, Christensen and Eyring explicitly called on higher education to see itself anew, and they identified internationalization, supported by distance education technologies, as an emergent priority. They cited the case of higher education in the Salt Lake Valley of Utah as an example. Four different types of universities, with four distinctly different missions and visions, provided diversified types of higher education to over 30,000 people locally and an unknown number across the globe. Each institution included internationalization in some form within their mission, vision, or values. Each realized internationalization differently within their own contexts, and in ways that assumed an emerging global landscape in which students would live their lives.

Christensen and Eyring laid out a proposal for what it would take to "change the DNA" of higher education. What they describe is building a generative, global landscape of higher education, not a new iteration of a ladder of ascension in service to a nation or region, as the next evolutionary stage, at the macro level, in higher education.

We propose that the source for action in internationalization is not the globalization of markets and transactional exchanges between institutions within different nations and cultures; the source of action is co-creating the global landscape of higher education within a global ecosystem. Rather than viewing internationalization through the lens of market transactions, this ecosystem approach facilitates deeper institutional transformation by encouraging collaborative relationships and shared value creation among the international education community.

Postmodern Change Theory and Creating the Global Future for Higher Education

Transformative change involves surfacing and changing underlying assumptions and corresponding espoused values and beliefs, it affects the entire institution in deep and pervasive ways, it is intentional to generate purposeful and desirable changes, and it occurs over time (Eckel & Kezar, 2003). Yet many attempts at change in higher education are thwarted by, among other things, structural (Becher & Trowler, 2001; Clark, 1983; Meister-Scheytt & Scheytt, 2005; Sporn, 1996; Teichler, 2006,) and cultural constraints (Bartell, 2003; Kezar & Eckel, 2002; Sporn, 1996; Tierney, 1988, 2006).

To plan for transformative change, it is not enough to make visible only the dominant culture. "The cultures of many colleges and universities are composites of various subcultures that are defined by their own values, activities, norms, and beliefs" (Eckel & Kezar, 2003, p. 28). In institutions of higher education, multiple cultures co-exist, and within the university community, the culture is shaped by internal factions (administrators, faculty, students, board members, and support staff) as well as external constituencies and factors. Whether it is the dominant culture or sub-culture, culture is developed in a historical process and conveyed by language and symbols (Bartell, 2003, Cook & Yanow, 1993; Tierney, 1988).

A key part of organizational change is "the importance of helping people to think differently; creating new understandings and meanings is essential to deep and pervasive change" (Kezar & Eckel, 2002, p. 18). "Those who would change a modern academic system need to know that desired changes will attenuate and fail unless they become a steady part of the structure of work, the web of belief, and the division of control" (Clark,

1983, p. 114). Therefore, how one thinks about internationalization will ultimately support or impede organizational change. In short, organizational change requires its membership to learn to do things differently.

This context of transformative change and Stein et al.'s (2016) critique provide a perspective on the landscape in which internationalization is acted out, and the landscape that is emerging that can be examined through Scharmer's (2019) theory of change in action and matrix of social evolution.

Identifying and Leading from the Source

In 2009, C. Otto Scharmer published "Theory U: Leading from the Future as it Emerges". In it, he proposed a theory of awareness-based change, enacted by people, groups, organizations, and societies, operating in systems at the micro, meso, and macro levels, through four different "social field states of attention and awareness" (Scharmer, 2009). The intersection of the level of action in systems with the field states of attention and awareness produces a matrix of social evolution (Scharmer, 2018, pp. 33–39). For him, understanding how to be present in the emerging future is an essential aspect of leading transformative change at any level.

Scharmer's matrix of social evolution aligns with and influences theories of human learning and development (Bronfenbrenner & Morris, 1998; Vygotsky, 1978; Kegan, 1994; Kegan & Lahey, 2009, 2017), and organization and culture (E. H. Schein, 2021; Bolman & Deal, 2021). His framing of what is needed to lead from an emergent future aligns with leader development theory (Day et al., 2009; Kouzes & Posner, 2006; Buller, 2015).

Scharmer has applied his theory and tested it across multiple sectors (government, business, health, education, NGOs, and banking). In higher education, the espoused beliefs and available cultural artifacts (i.e., mission and values statements, diversity and inclusion offices, cross-national research networks) reveal a deep divide between the intent to act from the empathic-relational social field of awareness, and the need to express the value of higher education as a driver of enhancing a person's capital value in a labor market (i.e., "upskilling", promotion, new career path) and contribution to the public good through workforce development for the region or nation (see National Academy of Medicine, 2021, Chapter 1).

These competing commitments and needs create what Kegan and Lahey (2009) called "an immunity to change" across the micro, meso, and macro levels of most institutions. That immunity is evidenced in internationalization as a practice of an inability to self-consciously organize around the developmental needs of students as people and create what Scharmer calls "a living system" that works together to design and create a sustainable higher education experience for all people. This system would act to counter what Scharmer and Kaufer (2013) identifies as the three major divides created through market-centered social construction: the ecological divide, the social divide, and the spiritual-cultural divide.

The complex landscape of higher education requires a fundamental reimagining of institutional structures, culture, power dynamics, and the worth of every person. Transformational change is not merely about implementing new policies, but about fundamentally reshaping how academic institutions understand their *global* role and purpose in creating a landscape in which the emergent negotiated coordination of shared interests of diverse societies can thrive and evolve (Table 11.3).

This transformative change approach must acknowledge the intricate interplay between the dominant imaginary that sets the limits for how we imagine organizational culture, leadership practices, and visioning, as well as the interplay between the internal and external environments of higher education. By focusing on newly imagined deep structure and culture universities can embrace internationalization as a transformative mission. Luckily, emerging postmodern philosophy, theory, and models exist to support such a change.

Developing Leaders of Transformative Revolutionary Change: A Postmodern Model Supporting Internationalization as the Fourth Mission of Higher Education

As of 2021, there is a convergence of understanding of what leadership is, where and when it happens, and who is able to lead. We will not recapitulate that history here, except to say that it mirrors the shift from modern empirical frameworks to postmodern holistic frameworks for understanding people and behaviors. Bolman & Deal (2021, pp. 348–354) provide a concise and elegant summary explanation of how the consensus ultimately emerged.

As a result of their inquiry into leadership, they conclude that leading is an activity characterized by building and sustaining multilateral relationships to attain complex and competing aims. Leading is distributed deeply in both the vertical and lateral structure of shared work. Situations and their context shape what needs to be decided. Leading is done in relationship and is negotiated between the leader and constituents. And leading is not managing, although leaders may also be managers.

Day et al. (2009) propose an integrative theory of leader development that is consistent with leading as a situated activity that requires capacity to build negotiated relationships around shared goals and outcomes. A designed program of leader development guides the leader as developing

TABLE 11.3 The Leader's Field of Attention and Potential Impact on an Internationalization Mission in Higher Education

Bolman and Deal's (2021) Organizational Frames

Scharmer's (2013) Leader's Social Field of Attention Stage.	Structures	Human Resource	Source of Power	Symbolic
1.0 Traditional Higher Education Internationalization is viewed as a discipline, field, or practice. Internationalization is practiced primarily for the benefit of the institution and its mission (Center-focused)	Internationalization is integrated into the historical missions of higher education. Vertical authority is defined by faculty rank and administrative title. Laterally, the work is led by individual faculty or departments and integrated into programs.	Individual faculty or faculty in departments are the primary drivers of internationalization practice Institutional investment in internationalization is on a case-b-case basis, and practice is rewarded via codified productivity criteria for promotion and faculty tenure.	*Hierarchy*: Center-driven, with faculty at that center. Internationalization is valued in proportion to the extent that the work meets the defined aims of the historical academic mission, and rewarded through centrally established criteria for productivity.	The value of internationalization is symbolized by faculty numbers, faculty rank, faculty tenure, and the quantity and quality of publication and influence of esteemed emeritus faculty and alumnae.

(*Continued*)

TABLE 11.3 (Continued)

Bolman and Deal's (2021) Organizational Frames

Scharmer's (2013) Leader's Social Field of Attention Stage.	Structures	Human Resource	Source of Power	Symbolic
2.0 Ego-centric Market-Driven Higher Education Internationalization is viewed as adding value in a competitive market. It is deployed strategically by an institution to build market share and enhance reputation. Internationalization is driven by consumer interest and workplace value.	Internationalization is authorized as a decentralized initiative or goal. It is administered laterally through project teams and task forces. The institution coordinates with peripheral market stakeholders to meet joint aims served by internationalization.	Faculty and staff with defined expertise in the discipline and practice of internationalization drive the work on behalf of the university. They coordinate with stakeholders to secure funding streams (grants, tuition) and define a "market value" that results in revenue and prestige. Reward systems based on contribution to market relevance and value. Professional affiliations provide professional development, career advancement, access to resources, opportunity.	*Market Success:* Local and regional market relevance empowers internationalization. Success is determined by market share (student credit hours) and the degree to which internationalization meets joint aims. Economic pressures from state and national government policy and from markets demands.	National and international recognition for institution and its peripheral stakeholders (cross-national collaborations, global study and practice initiatives); awards and recognition for impact of internationalization; internal and external prestige.

Leadership **239**

Higher Education Networks and Negotiation
Internationalization is understood through the perspectives of multiple stakeholders. Core principles and standards define education and institutional practice in internationalization, and there are evaluation models of the effectiveness of internationalization as a practice.

Internationalization is part of a multicentric, multiinstitutional network with shared understandings and goals, focused on innovating across the network. Institutions advance multiple models for internationalization, to meet stakeholder aims. Institutions may have matrix (more than one reporting structure) or networked lateral structures, with minimal shared vertical authority, policy, and process.

Expert faculty and staff design and govern the educational frame of internationalization. Core principles and standards define expected practice in internationalization. Development of individual and group capacity for specialized work in internationalization prioritized in budget and reward systems across the network. Internationalization may be recognized as a "fourth mission" of higher education.

Networked Relationships: Shared aims for student learning and development drive internationalization across multiple connected higher education networks (i.e., the triumvirate of state, local, and professional accreditation bodies) Internationalization enables innovation in teaching, scholarship, and practice, in all academic fields and practices.

Individual prestige and national recognition are symbolized by the impact of program graduates on joint aims. Symbols include industry or community awards, reputation for impact on global and local aims, and cross-sector impact of graduates-as-leaders on decisions and actions intended to attain specific aims of internationalization.

(*Continued*)

TABLE 11.3 (Continued)

Bolman and Deal's (2021) Organizational Frames

Scharmer's (2013) Leader's Social Field of Attention Stage.	Structures	Human Resource	Source of Power	Symbolic
Eco-System Awareness-based Collective Action and Judgment Internationalization engages higher education in emerging possibilities that diverge from the status quo and contribute to the four missions. The aim is to develop and sustain a global landscape of internationalized higher education.	Internationalization frames a field of emerging possibilities for how higher education is understood and practiced. These emergent possibilities emerge through the synergies created by the global landscape of internationalized higher education.	Internationalization is an integral *fourth* mission of higher education. Intentions consistent with the aims of internationalization drive faculty and staff development, and new roles and authorities emerge to support the mission. Teaching, research, service, and internationalization collectively create a new field (imaginary) of possibilities in higher education.	*Emerging Field:* The emergent possibilities made present through internationalization is the driver of higher education, based on a vision for the whole (higher education, global society, the earth as ecosystem)	Symbols focus on sustainable practices and innovation of new social structures to support internationalized higher education as a global value are also emergent. The emphasis is on global eco-system outcomes and collective action.

adult learner through a spiral process of development. The process builds leader expertise and capacity, resulting in a practice of leading from a source of wisdom. Wisdom is defined as expert practice in leading people that aligns moral reasoning and judgment with self-knowledge, self-regulation, and the capacity for reflective judgment. Wisdom emerges as an outcome of a spiral process of maturation through learning, development, and practice. Day et al. understood the process to be education and development, as opposed to training.

Petrie (2014) proposed that leader development responsive to the new context of leading (volatile, uncertain, complex, and ambiguous, or VUCA) be designed as an accelerated process of maturity development, specifically employing strategies that address immunity to change (Kegan & Lahey, 2009). In response, Carvan (2015) proposed that the multiple emerging models of leader development met Hoare's (2011) definition of a "nexus on the borders of disciplines" and noted that situated models of education and learning theory were essential to the design of leader development for the VUCA context.

Carvan recommended the use of Bronfenbrenner's Process-Person-Context-Time (PPCT) model to frame the underlying bio-ecological context of vertical development. The PPCT model was designed to test Bronfenbrenner's bioecological theory of early development. In isolating and testing the components of experiential learning designed according to principles of the bio-ecological theory of development, Bronfenbrenner and Morris (2006) were able to establish that the impact of designed developmental experiential learning is dependent on the interaction of objective and subjective aspects of process, people, context, and engaged time. Deliberately developmental experiential learning designed to optimize the interaction of these components could increase the impact of vertical development designs.

Applying the PPCT model to designing experiential learning environments for leader development creates a replicable framework that situates the social action of leading in the context of transformative change and frames the learning environment most likely to individually and collectively accelerate people's development of the generative capacity to lead systems transformation. Applying Carvan's framework for education and development to lead social action leads to the following model for developing deeply situated capacity for leading internationalization.

Developing Leaders for the Internationalization Mission of Higher Education

At the foundation, the spiral of adult development would be a spiral of downloading, suspending, seeing through new eyes, redirecting attention, sensing the new reality, letting go, and making present the newly imagined future, from the source of taking action. Moving from "me alone", to "I" across the borders, to "we" are working from "where we are" to "all of us" coordinating from where we sit is the journey of maturity, and it can be accelerated.

The **process** of leader development must develop "leaders in place", or people who can lead in service to the internationalization mission from different subcultures and levels within higher education. **People** in the process are active agents in the design of their own learning and development, within an education designed to teach them the art and practice of self-transformation and leadership. The **context** for development is internationalization of higher education as a mission, and the resources that people bring to the process are their existing state of mature understanding of themselves, of internationalization, and of the practice of leading.

The **engaged time** for each instance of development is a crucial component and is determined by the intended learning and practice outcomes. The cycle of experiential learning and development of leading in service to a mission can be integrated into time at work instead of apart from work or study.

The **form** of the developmental process is consistent with Day et al.'s spiral of identity development. Each spiral is an experiential learning experience with identified learning outcomes, goals for developing self-awareness, self-regulation, and self-efficacy. The educational experience is designed for a cohort, but each journey is individualized through assessment, peer group mentoring, review, reflection, and coaching. Cohorts create opportunities to practice relationship-building and newly acquired practices. The practices of attending, listening, conversing, dialogue, inquiry and generating "flow" are integrated into the work of the cohort as a cohort.

In addition, the ecology of the experience would include the integration of a blend of technologies that engage people in nationally, regionally, culturally, and linguistically diverse cohorts. Immersive simulated and actual experiences co-exist and allow comparison of practices and insights.

The **content** of the learning experience is knowledge of theory, art, and practice in: leading, internationalization as a mission, systems and change, complexity, and maturity development.

The **direction of learning and development** is toward a mature practice of self-aware, self-directed learning, development, and transformation. The capacity to practice self-transformation is essential to lead internationalization as the fourth mission of higher education and co-creating the transformed global landscape of higher education in the process.

The **ecology** in which this development takes place is global and transcends the borders of any single institution. It can be situated within a nexus for leader development created and operated by professional organizations, community stakeholders, and networks for internationalization.

Conclusion

The question is not whether to act, but how the internationalization community can rise to meet this crucial moment in the history of higher education and its enduring contribution to human social evolution.

This chapter is more than a theoretical exercise or academic discussion—it is a call to lead in the co-creation of the emerging global landscape of higher education. In 2013, Scharmer and Kaufer proposed an idealized "University 4.0" that would provide an ecology for developing global action leadership across a diverse field of change makers. They envisioned the ecology of global higher education and are acting now to realize that vision.

Internationalization as the fourth mission is necessary for the re-creation of higher education for the emerging future. Internationalization envisions the postmodern global landscape for higher education as emerging from the fractures in our existing system, which is creating an ecological divide, a social divide, and a spiritual-cultural divide that requires leaders who can generate new systems. It is grounded in the global ecosystem that sustains humanity in all its social and cultural complexity. The call to *lead* internationalization is situated in this context.

We are all sitting uncomfortably on that boundary of possibilities. Luckily, since humans have already framed the new imaginary of a global system of awareness-based collective action (i.e., postmodernism) we have the capacity to make it real. The primary reason that social evolution is so varied is because of the diversity of human thought and action, the capacity for humans to construct and deconstruct models, and the capacity for humans to leave societies that do not work for them and to build others. However, the extent of expansion of human populations with different ideologies encompasses the known boundaries of the planet on which we live. *There is nowhere else to go.* And humans must adapt to this new context.

It is this characteristic of cultural change that requires a transformative, frame-breaking change in education as learning, and internationalization can frame the necessary idea that drives a collective capacity to "act in a moment" to change an imaginary construct into reality.

This moment is now.

Implications for Ethical Policies and Practices

1 Reframing Economic Value: Policies and practices need to shift away from viewing internationalization primarily through an economic or market lens (human capital development) and instead emphasize its broader educational and societal purposes.

2 Cultural Transformation: Universities need to implement practices that support deep cultural change, moving from traditional hierarchical structures to more collaborative, network-based approaches that reflect postmodern values. This includes rethinking power dynamics and decision-making processes.
3 Leadership Development: Universities should establish policies for developing leaders who can operate in complex, global contexts and that foster self-awareness, systems thinking, and the ability to lead transformative change.
4 Sustainable Practices: Policies must balance the drive for internationalization with environmental and social sustainability that promote responsible global engagement.
5 Student-Centered Focus: Policies and practices need to prioritize student development and learning outcomes over market-driven metrics, ensuring that internationalization serves its fundamental educational purpose.

References

Adamson, L. (2009). From human capital to human capability: Rethinking social investment in education. *International Journal of Educational Development*, 29(5), 565–575.

Agnew, M. (2008). Historical review of changes in university culture and their impact on organizational development [Unpublished doctoral candidacy examination]. University of Calgary.

Bartell, M. (2003). Internationalization of universities: A university culture-based framework. *Higher Education*, 45, 43–70.

Becher T., & Trowler, P., (2001). *Academic tribes and territories: Intellectual inquiry and the culture of disciplines*. The Society for Research into Higher Education & Open University Press.

Becker, G. S. (1964). *Human capital: A theoretical and empirical analysis, with special reference to education*. University of Chicago Press.

Bloland, H. (2005). Whatever happened to postmodernism in higher education?: No requiem in the new millenium. *The Journal of Higher Education*, 76(2), 121–148.

Bolman, L & Deal, T. (2021). *Reframing organizations: Artistry, choice, and leadership* (7th ed.). Jossey-Bass.

Bronfenbrenner, U., & Morris, P. A. (1998). The ecology of developmental processes. In W. Damon, & R. M. Lerner (Eds.), *Handbook of child psychology: Theoretical models of human development* (5th ed., Vol. 1, pp. 993–1028). John Wiley & Sons.

Bronfenbrenner, U., & Morris, P. A. (2006). The bioecological model of human development. In W. Damon, & R. Lerner (Series Eds.), & R. M. Lerner (Vol. Ed.), *Handbook of child psychology: Vol 1: Theoretical models of human development* (6th ed., pp. 793–828). Wiley. (Read pp. 793–803).

Buckner, E. & Stein, S. (2020). What Counts as Internationalization? Deconstructing the Internationalization Imperative. *Journal of Studies in International Education*, 24(2) 151–166.

Buller, J. L. (2015). *Change leadership in higher education: A practical guide to academic transformation*. Jossey-Bass.

Cai, Y., & Leask, B. (2024). Rethinking internationalization of higher education for society from an outside-in perspective. *Journal of Asian Public Policy*, 1–19. https://doi.org/10.1080/17516234.2024.2406093

Carvan, M. (2015). Leadership education for the volatile, uncertain, complex, and ambiguous now: A challenge to the field. *Journal of Leadership Education*, 14(4), 3–10.

Christensen, C. M. (2011). *Disrupting class: How disruptive innovation will change the way the world learns* (2nd ed.). McGraw-Hill.

Christensen, C. M., & Eyring, H. J. (2011). *The innovative university: Changing the DNA of higher education from the inside out*. Jossey-Bass.

Clark, B. (1983). *The higher education system: Academic organization in cross-national perspective*. University of California Press

Cook, S. D. N., & Yanow, D. (1993). Culture and organizational learning. *Journal of Management Inquiry*, 2(4), 373–390.

Crişan, A. (2019). Higher education and the challenges of postmodern society. *Journal of Educational Sciences and Psychology*, 9(2), 10–16.

Daley, L. (1961). The medieval university 1200-1400. Sheed and Ward.

Day, D. V., Harrison, M. M., & Halpin, S. M. (2009). *An integrative approach to leader development: Connecting adult development, identity, and expertise*. Routledge.

De Wit, H. & Altbach, P. G. (2021). Internationalization in higher education: Global trends and recommendations for its future. *Policy Reviews in Higher Education*, 5(1), 28–46. https://doi.org/10.1080/23322969.2020.1820898

Eckel, P., & Kezar, A. (2003). *Taking the reins: Institutional transformation in higher education*. Praeger Publishers.

Frank, D., & Gabler, J. (2006). *Reconstructing the university*. Stanford University Press.

Friedman, M. (1955). The role of government in education. In R. A. Solo (Ed.), *Economics and the public interest* (pp. 123–144). Rutgers University Press.

Hoare, C. (2011). Continuing to build a discipline at the borders of thought. In C. Hoare (Ed.) *The Oxford handbook of reciprocal adult development and learning* (2nd ed., pp. 3–15). Oxford University Press.

Kegan, R. (1994). *In over our heads: The mental demands of modern life*. Harvard University Press.

Kegan, R., & Lahey, L. L. (2009). *Immunity to change: How to overcome it and unlock potential in yourself and your organization*. Harvard Business Press.

Kezar, A., & Eckel, P., (2002). Examining the institutional transformation process: The importance of sensemaking, interrelated strategies, and balance. *Research in Higher Education*, 43(3), 295–328.

King, P., & Arlig, A. (2022). Peter Abelard. In *Stanford encyclopedia of philosophy*. Retrieved November 29, 2024, from https://plato.stanford.edu/entries/abelard/

Kouzes, J. M., & Posner, B. Z. (2006). *The leadership challenge* (4th ed.). Jossey-Bass.

LaMont, C. (1997). *The philosophy of humanism* (8th ed.). Humanist Press.

Marinoni, G., & Cardona, G. (2024). IAU 6th Global Survey on Internationalization of Higher Education: University internationalization in a changing world. International Association of Universities (IAU). https://www.iau-aiu.net/IMG/pdf/2024_internationalization

Meister-Scheytt, C., & Scheytt, T. (2005). The complexity of change in universities. *Higher Education Quarterly*, 59(1), 76–99.

Morrow, A. (2006). Critical theory, globalization, and higher education: Political economy and the Cul-de-Sac of the postmodernist cultural turn in Rhoads and Torres. In R. A. Rhoads & C. A. Torres (Eds.),*The university, state, and market: The political economy of globalization in the Americas*. Standford University Press.

National Academy of Medicine. (2021). *The future of nursing 2020–2030: Charting a path to achieve health equity.* Consensus study from the National Academy of Medicine. Chapter

Nguyen, T. H. (2010). Vietnam and the making of market-Leninism. *The Pacific Review, 23*(3), 375–395.

Noddings, C. (1995) *Philosophy of education.* Westview Press, Inc.

Palacios Lleras, M. (2004). *Investing in human capital: A capital markets approach to student funding.* Cambridge University Press.

Pashby, K., & De Oliveira Andreotti, V. (2016). Ethical internationalisation in higher education: Interfaces with international development and sustainability. *Environmental Education Research, 22*(6), 771–787. https://doi.org/10.1080/13504622.2016.1201789

Petrie, N. (2014). Vertical leadership development – Part 1: Developing leaders for a complex world. Center for Creative Leadership.

Rashdall, H. (1936) *The Universities of Europe in the Middle Ages.* Clarion Press.

Schachner, N. (1938). *The medieval universities.* University Press.

Scharmer, C, & Kaufer, K. (2013). *Leading from the emerging future: From ego-system to eco-system economies* (pp. 241–247). Berrett-Koehler Publishers, Inc.

Scharmer, C. O. (2009). *Theory U: Leading from the future as it emerges* (1st ed.). Berrett-Koehler Publishers.

Scharmer, C. O. (2018). *The essentials of theory U: Core principles and applications.* Berrett-Koehler Publishers.

Scharmer, C. O. (2019). Vertical literacy: Reimagining the 21st-century university. *Journal of Awareness-Based Systems Change, 1*(1), 52–68.

Schein, E. (2021). *Organizational culture and leadership.* Jossey-Bass.

Scott, J. (2006). The mission of the university: Medieval to postmodern transformations. *The Journal of Higher Education, 77*(1), 1–39.

Smith, A. (2017). *An inquiry into the nature and causes of the wealth of nations*, Vol. 1 of 2 (Classic Reprint). FB&C Limited.

Sporn, B. (1996) Managing university culture: An analysis of the relationship between Institutional culture and management approaches. *Higher Education, 32*, 41–61.

Stein, S., Andreotti, V., Bruce, J., & Suša, R. (2016). Towards different conversations about the internationalization of higher education. *Comparative and International Education, 45*(1) 1–18.

Stier, J. (2004). Taking a critical stance toward internationalization ideologies in higher education: Idealism, instrumentalism, and educationalism. *Globalisation, Societies and Education, 2*(1), 1–28. https://doi.org/10.1080/14767720420000177069

Teichler, U. (2006). Changing structures of higher education systems: The increasing complexity of underlying forces. *Higher Education Policy, 19*(4), 447–461.

Tierney, W. (1988) Organizational culture in higher education: Defining the essentials. *Journal Higher Education, 59*(1), 2–21.

U.S. Department of Education. (2006). *A test of leadership: Charting the future of U.S. higher education.* A report of the commission appointed by Secretary of Education Margaret Spellings. Author.

Vygotsky, L. S. (1978). *Mind in society: The development of higher psychological processes.* Harvard University Press.

Wheatley, M. J. (2021). *Who do we choose to be? Facing reality, claiming leadership, restoring sanity.* Berrett-Koehler Publishers.

Williams, J. J., & Marsh, B. (2008). In the marketplace of academic ideas: The future of higher education in the twenty-first century. *Social Studies Review, 47*(2), 12–16.

Williams, T. (2023) Anselm of Cantebury. In *Stanford encyclopedia of philosophy.* Retrieved on November 29, 2024 from https://plato.stanford.edu/entries/anselm/

12
CONCLUSION

Looking Back, Looking Forward

Melanie Agnew and Jos Beelen

How Did We Get Here?

Universities began as inherently international institutions, with medieval structures organized around "nations" that protected and supported international students and scholars. This early model emphasized knowledge exchange and cross-cultural understanding, standing in stark contrast to the contemporary landscape which reveals a profound drift from these foundational purposes.

The evolution of higher education internationalization from these medieval origins to its current state reveals what we term "internationalization drift"—a fundamental deviation from internationalization's original educational and societal purposes toward increasingly market-driven objectives against a backdrop of neocolonialism and neoliberalism.

This transformation occurs within a complex framework shaped by three interconnected domains—state, market, and education—often referred to as the "triple helix." English continues to serve as the dominant language across these spheres, reinforcing historical power dynamics between the Global North and South. Two key factors have accelerated this shift: government policies explicitly tying higher education to economic development and global competitiveness, and chronic institutional underfunding pushing universities to treat education as a marketable commodity rather than a public responsibility.

Higher education's original mission focused on preparing the next generation of leadership in service to society. Today, however, market imperatives dominate global engagement to such an extent that internationalization no longer serves this capacity. Instead, we see growing emphasis on competition rather than cooperation, and self-interest rather than societal benefit, evidenced at all levels of global engagement.

Where Are We Now?

The current landscape of higher education internationalization can be understood through analysis at three distinct yet interconnected levels: micro, meso, and macro. The Cultural Readiness for Internationalization (CRI) model described in Chapter 1 provides a framework for analyzing global engagement across these three levels while considering the interplay between internal culture and external environment.

Throughout this book, the authors demonstrate how market ideology permeates every aspect of higher education. Below are several key examples of this influence organized around the micro, meso, and macro levels.

Micro Level (Faculty)

At the micro level, international students and their families face exploitation through commission-based recruitment agents and universities' pursuit of tuition dollars. Mobility programs often privilege elite students, prioritizing career advancement and social mobility while ignoring environmental impacts—even short-term programs contribute to our planet's challenges. These market-driven practices reveal a broader pattern of how economic forces shape academic priorities and opportunities.

This prioritization of market interests is particularly evident in the disparity between hard and soft disciplines in higher education. Hard disciplines (such as technology and engineering) receive greater financial support due to their direct alignment with market demands. This creates a self-reinforcing cycle where faculty in these fields gain access to more research opportunities and this, in turn, accelerates their progression through tenure and promotion pathways. In contrast, the humanities, and other soft disciplines (like education and philosophy), despite their crucial role in fostering democratic ideals and promoting global understanding, face chronic underfunding. This resource disparity has created an imbalance that threatens the intellectual and cultural diversity within universities.

Meso Level (Deans)

The preferential treatment of market-aligned disciplines poses significant risks to higher education's broader mission. Schools and colleges within universities receive dramatically different levels of funding based on their perceived market value rather than their societal importance. Schools of Business or Engineering, for instance, command substantially higher funding than Schools of Education, Humanities, or Social Work—not because of their inherent value to society, but due to their stronger market alignment and revenue-generating potential.

This funding disparity manifests in multiple ways—higher faculty salaries, better facilities, more research support, and greater institutional investment in growth. Moreover, these market-aligned disciplines often pursue prestigious accreditations that, while ostensibly ensuring quality, primarily serve to enhance institutional reputation, rankings, and strengthen market viability. For example, in the United States business schools aggressively seek AACSB accreditation not just for quality assurance, but because it drives rankings, attracts higher-paying students, and justifies premium tuition rates, further widening the resource gap between disciplines.

This market-driven approach to resource allocation and reputation-building threatens the fundamental mission of universities as institutions serving broader societal needs. It risks creating a two-tiered system within universities, where market-aligned disciplines thrive while other essential fields struggle to maintain quality and relevance. The long-term consequences could include reduced capacity for addressing complex social challenges, diminished cultural and intellectual diversity, and a narrowing of higher education's contribution to human development.

Macro Level (Senior Leadership)

At the macro level, market ideology dominates higher education through multiple interconnected mechanisms that shape institutional behavior and outcomes. Reputation metrics, rankings systems, assessment frameworks, and accreditation requirements are just some of the drivers that reinforce market-oriented decisions and establish normative frameworks. These mechanisms systematically disadvantage and often oppress individuals and institutions based on their identities, geographical locations, and access to resources. The commercial manifestations at the macro level of how institutions approach internationalization are particularly evident. Revenue-based metrics heavily influence strategic planning, implementation, and evaluation processes. Universities increasingly prioritize activities that generate income or improve rankings positions over those that advance educational quality or social benefit.

The Interplay Between the Internal and External (Triple Helix) Environments

Understanding these complex dynamics requires examining how micro, meso, and macro levels interact within higher education's ecosystem. The triple helix framework provides a valuable lens for analyzing these interactions, revealing how individual experiences, institutional structures, and systemic forces are shaped by both historical colonialism and modern neoliberal policies. This framework helps explain how market pressures ripple across all levels—from individual faculty and students to departments and schools, and ultimately to entire institutions and systems.

Through this lens, we can see how Western academic perspectives and methodologies continue to dominate, while non-Western knowledge systems remain marginalized. International service programs, despite good intentions, often reinforce rather than dismantle colonial relationships between institutions and regions. Even virtual exchange programs like COIL, discussed in Chapter 4, may inadvertently reproduce existing inequities without careful design and implementation.

University Missions

The triple helix framework helps us understand how these challenges are not isolated problems but rather manifestations of a deeper structural shift in how higher education relates to state and market forces. The dominance of Western perspectives, the marginalization of non-Western knowledge systems, and the persistence of colonial relationships despite good intentions all point to a fundamental misalignment between higher education's societal mission and its current market-driven practices. This misalignment threatens not just educational quality and access, but the very capacity of universities to serve their essential multi-purpose role in addressing today's dire global challenges.

Higher education's essential role emerges as a complex web of interconnected responsibilities that serve both immediate and long-term societal needs. At its foundation lies the critical task of developing future leaders who will serve society—not just as technical experts or business professionals, but as individuals capable of understanding their self in relation to their essential leadership role.

Universities serve as centers where technical and humanistic approaches to knowledge creation converge, preserving diverse perspectives including often-marginalized non-Western knowledge. This work develops critical thinking, ethical reasoning, and cultural understanding needed for addressing global challenges. Higher education's core mission includes preserving cultural and intellectual diversity, especially protecting humanities and other fields that may not align with market demands but are vital for society. This means safeguarding different ways of knowing and understanding the world. As public institutions, universities must prioritize societal benefit over commercial interests, fostering cooperation rather than competition. They must function as independent centers of learning capable of addressing complex challenges while promoting cross-cultural understanding.

The foundational missions of higher education contrast sharply with current market-driven internationalization trends. The challenge is balancing these essential societal roles while navigating economic and political pressures. Internationalization as higher education's emerging fourth mission is essential for reimagining universities' role in an evolving global landscape. This reconceptualization emerges from recognizing fundamental fractures in our current system. It demands new forms of leadership capable of critically navigating complexity while fostering genuine transformation at multiple levels—individual, institutional, national, international, and global.

The Cultural Readiness for Internationalization (CRI) model offers a promising framework for this transformation. By prioritizing institutional cultural readiness, operationalizing cultural strength and orientation, and utilizing critical approaches, the model enables institutions to plan and measure progress while ensuring coordinated implementation. Its foundation in ideology, organizational culture, and systems theory makes it adaptable across diverse institutional contexts. The model's emphasis on cultural analysis stems from the premise that a receptive institutional culture is crucial for successful internationalization.

Steering through the Storm

Traditional management approaches no longer serve the needs of our postmodern context. Leaders must guide higher education to meet contemporary global challenges while maintaining its foundational educational mission. They must learn to lead through increasing uncertainty in the global education landscape while simultaneously driving deep cultural change within their institutions. This dual focus requires leaders who can both respond to immediate challenges and foster long-term transformation.

We need to think about "leading" differently.

Leadership emerges through building and maintaining multilateral relationships to achieve complex, competing goals. It operates across both vertical and lateral organizational structures, with context-shaping decisions and relationships negotiated between leaders and constituents.

Learning to lead can be viewed as a spiral learning process building toward wisdom—defined as expert practice aligning moral reasoning with self-knowledge and reflective judgment. This learning process focuses on education rather than training.

Effective leadership development must cultivate leaders across all levels and subcultures of higher education who can advance internationalization goals from their respective positions. Participants actively shape their own development journey within an educational framework designed to foster self-transformation and leadership skills. The development occurs within the specific context of higher education internationalization, building upon participants' existing self-awareness, understanding of internationalization, and leadership experience.

Countering the drift toward market-driven internationalization requires bold and courageous leaders. This demands skillful navigation of the interplay between institutional culture, market forces, and broader societal dynamics. Leaders must understand how these forces interact and influence each other, developing strategies that maintain educational integrity while acknowledging economic realities.

Leaders cannot be developed through conventional management training alone. They must become adept at reading and responding to complex global contexts while maintaining a clear vision of their institutions' educational and societal missions. This means developing both practical skills for managing uncertainty and deeper understanding of cultural change processes, creating a leadership approach that can effectively guide institutions through transformation while staying true to their core educational purposes.

Action is inevitable. The real challenge lies in how the internationalization community will step up to this historic moment and strengthen higher education's role in human social evolution.

Transforming Higher Education

The transformation of higher education demands a reconceptualization that goes far beyond surface-level changes. This reimagining must address every aspect of the institution—from organizational structures and cultural foundations to power relationships and human dignity. Such fundamental change extends well beyond policy reforms, requiring universities to fundamentally shift how they envision their internationalization mission.

Success in this transformation requires sustained commitment to several interconnected principles. Universities must maintain high educational quality and measurable student learning outcomes while simultaneously ensuring engagement is truly inclusive across all populations. They need to build genuine partnerships based on reciprocity rather than dominance, while fiercely protecting academic freedom and institutional autonomy. Supporting diversity across disciplines becomes crucial, particularly in preserving and strengthening areas like humanities that may not align directly with market demands. Throughout this process, institutions must maintain a commitment to continuous improvement, constantly evaluating and adapting their approaches based on evidence and changing global contexts.

These principles cannot exist in isolation—they must work together to create a cohesive framework for transformation. When educational quality aligns with inclusive engagement, when reciprocal partnerships support disciplinary diversity, and when academic freedom enables continuous improvement, universities can begin to realize their potential as truly international institutions serving global society.

Universities can leverage contemporary theoretical frameworks and philosophical approaches aligned with postmodern perspectives to examine and reshape their core organizational structures and cultural foundations. Rather than working within existing constraints, institutions can use these emerging models to move beyond surface-level adjustments and achieve deeper structural and cultural change.

Meeting the Moment: Where Do We Go from Here?

The future of higher education internationalization depends on our collective ability to reimagine its fundamental purposes and possibilities. This moment calls for more than incremental adjustments—it demands transformation that addresses deeper structural issues around power, equity, and restorative justice. Internationalization as higher education's emerging fourth mission is essential for this reimagining, particularly as we confront three critical divides—ecological, social, and cultural.

This approach to internationalization must be fundamentally rooted in understanding higher education's place within the broader global ecosystem—one that sustains humanity in all its diverse social and cultural manifestations. The imperative extends beyond traditional academic boundaries, calling for responses to systemic divisions while nurturing the interconnected web of human experience and knowledge.

Through thoughtful application of frameworks like the CRI model and emerging postmodern approaches, higher education can progress toward more ethical and inclusive forms of internationalization. Success demands balancing pragmatic concerns with educational values, market pressures with societal needs, and institutional priorities with global responsibilities. This balance requires sustained commitment to both practical change and philosophical transformation.

We have seen consistent calls to values in internationalization and other critical approaches, such as those by the Critical Internationalization Studies Network. What these have in common is that they identify neoliberal practices, inequalities, and default exclusion mechanisms in higher education. Critical approaches can guide universities, but it is possible for universities to engage with philosophical transformation while not aiming for or achieving practical change. For example, universities embrace inclusivity in teaching and learning but misconceptions proliferate. Lack of support of academics in their disciplines complicates practicing internationalization of the home curriculum that reaches beyond activities and actually achieves its intended outcomes.

A Call to Action

The challenge of leading internationalization in this context requires addressing not just institutional transformation, but the healing of fundamental divides through the creation of new educational paradigms. This positions internationalization not merely as an additional function of higher education, but as a transformative force capable of bridging divides while fostering sustainable and inclusive global engagement.

The moment is here. The action is now. Our response to this historic opportunity will determine whether higher education can fulfill its vital role in addressing global challenges while fostering cross-cultural understanding and cooperation. The path forward requires us to collectively lead with courage to imagine new possibilities, to commit to deep transformative change, and to create a more equitable and sustainable future for internationalization and those we serve.

INDEX

Note: **Bold** page numbers refer to tables and *italic* page numbers refer to figures.

Academic Cooperation Association 97
academic disciplines: approaches to global learning 57, **58–59**; challenges in internationalizing the curriculum 62–63; disciplinary categories 57, **58**; hard-applied disciplinary category 61; hard-pure disciplinary category 60; knowledge production 56–57; soft-applied disciplinary 62; soft-pure disciplines 61
Academic Freedom Index 47
activist network 75
Adamson, L. 231
Africanization 116, 118–119
Agnew, M. 57, 63, 114, 178, 197, 199, 204–205, 207–208
Aldrich, C. 83
Almeida, J. 75
Altbach, P. 35, 206, 224
Altinay, F. 203
American Association of University Professors (AAUP) 47
anti-oppressive approach 9, 201
anti-oppressive internationalization 9, 10, 199, 212
Anzaldúa, G. 169
Arendt, H. 178
Argyris, C. 17

articulations of internationalization: artifacts 11, **12**; disciplines 57, 60, **60**; personal motivations 9, **10**; underlying assumptions 11, **13**; values and beliefs 11, **13**

Baer, H. A. 95
Bailey, L. 30
Bamberger, A. 30, 93–94, 145
Barnawi, O. Z. 94
Bartell, M. 203, 206
Bauman, Z. 165, 177
Becher, T. 57
Becker, G. S. 231
Beck, K. 95
Bedenlier, S. 91
Beelen, J. 73–74, 80, 83
Bernardo, A. 97
Berry, H. A. 144
Bhandari, R. 115
Biesta, G. 197
Black Reparations in the Era of Globalization (Mazrui) 119
Bloland, H. 224
Bolman, L. 236
Borger, J. 83
Brandao, A. 177
Brandenburg, U. 115, 144, 241
Brooks, R. 96

Buckner, E. 197, 208–209
Bulnes, C. 64, 84

Cai, Y. 30
Canagarajah, S. 117
Carvan, M. 241
Chasi, S. 28, 121, 123, 125–126
Chen, L. 94
Chisholm, L. A. 144
Christensen, C. M. 224, 233–234
Cleaver, F. 146
Clifford, V. 60
Climate Action Network for International Educators (CANIE) 31
cohesive and externally oriented culture 8
cohesive, internally focused culture 8
COIL/Virtual Exchange 81–84
Collaborative Online International Learning (COIL) 38–39, 76, 81–85, 97, 170, 180, 250
collaborative partnerships: educational aims 178; epistemic partnership 179–180; equitable partnerships 178; ethical policies and practices 180–181; future transcultural planning (2024–25) 174–177, *175–176*; institutional 167–169; nests of possibility 167; overview 165–166; partnership and engagement framework stages 166–167; peer research 179; process narrative 169–170; shared epistemic production 179; transcultural interdisciplinary collaboration 170–174; transdisciplinary collaboration, partnership, and identity 177–179
colonial policies 49
Comprehensive Internationalization 26
Cooperative Extension System (CES) 135, 139–144, *142*
COVID-19 pandemic 77, 82, 124, 169
Cozart, S. M. 80
Crişan, A. 224
Critical Internationalization Studies Network 30
Critical Media Literacy (CML) 83
cultural readiness for internationalization (CRI) 4–5, 114, 135, 149, 153; assumptions and sense-making 17–19, *18*; change model 4–5, *5*; cultural cohesion and orientation 6–8, *7*; enabling environment 19, 20–22, 23; ethical policies and practices 24; ideologies 8–9, *10*, *11*; organizational culture 11, *12–13*, 14–15; overview 3–4; strategic contribution 23; university culture 15–17, *16*
curriculum internationalization 38, 41, 56, 62, 76
Czech mobility: climate case 101–102; colonial dimensions 99–100; ethical practices and policies 108–109; international student mobility 98, **98**; neoliberal dimensions 100–101; overview 98–99; participatory dimension 104–107; representational dimension 102–104
Czech National Agency 98

Daley, L. 219
Davlasheridze, M. 141
Day, D. V. 236
Deal, T. 236
Deardorff, D. K. 203
Declaration of Principles on Academic Freedom and Academic Tenure 47
decolonialism 49–50
Decolonising Our Universities 49
de-internationalization 26
DeLaquil, T. 92
de Louw, E. 64, 84
De Oliveira Andreotti, V. 146
De Sousa Santos, B. 170
DeWinter, A. 84
De Wit, H. 26–28, 31, 35, 77, 92, 115, 126, 134, 203, 205, 207, 224
Dutch Ministry of Education and Culture 36

ecology 242–243
Egron-Polak, E. 115
engaged time 241–242
equitable partnerships 156, 178
Erasmus Student Network (ESN) 96
Euro-American-centrism 28
European Association for International Education (EAIE) 35, 208
European Commission 174
Eyring, H. J. 233–234

Farag, A. 83
Fraunhofer-Gesellschaft model 139
Freire, P. 118
Fricker, M. 165, 170
Friedman, M. 231
Frieß, W. 78, 107
future transcultural planning (2024–25): asynchronous component 175; ongoing research 174; project components 175, *175*; skills *176*; synchronous virtual session 176–177
fuzziness 26

Gao, C. Y. 204–205
Gasset, J. O. 170
Global Challenges University Alliance 202
The Globalisation of Internationalisation: Emerging Voices and Perspectives 120
Global Knowledge Economy 199, 201
Global Learning at The Hague University of Applied Sciences 39
Global North 30, 38–39, 76, 82, 84–85, 95, 99, 114–115, 120, 122–123, 134, 147
Global Public Good articulation 199, 201, 212
Global South perspective: academic discourse 120–121; decoloniality and gender 117; decolonization and border thinking 117–118; decolonize curricula 117; development of higher education theory 126; dialogue and declaration 121–122; epistemic recognition and respect 116–117; ethical policies and practices 128–129; future scholarship 127–128; inclusion and recognition for indigenous languages 117; injustice and social justice 119; internationalization in South Africa 123; scholarship from South Africa 119–120; southern philosophies 118; 2022 definition on scholarship 123–126, **124**, *125*; university structure 117; Western scholars 121
Goetz, S. J. 141
Google news 48
Google Scholar 123
Gregersen-Hermans, J. 80

Hagenmeier, C. 120, 127, 129
hard-pure disciplinary category 60–61
Hartman, E. 30
Heleta, S. 28, 76, 121, 123, 125–126
Higher Education Act of 1965 232
higher education internationalization (HEIs): call to action 254; CRI model 248; ethical policies and practices 214–215; evaluation models and frameworks 202–203; integrating equity and reflection 207–214; internal and external (triple helix) environments 249–250; macro level (senior leadership) 249; macro-level (senior leadership) indicators 206; marketization of internationalization 198; meeting the moment 253–254; meso level (deans) 248–249; meso-level (deans) indicators 205–206, **211**; micro level (faculty) 248; micro-level (faculty) indicators 204–205, **210**; organizational development phases and multilevel indicators 203–206; steering through the storm 251–252; sustainable development goals 198–202; transforming higher education 252–253; University missions 250–251
Hoare, C. 241
Hofstede 103, 175
Huang, F. 94
Hudzik, J. 96, 115, 203
"Human Capital: A Theoretical and Empirical Analysis, with Special Reference to Education" 231
Hunter, F. 115

IAU 2024 Global Survey Report 220
inclusive internationalization, dimensions: overview 91; participatory dimensions 97; representational dimensions 96–97; theoretical dimensions 92–96
incohesive culture with an external orientation 7
incohesive, internally focused cultures 6
intelligent internationalization 26
International Association of Universities (IAU) 76, 208, 220

International Community-Centered University Service (ICCUS) model 150, *151*, 152–153; accountability mechanisms 152–153; benefits 150; control programs 150, 152; cooperative extension system **154**; CRI model 153, 155; overview 149–150
international development, HEIs: accountability mechanisms 149; beneficiaries of service 147; control programs 147–149, *148*; critical voices in the internationalization of service 145–147; defining 135–137; ethical policies and practices 157; ICCUS model 149–155; IHES theoretical framework 144; overview 134–135; service-learning 144–145; system of land-grant institutions (LGIs) 138–139; third mission of higher education 137–138; U.S. land-grant universities and the third mission 139–144, *142*
International Education Association of South Africa (IEASA) 29, 127–128
International Higher Education for Society (IHES) 30, 115, 144–145
internationalization drift 3, 220
internationalization of curriculum (IoC) 205
internationalization of higher education: affirming academic values 29; being included in and excluded 32; critical and comparative process 28; critiques of internationalization 29–31; critiquing critical internationalization 32, **33–34**, 35; definitions 27–28; ethical policies and practices 42; Euro-American-centrism 28; international students 36–37; mobility 31; in Netherlands 35–41; overview 26–27; studies network 32
Internationalization Quality Review Process (IQRP) 205
International Online Collaboration Competencies (IOCCs) 84
international student recruitment partners: agent-facilitated mobility 191–192; CRI model 183; engaging agents 187–189; ethical agent-based internationalization 185–187; ethical policies and practices 193; for-profit third-party education agents 184; monitoring agent behavior 190–191; overview 183–185

Jacobs, L. 120–121, 127
Janebová, E. 97, 100, 107
Jithoo, D. 127, 129
Johansson, A. 79, 81
Johnstone, C. 94–95, 97, 107
Jones, E. 73–74, 76, 78, 92, 115
Jooste, N. 119

Kaufer, K. 236
Kegan, R. 235
Killick, D. 80
Klamer, R. 84
Knight, J. 3–4, 28, 31, 114, 203, 205–207
Knowledge Transfer Partnerships 139
Kolm, A. 84
Kostrykina, S. 115

Laakso, L. 120
Lahey, L. L. 235
land-grant institutions (LGIs) 138
Landorf, H. 57, 63–64
leadership: developing leaders 241–242; direction of learning and development 242; ethical policies and practices 243–244; fourth macro mission of higher education 224, **225–228**, 229–230; global future for higher education 234–235; global landscape and the source of action 233–234; humanism 223; identifying and leading from the source 235–236; internationalization resurfacing to center 220; modernist market 231–233; physical campus 229; postmodernism 223–224; scholasticism 221–222, **222**; time of drift 230–231; transformation of the university mission 221; transformative revolutionary change 236, **237–240**, 241; university missions 220–221; university's organizational structure 219–220

Leal, F. 119
Leask, B. 30, 74, 76, 81, 85, 115
Le Grange, L. 118
Le Ha, P. 94
Liquid Modernity 177
Liu, W. 27
Lugones, M. 117

Mace, M. 85
macro-level (senior leadership) indicators 206, **213**, 249
Marginson, S. 3–4, 28, 32, 115
Maringe, F. 127, 129
Marshall Plan 135–136
Mazrui, A. A. 119
Menchu, R. 118
meso-level (deans) indicators 205–206, 248–249
Mestenhauser Institute for International Collaboration 103
Mestenhauser, J. 79, 114
micro-level (faculty) indicators 204–205, 249
Mignolo, W. D. 117, 201
misconceptions of internationalization at home: accessibility and inclusion 83–84; alternative to mobility 77; COIL/Virtual Exchange 81–84; disengagement of academics 79; disengagement of educational developers 80; inclusive by default 78; internationalization and decolonization 81; with international students 78; leadership 80–81; pars pro toto effect 78; professional development 79–80
Mitchell, L.-M. 121
Molotov Plan 136
Morrill Acts 139–140
Morris, P. 30, 241
Mucha, A. 78, 107
Mukwambo, P. 124

The National Agency Report 106
National Taskforce Inclusive Internationalisation 37
Naude, P. 119
Ndaipa, C. J. 125
Ndlovu-Gatsheni, S. 116
Nelson Mandela Metropolitan University (NMMU) 119

Netherlands, critical internationalization: awareness of unintended consequences 40; on balance 41; critiquing rankings and competition 39–40; decolonization in Dutch higher education 40–41; inclusivity in study abroad 37–38; internationalization at home 38–39
Nuffic 37–39

Obadire, S. 127, 129
Official Development Assistance (ODA) programs 136
Onculeri 171
Organization for Economic Cooperation and Development (OECD) 136
Oyěwumi, O. 117

Pashby, K. 146
Pattison, S. 97
peer research 178
Pekol, A. 29–30, 99
Perez-Encinas, A. 78, 84
Perspectives on Comprehensive Internationalization of Higher Education (Dorasamy & Mugano) 127
Peter, J. 127, 129
Petrie, N. 241
Policy Framework for the Internationalisation of Higher Education in South Africa 120
Process-Person-Context-Time (PPCT) model 241

Quadruple Helix model 139

Ramose, M. B. 118
Rashdall, H. 222
Reich, R. 48
Reisberg, L. 206
relational translocalism 116, 199, 200, 201, 211–212
Rudzki, R. E. J. 203
Rumbley, L. 94, 115, 206

Salmi, J. 206
Santos, B. D. S. 205
Schachner, N. 219, 222
Scharmer, C. 236
Scharmer, O. 235

Schein, E. 198
Scholasticism 198
Scienceguide 41
Scott, J. 224
Sehoole, C. 120
shared characteristics 178
shared epistemic production 179
Shields, R. 94
Singh, T. 127, 129
Smith, A. 231
soft-applied disciplinary 62
soft-pure disciplines 61
Soria, K. M. 85
Soulé, M. V. 81
South African Higher Education Internationalization 127
South African Policy Framework for Internationalisation of Higher Education 28
Spellings, M. 233
Sporn, B. 6
Stein, S. 9–11, 28, 32, 60, 65, 76, 91, 115, 192, 197, 199, 202–203, 206–209, 211–212, 231, 235
Stier, J. 8–9
Stohl, M. 203
Streitwieser, B. 92
Sumner, W. G. 207
Sustainability Development Goals (SDGs) 137

teaching and learning: definitions and their reception 74–75; ethical policies and practices 85–86; internationalization at home 75–77; misconceptions of internationalization at home 77–84; notion of home 76; revised definition 74; terminology 73; 2015 definition 75
Technical and Vocational Education and Training (TVET) 42
Teferra, D. 76, 119
Teichler, U. 206
theoretical dimensions: anti-neoliberalism 93–94; climate-centric critique 94–95; decolonization 93; inclusive internationalization 92–96; neoliberal internationalization 92
"Theory U: Leading from the Future as it Emerges" 235
Torres, C. A. 118
triple helix 247, 249–250

Troisi, J. 85
Trowler, P. 57
Truman, H. S. 135–136
Tull, K. N., Blackman, M. 169
"21 Day International Challenge" 146

Ubuntu 118–120
United Nations Sustainable Development Goals 199
university governance and internationalization: academic disciplines 56–63; academic freedom 50, *50*; academic freedom and institutional autonomy 47; anarchical governance 53–54; appropriation, occupation, and control 49–50; bi-cameral governance system 52; contemporary challenges 47–48; critical analysis of disciplinary approaches 65–66; disciplinary challenges and inequities 66–67; ethical policies and practices 67–68; external environment and its impact 47–48; faculty disciplines 63–65; hierarchical governance 52–53; models of bi-cameral governance 50–51, *52*; monarchical governance 54–55; oligarchic governance 55–56; overview 46–47; triple helix of control 48
U.S. Cooperative Extension System 149

Van Balkom, W. D. 114, 197, 199, 204–205, 207–208
Van den Hende, F. 38, 79–80, 85
Van Gaalen, A. 203
Van Mol, C. 78, 84
Van Stapele, N. 83
Vavrus, F. 29–30, 99
Velvet Revolution 99
virtual internationalization 26
von Humboldt, W. 223

Weissova, L. 79, 81
Wei, Y. 94
Whatley, M. 83
Wimpenny, K. 80–81, 93, 125
Wingrove, P. 35, 37
Wolhuter, C. 120

Yip, G. S. 205

Zumeta, W. 103

For Product Safety Concerns and Information please contact our EU representative GPSR@taylorandfrancis.com
Taylor & Francis Verlag GmbH, Kaufingerstraße 24, 80331 München, Germany

www.ingramcontent.com/pod-product-compliance
Lightning Source LLC
Chambersburg PA
CBHW051112230426
43667CB00014B/2542